LIVING
OPRAH

LIVING OPRAH

*My One-Year
Experiment to Walk the Walk
of the Queen of Talk*

ROBYN OKRANT

CENTER
STREET®

New York   Boston   Nashville

This book is based upon personal experience. My interpretations and conclusions are not necessarily those of or endorsed by Oprah Winfrey.

Center Street
Hachette Book Group
237 Park Avenue
New York, NY 10017

www.centerstreet.com

Center Street is a division of Hachette Book Group, Inc.
The Center Street name and logo are trademarks of Hachette Book Group, Inc.

Printed in the United States of America

First Edition: January 2010
10 9 8 7 6 5 4 3 2 1

Library of Congress Cataloging-in-Publication Data

Okrant, Robyn.
   Living Oprah : my one-year experiment to walk the walk of the queen of talk /
Robyn Okrant. — 1st ed.
      p. cm.
   Summary: "On January 1, 2008, a 35-year-old average woman embarked on a year-long journey with Oprah as her guide. Robyn Okrant decided to follow every piece of advice offered in Oprah's show, magazine, and website. Living Oprah is the account of what it's like to 'live Oprah'" — Provided by the publisher.
   ISBN 978-1-59995-239-0
   1. Winfrey, Oprah—Influence. 2. Okrant, Robyn. 3. Women—United States—Biography. 4. United States—Social life and customs—1971- 5. Popular culture—United States. I. Title.
   PN1992.4.W56O39 2010
   791.4502'8092—dc22

                                                                              2009035036

*to Grandma Shirley, who was in my heart during every twist
and turn of this wild roller-coaster ride*

and

*to Grandma Ethyle, Queen of Book World, who would
have been so proud to put this book on her shelf*

BURSTING WITH GRATITUDE

for the community of bloggers and blog readers who made up my extended family in 2008. I am so grateful for your morale-boosting comments and for checking in on me regularly.

for superwoman, Susan Schulman, bitingly funny, supportive, protective, and beyond knowledgeable.

for my editor, Michelle Rapkin, whose empathy and kindness are perfectly balanced with her strength and honesty. Oh, and I think she might be able to read my mind.

for three of the best friends a gal could hope for: Grace Bulger, Jefferson Burns, and Scott Woldman. I admire each one of you and love you very much.

for Anne Ford, who lit this crazy fire.

for Kerry Maiorca at Bloom Yoga Studio, and the generous instructors, staff, and students who make it my second home.

for my inspiring mother and father: words cannot express my gratitude for your encouragement and love. I can convey my feelings for you only through interpretive dance.

for the best sistah a girl could wish for, Elisabeth. Your challenging questions have kept me on my toes. You are one smart (vegan, high-fiber, gluten-free) cookie.

and lastly, but never leastly, for my Jim. How on earth would I have survived this without you? Impossible! You are a delicious combination of patience and encouragement, smothered in spicy salsa, wrapped inside an adorable tortilla. I can almost promise I'll never put you through anything like this again.

CONTENTS

LIVING
OPRAH

JANUARY:

What have I gotten myself into?

Time spent this month: 98 hours, 46 minutes
Dollars spent this month: $707.01
Advice from Oprah that I've passed on to other women: to Buy
 Dr. Christiane Northrup's Women's Bodies, Women's Wisdom.
 I truly felt more empowered to become my own health advocate
 while reading this book.
Words that stuck: "You're doing what?"—Mark Okrant, my dad,
 when I first told him about Living Oprah

JANUARY 1, 2008
 I can feel adrenaline pumping through my body. I'm moving and talking a mile a minute. I've got the same buzz that I usually feel on opening night of a new play, although it's noon and I'm not going onstage. Wasabi, our cat, dashes by me, terrified by the loud noise as Jim turns on our ancient vacuum cleaner.

My husband and I are putting the last-minute touches on our annual New Year's Day foodfest and movie marathon. It's been many years since I've enjoyed a late night party, but I still love to celebrate the dawning of a brand-spanking-new year with close friends. So, while I'm generally fast asleep around 11 PM on the 31st, I wake up bright and early on January 1 to clean the house, prepare mountains of food, and decorate. I realize most people are probably sleeping in and enjoying their day off, but when my alarm rings at 8 AM, I turn into a worker bee. The clock is now creeping closer to 1 PM—party time—and we're almost ready for folks to come over to lounge around our home in their comfiest clothes, drape themselves on the couches that we've finally paid off, enjoy some movies, and chat the day away until long after sunset. Oprah might have called us all "schlumpadinkas" had she witnessed our casual clothing. But how can you enjoy hours of eating without elastic waistbands? As usual, I've put out enough food to sink a ship.

I'm especially excited about this year's event as I'm unveiling my Living Oprah project, which launches today, to those closest to me. I can't wait to hear my friends' feedback, and I've visualized their reactions throughout my morning preparation. In my imagination, their responses run the gamut from impressed to *very* impressed, and I am feeling confident as I bring a dish of blueberry bars into the dining room to place on the buffet table.

The only problem is, I can't seem to get the dish to fit without making the array look squashed. As I juggle everything to make space for the platter, I start to regret that I don't own an actual dining room table. The old hand-me-down drop leaf that was in Jim's bachelor pad before we were married might not have been pretty, but it did its job—until today, that is. I take a step back to assess the awkward-looking presentation. I imagine celebrity party planner and regular *Oprah* contributor Colin Cowie shaking his head in disgust. Tension builds between my shoulder blades. I want this day to be perfect, but the table is sagging under the weight of the food and the whole affair looks a little unsteady. I try to chill out. It might not look like a spread in *O, The Oprah Magazine*, but hopefully (fingers crossed) everything will taste great. Generally confident about the food I present when I entertain, I gasp when I spot the layer of green slime inside the blueberry bars.

I was certain the pureed spinach I folded into the fruit preserve mixture would be invisible to the naked eye after the bars were baked, but there it is, plain as day. That's right, I said spinach. In a dessert. It's not what I'd usually put out as a treat, but when I planned this year's menu, I created it based on recipes and ideas I found on Oprah.com. As I clicked through the website, perusing delicious-looking dishes, I happened upon this one for Blueberry Oatmeal Bars (with Spinach) from Jessica Seinfeld. The wife of the famous "have you ever noticed/don't-you-hate-it-when/what is the deal with" comedian appeared on *Oprah* in 2007 to promote her cookbook and discuss tips for hiding vegetables and other healthy items in comfort food. Oprah gushed over Seinfeld's creations, and although I was wary I followed the instructions to the letter and hoped for the best.

Jim offers a really helpful question. "What if you can't just see the spinach, you can actually taste it?"

Gross.

"Will you eat one?" I hold a bar up to his face.

He looks like cornered prey and shakes his head. "I better make sure we have enough ice," he says and skitters off to the kitchen.

Coward.

I shove a blueberry bar in my mouth and chew quickly, alert to any hint of off-putting flavor. Actually, it tastes pretty good, it only looks unsavory. I close the blinds a bit, hoping it'll be too dark in the dining room to see the spinach. I guess if my friends hate the bars, I can just pass the buck. It's not my recipe, after all.

Wasabi, frightened by the sound of our doorbell, bolts under the love seat as our first guest arrives.

Some time later, plied with Oprah-approved food and drink, my friends seem cheerful and ready to hear my plan for the coming year. I tell them it all started just a few weeks earlier (cue the flashback music) when I was sitting in a cramped video-editing suite with my friend Anthea, who was also my partner on a final project for our graduate school film class. We were trying to make heads or tails of our video, which combined two aspects of our mutual interest in women in pop culture: specifically, my fascination with self-help gurus and their followers, and Anthea's focus on various female stereotypes. We had been discussing Oprah Winfrey for the better part of an hour. Let's face it, we'd have to be living on the far side of the galaxy not to draw a connection between the Queen of Talk and the subject matter of our project. She is at the pinnacle of the self-improvement, popular culture mountain.

We were gabbing about Oprah's abundant advice on how to improve our health, relationships, homes, finances, spiritual lives, fashion sense, and the list goes on and on. Winfrey inspires masses of women all over the world. And yet, it dawned on me, for every Oprah fan I've come in contact with, there has also been someone who can't hide her vitriol about the media sensation. I wondered why.

And more important, why do so many women put an immense amount of pressure on themselves to live up to the Oprah ideal? I was buzzing with excitement (and my fourth extra-large Earl Grey tea) to find out. Could Oprah's guidance truly lead a woman to her "best life," or would it fail miserably? Is it even possible to follow someone else's advice to discover one's authentic self? I told Anthea I thought it would be a great social experiment if someone actually tried to adhere to every suggestion that Oprah offered.

Like many of my ideas that seem brilliant (to me) at first conception, yet impossible and bordering on insanity the longer I think about them, I decided this spark would probably fade into oblivion. But, for the life of me, I couldn't get it out of my head. On one hand, it seemed like an entertaining and somewhat ridiculous challenge, but on the other hand, it felt...important.

In our journey toward a more satisfying existence, we are faced with solutions from many disparate sources, and yet Oprah Winfrey stands out from the rest. Her well-known catchphrase and tagline is "Live your best life." In order to lead us toward this goal, Winfrey's advice is completely holistic. Her television program, magazine, radio show, and website offer a wellspring of guidance for the modern woman. When it comes to suggestions for better living, Oprah leaves no stones unturned.

Later in the year, when I was steeped in this project, folks curious about my experiment would ask, "Why Oprah? Why not Martha Stewart or Ellen Degeneres?" Choosing Oprah was a no-brainer for me. No one else reaches as deeply and thoroughly into every corner of a woman's existence. She does not teach us to decoupage, like Martha, or encourage us to lighten up and dance, like Ellen, but she does teach us how to live.

I've definitely taken her advice intermittently over the years. I poured myself into body-shaping, fat-smashing Spanx after she extolled their virtues on her show. Buh-bye, muffin-top! However, I was not an everyday Oprah viewer. I did not read her magazine or peruse her website. Until I began this project, I would have considered myself only a casual audience member.

Even so, I do have a long history with *The Oprah Winfrey Show*. When her talk show became syndicated in 1986, I would watch it with my mother. I was comfortable with Oprah's format immediately. After all, I watched her predecessor, Phil Donahue, throughout my childhood, and my mother even recalls viewing his show when she was pregnant with me. Some babies in the womb enjoy the concertos of Mozart and are read the poetry of Robert Frost. I was introduced as a fetus to topics along the lines of extramarital affairs, 1970s sexual taboos, and stunning celebrity gossip. I was trained before my birth to enjoy a good talk show.

Oprah was an immediate hit in our household, in part because of her gender. While Donahue might have been an outspoken supporter of feminism, and his show geared toward women, there was no getting around the fact that the dude was a man. He might sympathize with us, but he could never stand in our shoes. Well, technically he could, but my pink and gray Kangaroos with Velcro closures and side pockets would have looked ridiculous with his rumpled suit and tie.

On the other hand, Oprah, a plainspoken, strong-willed woman, ruled her own roost. And we suspected she really understood us because she was one of us. In those early years, as she covered the usual sensational talk show topics, she showed amazement when we did. She laughed when we laughed. She seemed uncomfortable when we were. And I held a warm spot in my heart for her because she seemed slightly awkward, not incredibly stylish, and not the stereotypical "beautiful" woman we were accustomed to seeing on TV. I certainly wasn't a beauty at that time in my life (don't argue with me, Dad, I have photographic proof), and I never saw anyone who looked like me on screen. Well, Oprah didn't exactly look like anyone on television at that time, either. She gave me hope. I figured if she could do it, who knows? Maybe I could do anything I set my mind to, as well. I felt a definite kinship to the rising queen of television.

That was many moons ago, and after decades in the business of talk, she's come a long way, baby. She's risen from a talk show host to become a media mogul, a corporate trailblazer, and a spiritual guru. Her fame and fortune shot through the roof, making her one of the most influential and well-known celebrities on the planet. Now I have to wonder, do Oprah and I still have anything in common, or have we drifted apart? While her bank account has bulged and her privilege has expanded into the realm of American royalty, can she still represent the average American woman? While her advice is certainly plentiful, is it still relevant?

I wanted to find out.

Several days after I devised my experiment, my husband and I stood in our pajamas, eating oatmeal in the kitchen. Wasabi was running in circles on the linoleum floor, a brown paper lunch bag over his head. I eyed my husband, trying to guess his mood. I knew that if I were to take on such an involved project, I'd need his complicity.

"How would you feel if—" And here is where I witnessed Jim shiver reflexively, as he usually does when I begin conversations by soliciting his feelings.

I took a deep breath.

"How would you feel if I spent some time doing everything Oprah says?"

He looked confused and gulped down his espresso. "Is this for school?"

"No, it's for me."

Jim slumped in minor disappointment as the cat extricated himself and started strutting around the kitchen, acting as if he'd actually meant to trap his head in a brown paper bag for the past five minutes.

Jim asked, "Would I need to do anything?"

I shrugged. "I doubt it."

And truly, at the time, I didn't think this experiment would impact him very much. I assured Jim that I could compartmentalize my activities by setting a couple hours aside each day to watch and read Oprah, do some Oprah-advised activities, look at her website, and move on with my day as usual.

That night, I was so excited I couldn't sleep. As Jim snored at my side, I lay with my eyes wide open, wondering in what time frame I should complete this experiment. While I'm no natural athlete, I'm no stranger to endurance events. I've trained hard over the years and have (barely) finished a multiple-day 500-mile bike ride, (stiffly) flowed through 108 yoga sun salutations at one time, and spent weeks (huffing and puffing) trekking, climbing, and crawling my way through the Nepal Himalayas. I am drawn to test my physical limitations and have found that long-term events help me discover what I'm really made of. So why not apply the same principle to a more intellectual pursuit?

A month of living according to Oprah's recommendations seemed too easy, and a few months seemed arbitrary. But a full year felt right: a cycle of seasons in which to explore Oprah's influence and my ability to follow directions without question. Could I possibly last an entire year—a leap year, no less—as Oprah's crash-test dummy, placing myself at the mercy of her advice without resistance?

I was certainly game to find out.

First and foremost, I decided on a title for my project: Living Oprah. I wish I had an amazing story about how I came up with that, but there isn't one. It just popped into my brain. It was simple, succinct, and struck the right chord for me.

But how would I keep myself accountable and inform my friends, family and, colleagues about Living Oprah? Although I was gun-shy about blogging, it seemed be the perfect medium. It's easily updatable, accessible to readers, and it's gloriously free. On December 14, 2007, I set up my blog: www.LivingOprah.com. I was nervous. I felt out of touch because I had no clue what any of the blogosphere lingo meant or what might be construed as dreadful blog etiquette. I already had to google common Internet abbreviations such as DH, IDK, and JMO. To all of these and more, I had to wonder, WTF? But I would learn. And besides, I was certain my audience would be comprised of my mom and...well, that's it...just Mom.

I was also anxious about making all my private thoughts public and I definitely didn't want to embarrass the daylights out of my husband. I decided the perfect solution would be to remain completely anonymous, going simply by the moniker LO, short for Living Oprah. Sure, my friends and family would know that I was committed to the project, but beyond that circle, people didn't need to know my name.

In the planning stages of Living Oprah, if you can call the last 17 days of December 2007 "planning stages," I thought I'd apply for grants and sponsorship to support my project financially. My husband and I weren't exactly rolling in dough, and we had to be careful and wise with our budget. He's an artisan who works for a tile manufacturer and I am a yoga teacher, and during the first half of 2008, I'd also be working on my graduate thesis at a very pricey art school.

So patronage seemed like the right way to go. Did I mention how expensive art school is? It costs a fortune to hone one's craft and earn a degree in a vocation almost guaranteed to provide a life of barely making ends meet, frequently doubting one's career choice, and taking a day job simply because it offers health insurance. I know many of you folks in the arts can relate. And if you aren't in the field, please tip your barista well.

Sponsorship and advertising for a Web-based project inevitably require banner ads and wacky animated links. I know they are a necessary evil on some sites, as click-thru advertising generates revenue, and while I could have used the money, I really didn't want the distraction. Also, I thought advertisers would have an impact on my project. What if a sponsor wanted to have some say in the content of my site? I couldn't allow that. Most important, since I would be attempting to determine how Oprah's advertisers impact her message to us, it seemed mighty hypocritical for me to use them.

I came to the conclusion that it would be too easy to have financial help. One of the reasons I decided to spend a whole year Living Oprah was to see if it's remotely feasible to live entirely as a celebrity guru says the average Jane should. To draw the most honest conclusion about whether the benefits outweighed the costs, I had to use my own means. I was interested (and a little scared) to see what psychological impact this would have on me, and felt I would be deviating from my project's intent if I avoided its financial demands.

With the decision made to fund this project on my own, I clarified exactly how I'd follow Oprah's advice for the year. I decided to turn to the Big Three: *The Oprah Winfrey Show*, *O, The Oprah Magazine*, and Oprah.com. If Oprah gave a directive of any kind through one of these outlets, I'd follow it. If one of Oprah's guests gave a piece of advice on her show, I'd act upon it only if Oprah personally backed it up. Additionally, if Oprah wrote a suggestion to us in her "Here We Go!" letter or her "What I Know for Sure" column in *O* magazine, I would take heed. In fact, if she made a suggestion anywhere in the public eye or ear, I latched on. I committed to taking all of her suggestions quite literally and would leave as little to interpretation as possible.

I would use Oprah.com in a slightly different manner. As it contains all Oprah-approved material, I'd refer to it as my encyclopedia for living. If I planned an event, desired advice on fashion, required remedies for stress, or even if I needed a way to ease strife in my marriage, I'd search Oprah's website for solutions and guidance.

Armed with my rules, my blog, and my remote control, I was ready to roll. The year 2007 was coming to a close. I bade a fond farewell to free will and embraced Living Oprah with open arms.

Back to my New Year's Day party (fade out the flashback music, bring the lights up to full)....

I've detailed the whole Living Oprah project to my guests and am witnessing a moment that harkens back to the old opening of the Richard Dawson version of *Family Feud*. My friends are frozen in a vignette: mouths full of Mushroom, Goat Cheese, and Caramelized-Shallot Pizza, looking alternatively distraught, anxious, and uncomfortable. Luckily for me, they could all win awards for their sense of humor, and the room soon erupts into laughter. But the hilarity too soon devolves into cautious giggles. They're worried about me. Will I have enough money to make all the purchases Oprah asks of her viewers? Will my marriage last? Jim busies himself with refilling people's drinks so he doesn't have to answer any questions that start with, "Jim, how do *you* feel about..."

My friends voice concern over whether there are enough hours in the day to live under Oprah's rule.

"That's one of the reasons I am doing this project," I tell them. "If it runs me ragged, then so be it."

There are many women in my life who look up to Oprah and feel inadequate in comparison to her. But why should we compare our lifestyles to that of one of the wealthiest and most powerful people in the public eye? I remember an episode of *Oprah* about germs and cleanliness. The TV hostess mentioned she prefers her bedsheets changed every other day. At that point in my life, I was digging around in the cushions of my sofa for enough quarters to do my laundry. I vividly remember wondering, while watching that show back in 2004, if Oprah could empathize with my priorities.

It's clear to me that she very much wants to share with her audience what she's learned over the years. She offers herself as a guide, a teacher, a role model. But is Oprah's ideal possible for women who don't have domestic help, who have families to manage, and who can barely make ends meet? Her show is filled with "musts" and "gottas" and "can't live withouts." These are incredibly strong words coming from such an influential media figure. Let's face it, when Oprah says jump, millions of people—mainly women—ask, "How high?"

My friend Joe looks concerned for me and offers his help. I've worked with him for years creating ensemble-based theater projects, and he knows how much I thrive on collaboration. I thank him but tell him I want to handle this one alone. "So many women around the world allow Oprah to dictate what we should read, watch, listen to, how we should cook, exercise, organize, and how we should vote. I want to find out if Living Oprah is actually the road to happiness and fulfillment. Besides," I tell him, "it's something I need to try on my own or else it'll feel like cheating."

Oprah is admirable. I find her career path from rags to riches awe-inspiring and can understand why many want to be just like her or at least learn how to put her secrets to success to work in their own lives. In the earlier years of her syndicated television program, women were able to relate to her struggles, her excitement at meeting celebrities, and her amazement at coming into contact with those living on society's fringe. We imagine that she can relate to us and we to her. However, with her overwhelmingly privileged lifestyle, can she still be the voice of the everywoman? Surely she can sympathize, but can she still speak for us? Well, she does. And we listen. We fall in love with her decorator, her doctor, her chef. Oprah defines how high we set the bar for ourselves, and based on her suggestions, we challenge ourselves to meet tough expectations.

It's vitally important for women to question the sources of influence and persuasion in our lives. We are inundated with get rich/get thin/get married suggestions every time we turn on the TV or walk by the magazine rack. And sadly, we tend to judge ourselves against seemingly impossible standards. I want to get to the bottom of why this cycle exists and find out how I'm complicit in it. I spend a lot of time worrying and bellyaching about it, but that's just a waste of time and energy. I want to better understand myself, other women, the self-help entertainment industry, and Oprah Winfrey.

My friends munch thoughtfully on their blueberry bars and I cringe to see Joe begin to inspect the layers of his.

One friend pipes up, "If this project kills you, can I have your kitten?" (Note to self: Adjust guest list for next year's party.)

We all laugh, turn the subject away from Oprah, and begin to debate which film should kick off this year's movie marathon. It dawns on me that I should have Netflixed *The Color Purple*.

Joe places his half-eaten bar on the edge of his plate, turns to me, and repeats quietly, "Seriously, if you need any help on this, let me know."

I can't understand why everyone is so anxious.

Jim puts his hand on my knee reassuringly.

"This is gonna be a piece of cake," I whisper to him. But my friends have me wondering if it'll be less like angel food cake and more like Oprah's 400-pound 50th birthday cake.

It's about five minutes until the start of the first Oprah show of 2008. I know it's going to be a rerun, but still, I sit bolt upright on my couch with my laptop, notebook, pens, pencils, highlighters, remote controls, and a nutritious snack. I could be mistaken for the suck-up student on the first day of school who sprints into the classroom, breathless, in order to sit in the front row and impress the teacher. Actually, if memory serves, that *is* what I did in high school. I can't imagine why I wasn't very popular.

My husband, rushing to leave for work, hurries back and forth in front of the TV. He keeps blocking my view and it's driving me crazy, so I'm forced to pull out that oldie but goody: "You make a better door than a window." He rolls his eyes at me and I remind him I'm not sitting around *enjoying* morning talk shows while he heads out to bring home the bacon, I'm doing *research*.

"This is going to be a long year," he grumbles but smiles sweetly before kissing me on the head and flying out the door.

I sigh out all my tension. Alone at last. Just me, the television set, and Oprah Winfrey.

Like I said, today's episode will be a rerun, as will the next couple of weeks' shows. No matter. If the show is on, I'll be watching, taking notes, and following directions. Just because an episode has had a previous airing doesn't mean I'm off the hook. It's possible that I'm a glutton for punishment. As I watch the show, I want to be slammed with Oprah's assignments, as if being swamped will prove my commitment to the experiment. And yet the thought of being bombarded by a steady stream of Oprah's directives produces a stubborn streak in me.

As if she senses my rebellion, I receive my first bit of advice from Winfrey: "You have to get things tailored. This whole idea that you can buy things off the rack...and they're supposed to fit you perfectly... It's ridiculous."

I guess I'm ridiculous. I can count on two fingers the number of times I've had clothing tailored in the past. My wardrobe of choice is generally low-key and low maintenance. Whether I'm teaching, going to the supermarket, or meeting a friend for dinner, I can usually be found leaving my front door in black yoga pants and cotton tank top, Jim lint-brushing cat hair off my butt. I scribble "tailor clothes" on my to-do list and grin broadly at the first assignment at the top of my otherwise blank legal pad.

It is quite easy to wish for more to do in the first days of January. School isn't yet in session and I have a lot of free time on my hands. This is unusual. I tend to fill up every moment of my day with activity and deadlines until, inevitably, I regret it. I always swear that if I can make it through my projects without keeling over, I'll never over-extend myself again. Even when I have downtime, I pack it tight with activity. If I were to draw a picture of what I look like on a day off, the image would depict me neatening up my living room, eating lunch, and watching old episodes of *Buffy the Vampire Slayer*. I would be moving back and forth between two knitting projects, planning my next yoga class, hitting refresh on my laptop to see if new e-mail arrived, all the while returning phone calls to friends and paging through a fitness magazine. This is how I'd define a relaxing afternoon. Doing everything I enjoy in life. All at once.

Maybe Oprah has some insights to share on the topic of self-care, and I might actually find some peace this year. I'm 35 now, and for the past five years or so, my chronic Superwoman syndrome has teetered dangerously close to becoming a key ingredient in a recipe for emotional disaster. But—and this is a big but—multitasking to the point that I can barely see straight has served me well, and it's hard to let go of a quality that's helped me out in so many ways. For instance, anyone who works in non-Equity Chicago theater knows when you sign on to be part of a production, you're inevitably expected to help build the set, hang posters up around town, assist with marketing, and if you're not required to be onstage, you'll probably end up working the box office at some point. This all takes place in the hours you're not in rehearsal or working your 40-hour-a-week day job. I've been scraping by as a writer, director, and actor in this environment for the past 15 years and as a result have turned into a human version of a Swiss Army knife. I fear if I ever lose my usefulness, I'll be replaced by a newer, sharper model.

I do trust in my ability to get a job done, and in the safety of my living room I feel ready to take on the world. I've read my January copy of *O* from cover to cover and already completed my first assignments from Oprah:

- "Quick, name five terrific things about yourself!" (I'm funny, I'm loyal, I'm a good daughter, wife, and friend, I can laugh at myself, I'm willing to take risks.)
- "Give yourself a time-out. Get into bed with a good book, the Sunday paper, or your favorite magazine...unplug the phone, and instruct, bribe, beg, command your family to grant you a few blissful minutes of rest..." (I spend an hour in bed reading the paper, wondering when I can get up and make good use of my time.)
- "...reinvigorate your appearance with some great advice on how not to look old..." (I learn that dressing too young for my age makes me look older and, as suggested, I pack up my graphic T-shirts and cargo pants and put them in the back of my closet for the year.)
- "...rethink your eating habits with some absolutely delicious and utterly original meals..." (The Smoky Halibut Paella with Brown Basmati Rice looks yummy but time-consuming.)
- "...just plain enjoy my interview with the dazzling Denzel Washington." (Done. With pleasure.)

The glossy pages of *O* reflected a lifestyle quite different from my own. As I paged through the lovely clothing, the jewelry, the adorable bric-a-brac, I felt like I was visiting a natural history museum and viewing a diorama of how the other half lives. I am ashamed to say I found myself wishing I could own a lot of this stuff (especially the most gorgeous $275 bathrobe I've ever seen and probably never will in reality). I had an honest to goodness emotional response to these images. Paging through the magazine's editorial pages and advertisements, in my mind's eye I chose the items I would buy if I could afford them. And because I am very generous in my imagination, I also thought about what I'd purchase for my mom (a gorgeous cashmere scarf), my sister, Elisabeth (cocktail rings for every finger), my girlfriends (super cute purses). As fun as it was to visit fantasyland in the moment, afterward, the excursion made me feel lacking. It made me very aware of what I can't have—what I didn't really think I even wanted before I saw those images. And instead of brushing it off easily, I actually felt bad. The magazine made these items look so much fun to own. But what fun is it to be reminded that I am not one of the people who gets to wear the $178 pair of miracle jeans that *O*'s fashion team celebrates for making every woman appear slim and sleek?

I felt so removed from the world I saw in these glossy images that I expected to be held at arm's length by the articles, as well. I was quite relieved when I read them, however. I had a preconceived notion that they would be fluffy or perhaps aimed at a very different demographic than my own. But, for the most part, I was wrong. Reading the magazine this year might prove enjoyable and, hopefully, constructive. While the material items chosen to grace the pages of the magazine were reminders that I didn't—or couldn't—belong to this club of women, the writing was far more inclusive and encompassing. I got sucked into self-help articles by Martha Beck and Suzan Colón and tell-it-like-it-is financial advice by Suze Orman. Just as Oprah's audience is mainly female, so are most of the contributors to the magazine. I was impressed by Oprah's ability to attract intelligent women willing to share their knowledge in the pages of her magazine. But I wished their work didn't have to be enveloped by photos of lipsticks, articles on "yoga for your face" and psychotainer/entertiatrist Dr. Phil.

When I had a fever as a little kid, my folks would crush my aspirin into a teaspoon of sugar water to disguise the flavor of the bitter pill. This seemed to be a grown-up version of the old aspirin trick. *O, The Oprah Magazine* hides life lessons within pages of sweet treats.

Maybe I shouldn't have a license to read magazines that are filled with pretty things. They tend to give me a bit of an inferiority complex. I tell myself I buy magazines for inspiration and entertainment, but in the end, I almost invariably compare myself and my life to what is shown in the idealized imagery. For several years I was on a complete magazine fast. I wouldn't even pick one up to pass the time in a waiting room, partly because I was working on my own empowerment and partly because I'm a germophobe. You might see a three-year-old copy of *Golfer's Digest* in my doctor's office, but I see enough bacteria to bring civilization as we know it to its knees.

But I digress....

Fashion magazines were the worst for me. Logically, I know those images don't reflect real women. Before I became a yoga teacher I was a graphic designer and understand the magical power of Photoshop. I know how to make a five foot four inch woman with curves look like a six foot two inch alien who could pass through a keyhole. Even with that comprehension, looking at those models and actresses still made me feel like my butt was a little squishier, my hair a little frizzier, and my teeth a bit more crooked than could ever pass for beautiful. Knowing I had this embarrassing tendency to allow an inanimate object make me feel crappy, I went cold turkey. And it felt good. I felt free from the desire to compare myself to some media-manufactured idea of beauty. But like a drug addict who never truly kicks the habit, one day I found myself in the magazine section of a convenience store, looking for a fix. Stupid *Vanity Fair* Young Hollywood issue!

I am very curious to see what my relationship with *O* will be over the next eleven-plus months. I am hoping I'll be able to see past the advertising and sweet treats in order to benefit from the wisdom of the contributors.

January 8, 2008
I discover a discrepancy between Oprah's priorities and my own. On a show that insists it is giving its audience bargain ideas to decorate ourselves and our homes, Oprah tells her guest, "I think in terms of investment... the best thing you can ever give yourself is to have beautiful surroundings."

I freeze. My husband and I are in the midst of robbing Peter to pay Paul to cover health-care expenses, and I am up to my eyeballs in student loan debt. I struggle to pay my bills and often create artwork at grad school based on the materials and time I can afford. Oprah seems to genuinely think she is helping us, but when she utters those words, all I hear is "Let them eat cake." In my world, the best investment I can make is staying healthy, getting a better education, and traveling to see my family.

I've already received comments through my daily blog and e-mails from my handful of readers who are upset by the divide between Oprah's world and their own. I speculate that it isn't a matter of jealousy due to her wealth. Folks are mainly irked that she continues handing out advice while they believe she has no idea what it means to live in their reality.

On the other end of the spectrum, I also hear from women who believe Oprah can do no wrong. They share their opinion that because of her philanthropic work and generosity to her audience, she is above reproach. While I don't believe anyone is above criticism, I can't disagree: Oprah does make a positive impact in the world and inspires many others to do the same.

Everyone who writes in is passionate about her or his point of view, and I feel energized by all the enthusiasm. I add poll questions to the blog each week to gain more insight about their perspective. And while it's challenging, I consider it my job to remain as neutral as possible. Although, truth be told, fence-straddling is not an event for which I'd win Olympic gold. I'm floored that anyone is even reading my blog, to be honest. As of today, I have 738 visitors checking out my website. Where have they all come from? I'll never question the power of a forwarded e-mail again, as my friends and family must have dispersed the announcement of my project to everyone in their address books. I feel like I'm hosting a coffee klatch on my computer, and I get a thrill every time I see I've received a new comment or e-mail.

January 14, 2008
Reruns are mercifully over. New topics, new guests, new obstacles to overcome. I'm like a kid in a candy store—which is ironic because this morning's episode is about how Americans are getting fatter and fatter. Oprah and her fitness expert, Bob Greene, are traveling to Mississippi, the fattest state in the country, to kick off their 2008 Best Life Challenge. They are encouraging the denizens of the town of Meridian to tackle their personal demons and take care of themselves, and the

at-home viewers are asked to do the same. We are told to download and sign our Best Life contract today.

While my heart goes out to the obese guests, I am distracted because Oprah looks disengaged. Is it because of her own weight struggles? This can't be an easy topic for her. I wish I weren't so strongly inclined to mention "Oprah" and "weight" in the same sentence, because I usually wish everyone would just leave her alone and allow her body to be her own business. I think the trouble is that Oprah has always invited us into her weight loss celebrations and has spoken with such certainty that *this* time she has it beat. When she does this, she gives an already overly nosy celebrity-watching culture a free pass to speculate on her dress size.

I have always felt empathy for Oprah because of her public battle with weight. It's because I've been in the same pain, had the same frustration, allowed my weight to yo-yo in an extreme manner. I've been fat and I've been thin. I've used food to numb the stress in my life. I've had trouble with my thyroid and wondered if my metabolism was on permanent vacation. I've felt inferior when I was heavier and on top of the world when I slimmed down. I've known logically that I should be able to love my body at any size, but struggled to do so. I can imagine that my humiliation factor would have gone up exponentially had my entire weight history been witnessed and judged by millions, frequently used as a punch line by late-night talk show hosts.

While Oprah might live in a glamorous world, beyond my imagination, she is also a painfully public display of a dangerous epidemic to which many of us can relate. In fact, according to the Centers for Disease Control statistics, 63 percent of Americans are overweight. We can see ourselves reflected in Oprah's struggles. Sadly, I think many judge her without understanding her life-threatening problem. And I have to wonder if her detractors get a smug satisfaction from seeing someone who lives a life of luxury be repeatedly defeated by a lifelong battle. Oprah's years of riding the weight roller coaster have been a lesson for me. I can't tell you how many times I've thought that if I just had enough money for a personal trainer, chef, dietician, and stylist I could have a great body and always look terrific. Well, Oprah has access to all this and more, and she still struggles. This is proof that the grass is not always greener on the other side of the TV screen.

I'm in pretty decent shape these days, but I'm curious to see how this Best Life Challenge will impact my eating habits and exercise routine. I've downloaded my contract. It states:

Get on board and make the commitment. Sign the contract—hang it wherever you need that extra bit of motivation. You're on your way to living your Best Life!

I hereby commit to living my Best Life. I will participate in a program of regular exercise, including a minimum of 80 minutes of activity over the course of four days each week. I will focus on challenging my abilities in the pursuit of elevating my physical performance. I will endeavor to be conscious of when I eat, and consistently terminate the consumption of all food two or three hours before bedtime. I will also be aware of why I eat, and will, to the best of my ability, eat primarily to satisfy my nutritional needs as opposed to my emotional needs. I will do my best to make healthful food choices by substituting foods that are nutritionally empty with those that are rich in nutrition.

Furthermore, I realize that this contract carries no promise of rewards, penalties or punishments other than those associated with the reflection of the strength of my character and of my health.

I sign my name on the contract. This all sounds doable, and I'm not as intimidated as I expected to be, although I am disturbed that the "strength of my character" is tied to how well I manage to diet and exercise. That seems harsh. I never judged Oprah's character based on her body. Regardless, 80 minutes of activity a week isn't too vigorous and is much less exercise than conventional wisdom suggests (30 minutes a day five times a week). I already exercise more than 80 minutes most weeks but will definitely benefit from showing up at the Y more consistently. The only thing that sounds like a real challenge to me is that I'll have to stop eating two to three hours before I hit the hay.

There are some days I don't get home from teaching until 9:30 PM. After my physically demanding job, I need to eat when I get in. Now I'll have to make certain I don't go to sleep before the allotted window closes. Staying up past my bedtime to fulfill this suggestion is not exactly making me dance a jig of happiness (unless dancing counts toward my contracted minutes of exercise, in which case, I'll jig).

Hold the phone! Oprah says she's not going to sign her contract for a couple days. She wants to drink champagne at an upcoming event, and as Greene informs us, once the contract is signed, we're not allowed to drink alcohol for at least a month or two. I look at my signed contract and groan to think of all the goodies I'll miss out on during my mom's big birthday bash tomorrow night. I'm not happy that Oprah isn't signing today with the rest of us. She admitted on the show that she needs to get back on track, and if we have to put our excuses aside (along with the sinfully delicious deep-fried pot stickers at my mom's favorite restaurant in Chicago), I wish Oprah would as well. I know it's ridiculous to connect my enjoyment of the Challenge to Winfrey's commitment, but I think it'd be more fun if she signed today. We all want the most popular girl in school on our team. I bet if she played her cards right, we'd even let her be captain.

January is coming to a close and I am very excited to learn what Oprah's Book Club selection will be. Her last choice, *Pillars of the Earth,* was a sweeping historical drama. As highfalutin as I'd like to think my literary choices are in general, I am a sucker for this genre. While I might have taken the cover off of *The Other Boleyn Girl* so nobody in my graduate-level writing classes knew I was reading the bodice ripper, I savored every word.

Pillars is a long book—my mass market paperback looked like a brick at 983 pages—but it's a quick and fun novel. I actually read my mother's copy when I was in high school, titillated by all the sex. It was just as much fun to reread when I was double the age but evidently no more mature, as I still eagerly awaited the next down-and-dirty-behind-the-pillar moment. By the time I started the Living Oprah project, Oprah's foray into Ken Follett's drama about horny medieval cathedral builders was coming to a close.

I am eager to hear what the next novel will be. My fingers are crossed for a contemporary author. I'd love to read something by a wry, clever, thought-provoking author such as (dare I dream it?) David Sedaris. Looking at the list of past selections, I see very few books that would provoke a big belly laugh. I think this might be the year. So the carpet is truly pulled out from under my feet, *yanked*, if you will, when Oprah heralds her newest Book Club selection, *A New Earth: Awakening to Your Life's Purpose*, by Eckhart Tolle.

Oprah says, "If you're interested in becoming all that you were created to be, if you want to begin to live your best life from the inside out, not looking at external ways for doing that, but how you really can begin to fulfill the potential of your life, this is the book for you."

Oy! This sounds like work, not pleasure—a sit cross-legged and ponder my inner demons kind of book, not a melt into a bubble bath and relax kind of book. As phenomenal as Winfrey makes this publication sound, I soon discover it isn't powerful enough on its own. Just like Butch Cassidy needed Sundance and chocolate cries out for peanut butter, Tolle's book also needs the perfect pairing. Oprah tells us, "You're gonna need one of these for reading *A New Earth*." She holds a bright yellow pen in the air, for all to see: the Post-It Flag Highlighter from 3M. Suspicious about how much a writing implement will enhance my spiritual growth, I add the product to my shopping list.

I'm always a bit wary when I hear that someone else believes that he or she holds the key that might unlock a previously sealed door to my enlightenment. Part of this is because of pride. I get prickly at the implication that (a) I don't know my life's purpose and (b) simply living my life isn't a valid enough journey without the wisdom of a questionably qualified outsider. Is it necessary to buy into someone else's plan to quicken my evolution as a human being? Somehow the writers of these books, the purveyors of these pearls of wisdom, were able to find a deeper sense of peace, joy, or enlightenment by seeking out and following their own path. I wish they would trust that we all have the ability to do the same. Right off the bat, Oprah's announcement makes me sullen and sulky.

Insult is added to injury. Not only will there be an absence of bodice-ripping in my near future, Oprah makes an announcement that we are also to sign up for a ten-week webinar that includes online classes every Monday night to be taught by Tolle and Winfrey. The course begins in March, and yes, like most classes, this one will also require homework — ten weeks of workbook pages to complete. I revert to my 15-year-old, stubborn, homework-avoiding, excuse-generating self. I don't wanna do homework! I don't wanna soul search! I wanna hang out with my friends! If I had a staircase in my home, there would be some *major* stomping up to my room and door slamming. This is not a good start to kick off my spiritual journey. Maybe I need to read this book after all.

As assigned, I immediately get myself a copy and sign up for the class. For the first few days I own *A New Earth*, I find myself glowering at the bright orange book and busying myself with other projects. I can't help but feel that cracking open the front cover will be like popping the top off a can of worms. Exhausting worms.

Speaking of the front cover, I have a weird feeling about carrying one of Oprah's Book Club picks around in public. Pre–Living Oprah, I never bought a book with the *O* seal on the jacket. Why? I can't quite put my finger on it. I've never been embarrassed that I watch her show, so I'm not entirely certain why I have such a strong feeling about these books. I think part of the reason is because Oprah is so tightly tied to pop culture and I didn't want to advertise that I allowed trends to drive my literary decisions. Also, before this year of Living Oprah began, I didn't really want to give the impression that I belonged to a "club" led by a talk show host. In fact, I would resent it if I went to a bookseller, found a book I was interested in, and discovered it was also part of Oprah's Book Club. I would even search the shelves for a copy that didn't have the telltale seal on the front cover. Why would I want to advertise for Oprah when I wasn't part of her organization? I never understood why people who didn't attend Harvard or have a child who attended Harvard would wear a sweatshirt with HARVARD emblazoned on it, so why would I carry a book with OPRAH'S BOOK CLUB on the cover when I wasn't part of the club? I'd rather wear a sweatshirt that said HARVARD on it. At least I've seen *Legally Blonde*. Twice.

Also, I always felt as if Oprah took sort of ownership of a book when her name was on the front cover and wonder what the Book Club would be without her branding on the jacket. I would bet money — hypothetical money of course, this is a recession — that it wouldn't be as powerful a merchandising tool. I believe that many people are drawn to a book not just because they heard Oprah mention it on her show but because it sits in a special section of their brick-and-mortar or dot-com bookstore. They buy it because they *do* want to be part of the club that I shy away from. They proudly display Oprah's stamp of approval on their book covers. I've seen women nod to one another and laugh on the Chicago El train when they realize they're both reading the same Oprah pick (this was years back and *She's Come Undone* was Oprah's favorite book).

But here's where I get really torn. Oprah is getting people reading, so why on earth should I complain? I spend countless hours commuting by Chicago's public transit system each week, and the majority of my fellow bus and train passengers are usually plugged into something electronic. They're not reading. But Oprah inspires people to appreciate the printed word. I love books. I am a writer. Therefore, shouldn't I love that Oprah loves books and authors? I feel I should be over the moon that there is a public figure suggesting that Americans should read. No other modern-day influential figure drives us toward specific literature like Oprah. The last time I had someone like her in my life, it was a crotchety literature professor in college who handed out a mile-long reading list to a room of groaning, hungover coeds.

Oprah's deciding a lot for us. She's creating our literature syllabus, and until this year I've never registered for her class. I wonder if I'll giggle with other commuters as we mouth to one another over our copies of *A New Earth*, "What page are you on?"

"Are you enlightened yet?"

"Keep reading, you'll love the part when you learn the meaning of life!"

Jim and I sit down to a dinner of Mustard Grilled Chicken and Roast Potatoes with Lemons. After searching for recipes on Oprah.com that would appeal to my husband, I spent a couple hours shopping, prepping, and cooking. The apartment smells fantastic. I cook most nights of the week, but I'm more of an improviser in the kitchen and tend to shy away from recipes. Because of my mad-scientist-meets-the-Swedish-Chef-from-the-Muppets cooking style, the results are sometimes fantastic, and other times we end up ordering Thai. Following a recipe isn't my cup of tea, but as I cooked tonight, I was relaxed knowing the end product had been tested and approved and there would be little room for failure. I adored the look on Jim's face when he came home from work to a welcoming smell wafting from the kitchen.

We dig in, and after just a few bites, Jim asks if I'll make this meal again. I am both thrilled and annoyed. I guess I wish he'd said something along the lines of, "Well, it's good, but it can't hold a candle to your cooking."

With a mouthful of potato, he casually mentions that a coworker of his mom asked why I'm making fun of Oprah. My heart leaps into my throat. It didn't occur to me that I was giving that impression. First off, I don't think I could spend an entire year making fun of anybody without all that negativity burning me to a piece of coal. A tiny, hard, angry, Robyn-shaped piece of black rock. What an ugly way to spend my days that would be. Nope. Not making fun of Oprah. Also, between you and me—don't tell Oprah—I'm a little bit afraid of her. Living in Chicago, sometimes you can feel her influence pulsating in the city, through the airwaves. She's like the Wizard of Oz. Except she really *does* have power and isn't some flaccid "man behind the curtain." Because she's such an omniscient presence in pop culture, media, and entertainment—and because I am an itty-bitty bug holding on as tightly as I can to make a career in the arts—I'm slightly scared she could squash me with one of her painfully uncomfortable Christian Louboutin heels.

Besides, this project is just as much a critique of myself as it is of Oprah. I am part of a celebrity-watching culture that puts one woman up on a pedestal even as it nudges another off a cliff. I am a consumer. I am a television watcher. I am a Web-surfing-Internet-junkie-Facebook-friend. And I am always seeking a deeper understanding of myself. Oprah's media empire caters to people like me. As much as I'd like to think of myself as my subversive, ideological, fearless teenage self, I'm just not. I'm a 35-year-old woman who frets about the newly forming wrinkles on my forehead all the way down to my carbon footprint. I have been shaped by pop culture, by the self-help industry, by fads, and by the media. Oprah is at the epicenter of influence, and her power is ever growing, ever flourishing with the times. As I witness Oprah dip into new media and deepen her stronghold over the world of infotainment, I wonder whether I am a creation of hers, or vice versa.

A note about the monthly accounting charts: I do not include behind-the-scenes project-related costs, such as the amount of money I spent on VHS tapes for the year, or the time I spent blogging everyday. These logistics were integral to Living Oprah, but they were obviously not advised by Winfrey. I felt it would be unfair to pad my monthly totals by adding them here.

Additionally, the charts show when advice and suggestions were received, although assignments may have been completed on a different date within 2008.

January 2008 Accounting

Date	Assignment	Cost	Time	Notes
1/1	Subscribe to *O, The Oprah Magazine. (LO)*	25.92	0h 5m	1-year subscription for $21.97 plus $3.95 for Jan. 2008 issue
1/1	Read *O* from cover to cover. *(LO)*		2h 30m	Mmmm...pretty things...
1/1	"Quick, name five terrific things about yourself!" *(MAG)*		0h 5m	I'm funny, I'm loyal, I'm a good daughter, wife, and friend, I can laugh at myself, I'm willing to take risks.
1/1	"Give yourself a time-out. Get into bed with a good book, the Sunday paper, or your favorite magazine...unplug the phone, and instruct, bribe, beg, command your family to grant you a few blissful minutes of rest...." *(MAG)*		1h 0m	I should do this more often, I'm sure, but it's not in my nature to put time aside for myself.
1/1	"Reinvigorate your appearance with some great advice on how not to look old..." *(MAG)*		1h 0m	I went through the 25 things on the "gotta go" list and tore through my closet. I think this will be an ongoing, yearlong project....I'm going to log the initial hour, but know with my taste, it'll be never ending! **(O)**
1/1	"Rethink your eating habits with some absolutely delicious and utterly original meals..." *(MAG)*		0h 0m	I rethought them. I think I eat very well but could spice things up and add more variety. **(O)**

1/1	"Just plain enjoy my interview with the dazzling Denzel Washington…" *(MAG)*		0h 12m	I just realized that sometimes she's going to tell us to *feel* a certain way. This is weird. I'll do my best.
1/1	Blueberry Oatmeal Bars. *(SHOW/WEB)*	18.31	0h 45m	*Deceptively Delicious* highlighted on *Oprah*. I visited her website and found this recipe.
1/1	Mushroom, Goat Cheese, and Caramelized-Shallot Pizza. *(WEB)*	38.39	0h 45m	This created several pizzas for about a dozen people. We kept making them fresh as people ate them. Big hit.
1/2	"One of the big secrets for women to understand is you have to get things tailored." *(SHOW)*	10.00	3h 15m	2 pairs of pants altered. I altered 2 dresses by hand (hem, strap length). Moved buttons on a blouse. I'm a terrible seamstress, but getting better.
1/4	Use cloth and reusable bags at grocery store. No more plastic. *(SHOW)*	8.98	0h 5m	I bought one bag at Trader Joe's, one at Whole Foods. We have others as well. We carry bags around with us "just in case." ($4.99 for one bag, $3.99 for another) **(O)**
1/4	Change lightbulbs to energy-efficient bulbs. *(SHOW)*	56.00	0h 15m	The $56 was for the initial purchase. As conventional bulbs burn out, we replace them. **(O)**
1/8	"I think in terms of investment, it's the best thing you can ever give yourself is to have beautiful surroundings." *(SHOW)*		1h 0m	I spend an hour beautifying and decide this will have to be an ongoing project for me. **(O)**

(cont.)

January 2008 Accounting (*cont.*)

Date	Assignment	Cost	Time	Notes
1/9	"I would just say to anybody, whatever secret you're holding, live your own truth." *(SHOW)*		0h 0m	This is a major one. I have to ruminate on it daily and also in the evening to make certain I fulfill living my "own truth." **(O)**
1/10	Sharon Salzberg meditation. *(WEB)*		0h 10m	Discovered this audio file when I searched Oprah.com for stress relievers. I liked the guided meditation very much and will do it again. **(O)**
1/10	Switch from overhead lighting to lamps. *(SHOW)*		1h 0m	This just took some rearranging in our home. It was like doing a Rubik's Cube, but finally figured it out. (Oprah-approved Nate Berkus suggestion on show)
1/10	Put stuff on my walls that becomes art once I hang it. *(SHOW)*	51.39	2h 0m	$5 for antique plate, $44.10 antique vent grills, $2.29 for picture kit to hang these. Also stuck some things around the house on our walls.
1/10	Add sea life to rooms. *(SHOW)*		0h 15m	Used stuff we had in closets and drawers: a nautilus shell, a sand dollar, and some stones we collected at the ocean. This is not my decorating style. (Oprah-approved Nate Berkus suggestion on show)

1/10	Add a fabulous chair to each room. *(SHOW)*	429.68	4h 30m	$160 in kitchen, $19.33 in bathroom, $40 in bedroom, $13.00 in front room, $197.35 in living room. I decided to call the yoga ball I use as an office chair "fabulous" so I wouldn't have to get something new. (Oprah-approved Nate Berkus suggestion on show)
1/10	Frame important notes. *(SHOW)*	1.00	0h 10m	I reused some frames I already had. Only needed to buy one from dollar store.
1/10	Add books about subjects you love to each room. *(SHOW)*		0h 10m	Just took a tiny bit of rearranging. We tend to do this anyway. (Oprah-approved Nate Berkus suggestion on show)
1/10	Make your rooms personal. *(SHOW)*		3h 30m	Our rooms are in a constant state of flux as we continue "personalizing" them. It's been fun. I stopped counting the time at the end of January and will simply make this ongoing. **(O)**
1/14	Sign Best Life Challenge contract. *(SHOW)*		0h 2m	Download, print, sign. This Challenge will be an ongoing project though the year. **(O)**
1/16	See the movie *Juno* ASAP. *(SHOW)*	10.00	1h 36m	Well, I had already seen it and thought at first that covered the assignment. Then I realized that Oprah's wording meant I still had to go see it ASAP, so I did.

(cont.)

January 2008 Accounting (*cont.*)

Date	Assignment	Cost	Time	Notes
1/17	Oprah hopes we will buy Christiane Northrup's book *Women's Bodies, Women's Wisdom.* (SHOW)	13.91	19h 15m	(15 minutes to find lowest price; approx. 1140 minutes to read) This was a *great* buy. I read this book from cover to cover and have returned to it several times.
1/17	Read Book Club selection *Pillars of the Earth.* (BC)		17h 0m	I had a copy but can't figure out where it came from. Did someone leave it at my house? Let me know.
1/21	Take Peter Walsh's online clutter test. (WEB)		0h 5m	I'm mortified.
1/23	Make Mustard Grilled Chicken and Roast Potatoes with Lemons. (WEB)	17.54	2h 0m	Jim loved this meal so much. It encouraged me to continue cooking in this way. ($17.54 was for all ingredients not already in my pantry...why is it I never have mustard? Is someone stealing it?)
1/23	"If visiting New York, visit the museums but then go to Dylan's Candy Bar." (SHOW)		0h 20m	I've never wanted a salad as much as I did when I left that store.
1/23	Oprah wants everyone to taste a MoonPie. (SHOW)		0h 1m	Done.
1/23	Oprah hopes we will watch *African American Lives* on PBS. (SHOW)		4h 0m	Really interesting. Wish Henry Louis Gates, Jr., would research my family tree.

Date	Task	Cost	Time	Notes
1/23	"Please don't tell Bob Greene" about all the junk Oprah ate on the show today. (SHOW)		0h 0m	I promise I won't. But should we be keeping secrets about our food and feeling shameful about it?
1/25	Read "Feel the Heat" article. (WEB)		1h 0m	Trying to build sexual energy in my marriage while working on my MFA thesis is not so sexy. Going to revisit later this year. Will keep the lessons in mind moving forward, though.
1/29	Read Gavin de Becker's *The Gift of Fear.* (SHOW)	9.00	3h 0m	Is it ironic to be scared to read this?
1/30	Purchase Post-It Flag Highlighter Pen from 3M. (SHOW)	8.49	0h 30m	Oprah *loves* these. They seem like a waste of packaging and materials to me.
1/30	Get Eckhart Tolle's *A New Earth.* ("Run out and get your book.") (SHOW/BC)	8.40	0h 10m	The first book I've owned with Oprah's Book Club seal on the cover.
1/30	Register for Eckhart Tolle online class. (SHOW/BC)		0h 5m	Wonder if Oprah will be teaching? Moderating? Studying with us?
Through-out month	Watch every episode of *Oprah.* (LO)		23h 0m	23 episodes
Through-out month	Do Best Life Challenge exercise. (BLC)		4h 0m	80 minutes a week × 3 weeks: 240 minutes
TOTAL		707.01	98h 46m	

Accounting Abbreviations: LO = Living Oprah project task; SHOW = The Oprah Winfrey Show; WEB = Oprah.com; MAG = O, The Oprah Magazine; BC = Oprah's Book Club; BLC = Best Life Challenge; (O) = ongoing project

FEBRUARY:

An enterprising month

Time spent this month: 67 hours, 8 minutes

Dollars spent this month: $669.31

Most inspiring suggestion: "Remember, it's not just about money. It's about what you can do for somebody else. Rally your friends, your family, neighbors, and pull off your own Big Give. Be creative." I'm excited and a little daunted by this call to action.

Poll results from LivingOprah.com: Have you ever followed health advice seen on Oprah's show, website, or magazine?

Yes (53%)

No, but I've passed info along to someone else (5%)

No (41%)

O NE MONTH down.

Weekends have become quite a relief for me. Although I am unwavering when it comes to following my project rules, I've given myself Saturday and Sunday off from blogging. Who knew that writing daily could be more draining than my Best Life Challenge exercise? The issue is not the consistency of writing the blog, but that I'm not yet entirely at ease exposing my feelings online. I want Living Oprah to be completely transparent this year, but I twitch whenever I divulge financial fear or other insecurities to the strangers who read my website. Still, it's becoming less difficult and the anonymity definitely helps. So does my job. Going to teach at the yoga studio is a relief from being constantly "on." After all, in order to avoid being kicked in the head when assisting students into handstand, I must focus on the present moment (and flying feet), not the Oprah project. The hours I spend teaching allow me to take my attention off myself and be useful to other people. Oprah is right—doing things for others makes me feel great and gets me out of my own head. It's the one time during the day that I'm not wondering if I'm measuring up or if people think my out-fit is unflattering. Also (and I'm really ashamed to tell you this), since watching the show daily and reading the magazines, I've been judging whether other women are dressing to Oprah's specifications. It's not as if before the project I walked around without comparing myself to other gals—I'm no saint—but now my eyes constantly dart around a room to see if anyone else is floundering as miserably as I am at this.

Last night while channel surfing, Jim pointed at the TV and said, "That shirt is totally cutting that lady in half. It's a really bad length for her body type."

"Excuse me?" Worried that my husband's fashion commentary might be a sign of an impending apocalypse, I froze for a moment. Then I calmly asked where he learned to say such a thing and he looked sheepish. "Oprah?" I asked.

He nodded and flipped the channel to a masculine-looking show about crime-scene detectives. Clearly this project hasn't only changed me, it's adjusted the very cells in Jim's brain. I'm a little nervous that maybe he's judging me every time we leave the house together. He used to be the lowest-maintenance man I'd ever met when it came to clothing. As long as it fit and had no visible stains or tears, he'd wear it. I am not even sure he would have noticed if I wore a ball gown or a garbage bag out to dinner in the past. Now I've given him a bite of the apple from the tree of style knowledge and created a weapon that could be used against me at any moment. Next time I ask him if my outfit makes my butt look fat, he might actually say yes. Eek.

Whether the topic is style or spirituality, I find myself wavering between being thrilled by each new assignment and having a sort of knee-jerk, stubborn response. My hackles rise if Oprah touches on an area I am more sensitive about, like my home or my outward appearance.

On the flip side of the coin, I get a little jolt of excitement when she offers suggestions that apply to physical and emotional well-being.

Being a health junkie, I am excited to learn that in early February, Dr. Mehmet Oz is is going to lay out his antiaging plan for us. While I am happy to hear that the good doctor is visiting the show, I struggle with the term "antiaging." Why is the natural process of growing older considered a disease that we're all trying to eradicate? What a waste of time and energy and money to fight the inevitable. Of course, you should know that even as I wave my PROUD AT ANY AGE banner, I'm a big, fat hypocrite. I wish that getting older in this country wasn't seen as a fate worse than death, but I totally buckle under the pressure. I've been dyeing my hair since I was about 14 or so, when premature grays began to sprout faster than I could pluck them. So while fighting visible signs that I am a human being seems utterly ridiculous, I'm not immune. Neither, it seems, are the folks at O magazine. Copious advertisements for turn-back-time products are sandwiched between articles.

I have this totally idealistic dream that one day we'll all accept how we look as we age and stop spending money for every serum under the sun. And I truly am willing to let go of all my fear and the time I spend looking at the skin on the back of my hands. But I'll only do it if you do it first. I don't want to be the only haggard-looking one out here. Maybe if we all count to three and drop our antiaging regimens at the same time, we can create a new normal for women and allow the weight of self-criticism to be lifted from our shoulders. Until then, while I still need to keep up with all you smooth-skinned gals, I'm slathering on the eye cream. Call me if you want to start a revolution.

I wish I could once and for all separate the goal of a youthful appearance from the value of a healthy body. The aspect of the antiaging war I truly appreciate is when it addresses living, dare I say it, our "best lives" as long and as healthily as we can. I've applied my share of sunscreen in my time, but I've done a lot of harm, too. I was overweight and had a destructive lifestyle from college through my mid-20s and now, a decade later, I'm no Dara Torres, but I'm in the best shape of my life. And I want to keep getting better.

When The Oprah Winfrey Show runs promos about Dr. Oz, I have a Pavlovian response (sans drooling). Even if I weren't Living Oprah this year, I'd tune in to any episode she aired promising a sip from the Fountain of Youth. I know I am in good company. Some of my blog readers discuss getting and staying healthy for their families, or because it gives them confidence, and still others coyly admit to a bit of vanity. I think it's a combination of all of these for me, and although I don't have kids who beg to get bounced on my knee, I still want to stop my joints from creaking. And most important to me, my constant battle against the progression of double major scoliosis fuels my fire to stay healthy.

I have what you might know as an S curve made up of two 60ish-degree angles in my spine. Remember that kid who was always made fun of in junior high because of her back brace? Well, that wasn't me but it probably should have been. I avoided nasty nicknames because I didn't wear a brace as a child. I simply bounded about the playground with a diagnosed but untreated condition. That was all well and good for a sprightly and otherwise healthy kid, but it led to chronic pain as an adult.

My scoliosis is idiopathic, which is the medical community's way of saying "We have no idea why you have what you have or why it's getting worse." Basically, I have two options. I could have my spine fused and rods inserted in my back so the curvature doesn't worsen. If I do this, I won't be able to bend or twist—not the most exciting prospect for a yoga teacher. Or I can keep myself as strong and healthy as possible, biding my time until I hear about wild advancements in noninvasive spinal procedures. While the chronic pain sometimes makes me want to give up and schedule surgery, I prefer to keep myself off the operating table. I'm not trying to garner even the tiniest bit of sympathy here, but I do want to draw a clear picture of why I am so rapt whenever a doctor or alternative medical practitioner appears on the TV screen. I have a secret hope that someone will have information I've never heard. And even though I have a pretty strong suspicion that I'll never learn anything new when I tune in, I still watch without fail.

One of the reasons I was drawn to Oprah as a subject for this project was my continual search for new ways to manage my pain, keep my self-esteem from faltering, and ease the stress and fear associated with scoliosis. I've investigated various therapies and modalities, some physical, some spiritual and emotional, to help me cope with this lifelong journey. Through my research, I observed that several healing methodologies boasted some connection to Winfrey. "As Seen on *Oprah*!" was boldly posted on health-related websites and advertisements. Even before I conceived of Living Oprah, all roads were leading to her. Back then, I was dubious that I might find true aid and solace in front of the television. But now, fully invested in this project, I have an excuse to drop my apprehension and open myself to the possibility that Oprah's favored health-care professionals can help me improve my quality of life.

As Dr. Oz steps onto Winfrey's stage, I allow myself to wish today, with wild abandon, that I might acquire surprising knowledge to stop the effect of time and gravity on my body. I am disappointed that the info I hear on Dr. Oz's antiaging episode is data I've read, watched, or heard before. But Oprah and her staff have a magical way of presenting material so it feels new. Many folks in her audience look completely amazed by the advice they are receiving, as if they'd never before heard the word "antioxidant" or knew they were supposed to exercise. And who knew—fiber is good for you!

And speaking of fiber, we've all been urged on the *Oprah* show to strive toward *S*-shaped fecal matter. Not only do I stare at myself in every reflection I pass to make certain I am acceptably dressed, but now I need to study the toilet bowl to make sure I'm a proper pooper. Clearly, there is no aspect of my life that can remain untouched by Oprah's guidance. So much for my promise to Jim that I could compartmentalize this project without allowing it to affect my life in a meaningful way. If I'm to do this successfully, I've got to surrender more self-control and self-direction than I thought.

I watch Oprah's studio audience like a hawk. Their reactions seem so over the top at times, especially when she gives them a present. I think they'd have the same scream-until-glass-shatters response whether Oprah gave them a new car, the secret to marital bliss, or a pack of gum. Plus I'm always blown away when I hear the roar of the crowd when Oprah walks onstage.

I wonder what it must do to a person's psyche to be applauded just for coming to work. I think it would make us all feel more worthwhile at our jobs if there was an eruption of cheers every time we entered the boardroom, the stockroom, the classroom. I have to imagine that if people consistently tell you that you are important, you start to feel important. Highly valued. I am curious how that changes the way you walk through life.

Although I haven't been overly interested in attending a live taping of her show recently, I think this is the perfect year to get my butt back into a seat in Winfrey's studio. I've been there a couple times in the past, early in my Chicago tenure. Like visiting the top of the Sears Tower, strolling around the Lincoln Park Zoo, and eating a piece of deep-dish pizza, I felt that seeing a taping of *Oprah* was a Chicago institution that was not to be missed. The first time was around 1995 or so. It's a hazy memory, but I recall the guest panel was made up of people who were considered outsiders in their respective communities. I do remember that back then the show was more interactive, and we were invited to step up to a microphone to ask our burning questions.

The other taping was around 2001. I also barely remember this one, but I know I wore an atrocious orange-plaid blazer and was made fun of by my friends for months. Oh—and there was a male guest on the show who wanted to have sex so many times each day that his wife barely had enough time to put on a pair of pants.

It's my understanding that it's nearly impossible to get tickets to the show now. There are online tales of people who swear they've been applying for tickets for years without luck. When I mention my desire to see the show on my blog, one of my regular readers, Little Merry Sunshine, sends me a personal account about how a friend of hers got tickets to the show. Armed with her good advice, I visit Oprah.com.

I live less than eight miles from the television studio and can be there at a moment's notice, so things are a bit easier for me than for most people. As LMS advised, I find a list of soon-to-be-taped shows that are in need of audience members. One stands out in particular as they are looking for fans of the original *Star Trek* series as well as *Boston Legal*. If it looks like a duck and walks like a duck, then surely Oprah is going to be hosting William Shatner on her show! I haven't seen an episode of *Boston Legal*, but I've seen every single *Star Trek*, mainly watching them with my dad on Sunday afternoons during my adolescence. We'd sit on the couch, each of us with a big bowl of Chunky Beef Soup and Minute Rice in our laps, ready to witness the age-old battle between humans and the rest of the universe. It was like dinner theater. Ah, I loved those papier-mâché sets, laughable aliens, and the lavender eye shadow (worn by both the women *and* the men on the show). I share this story on the ticket request page of Oprah's website and also mention that my love of sci-fi endeared me to my husband when we were dating.

I am surprised by a speedy response. O's people find my admission of sci-fi dorkitude charming, and they call me up because they might have seat availability. However, they need me to e-mail a photo before they can tell me if there is a ticket. I send one immediately. Why the photo? In my excitement, I neglect to ask. Maybe they are concerned I am a nut who will show up at the studio in head-to-toe Klingon makeup and weaponry. Please. If I were to go in costume, I would totally dress as Uhura.

I might not be going in *Star Trek* attire, but I will be dressing in my best *Oprah Winfrey Show* audience member costume. Also, to fit in with the rest of the crowd and look pretty for the camera, I decide to wear makeup to attend the taping. This yoga teacher's cheeks very rarely feel the touch of a powder brush, but I purchase cosmetics recommended on Oprah.com and spend quite a bit of time applying the layers of paint according to instructions on the website. I feel a little clowny, but my husband thinks it is all in my head. Still, the weight of it on my face makes me feel as if I am wearing a disguise.

And Jim? He wants to go with me to the show, and the audience wrangler sounds as if she'd prefer me to bring someone along. Unfortunately, our cat is scheduled to be neutered at the exact same time as the taping. My husband and I think about postponing the surgery, but we are warned by the vet not to wait, so Jim agrees to take one for the team. I become nervous about the prospect of going all by myself and know the fun factor won't be as high without my partner in crime. Sadly, there isn't any time to arrange for another companion. I am going stag.

On a cold and gray Chicago morning, I head down to the television studio. There is a small group of us invited specifically for the Shatner taping. After we check in, we're taken upstairs to the audience waiting area. This room appears to hold several hundred people, but there are just a handful of us here now. We're treated very nicely and offered beverages and snacks. We all carry the *Star Trek* memorabilia we were instructed to bring to the show. With our phasers, starship *Enterprise* models, and alien figurines, we certainly aren't going to be mistaken for guests on an *Oprah* episode about hip trendsetters. We look more like we'd be lining up for a taping of "I Was Beaten Up in High School."

Most of the staff who greet us upstairs are friendly and welcoming. They chat with us about *Star Trek* and refer to a couple of the notes we sent to request tickets for today's taping. They are super high energy. The women I meet on the production staff are all dressed quite similarly, as if the stylists from *O* magazine chose their outfits this morning. It is probably the norm for most large companies to have a shared corporate culture. I've only seen a tiny cross-section of Oprah's employees so far, but this society of women seems to be defined physically by neatly tailored clothes (trendy but conservative), splashy accessories, and perfectly groomed eyebrows (in opposition to the Bert look I've perfected).

Their body types, ages, and skin colors may vary, but their style doesn't veer too far from center. I make a quick trip to the restroom before the show starts, and as I wash my hands I check myself out in the mirror. I giggle a bit when I realize I'm dressed in the exact same manner as everyone else upstairs. I feel a bit awkward here at the show, but at least externally, I fit right in. I wonder if it's wrong to be comforted by this.

I head back up to my seat in the holding area. We are informed that Oprah is doing multiple shows today and are invited to watch her live interview with Valerie Bertinelli in the waiting room. As we turn our eyes to a flat-screen TV, we see Oprah ask the former child star about her weight loss secrets. She seems especially interested in the weighted vest Bertinelli wore while walking to lose 40 pounds. Winfrey tells her audience, "Let's go get that thing." I give a little yelp and then cover it with a cough. Just what every girl with curvature of the spine wants: to accessorize with weighted clothing.

When we are ushered into the actual studio, Oprah is heading in the opposite direction to change clothes. The Bertinelli and Shatner pieces will air on two separate days, and Winfrey must dress accordingly. On her way out, she walks past our group, says hello, and mentions something about her shoes. And I don't know how to say this in any way that doesn't make me sound like a creepy stalker, but she smells really nice. I avert my eyes as if somehow she'll be able to take one look at me and I'll pour out my life story to her, beginning with my conception and ending with Living Oprah. I am less scared about what Winfrey's response would be if she found out about my project than I am frightened by the prospect of being jumped by her adoring fans who can't take their eyes off her as she disappears from view.

My little group is seated two by two. A small area has been cleared for fans of the Shat (please don't blame this nickname on me, I didn't invent it), and we are placed in certain seats according to...what, exactly? I try to figure out how the staff decides who will be sent to the back of the house and who is placed closest to the stage. Does it have anything to do with the pictures we were asked to send or how we are dressed today? I feel as if I'm auditioning for a role, but I'm not sure what the director wants from me. I try to appear as eager, nonthreatening, and camera-friendly as possible. Clutched in my hand is a tiny alien figurine—a telepathic Talosian from the two-part episode "The Menagerie." I rub its oversized cranium for luck. One of Oprah's staffers taps me on the shoulder and points me toward my seat, right in the center of the second row. Victory!

I want to throw my head back and laugh. I am buzzing with energy and wish I could hear every conversation around me at once. I feel like I have infiltrated a clandestine organization: I am part anthropologist, part spy, part crazily excited to see Captain Kirk. I wait with a smile plastered across my face so large that I think my jaw might fall off. I feel important. Yes, at Security I was stripped of my iPod, my cell phone, and all the paper and pens in my purse, but it still feels good to be one of a special group in the *Oprah Winfrey Show* studio. The atmosphere is electric.

An employee of the show steps onstage and asks us questions about our love of all things *Trek* and gets us hopping with excitement to see

Oprah again. I wonder if the room is being pumped full of oxygen, like they do in Vegas, to keep us bright-eyed and bushy-tailed. I'm only half serious. The thrill in the crowd is all about O, not O_2. Winfrey walks onstage and we all begin to clap. We are instructed to react as if we hadn't seen her before, since this is supposed to look like a different day of taping. We all jump to our feet. The applause and cheering get louder and louder. A woman near me yells, "Thank you, Jesus! Thank you, Jesus!" I'm not even Christian, but it feels blasphemous.

Some people around me are going a little too far and I get uncomfortable and choked up. I feel foolish for becoming upset, but my adrenaline is rushing and I'm on an emotional high. That's putting it mildly. In truth, I am totally freaking out in this mob of screeching strangers. I wish my husband was here to make this a little less surreal for me. I'm wondering why everyone is falling over themselves to be seen by Oprah, and why a woman is actually thanking her Savior for this moment. And I'm wondering why I'm not brave enough to sit back down in my seat rather than reacting as if Mother Teresa, all four Beatles, Abraham Lincoln, and Gandhi have been beamed onto the stage. Instead, I take the easier route and allow myself to be swept up by the crowd.

Oprah looks as if she can't understand why we are losing our collective mind. She repeats to us, "Get over yourselves. Get over yourselves." I just clap and smile even bigger and hope she'll make eye contact. What is happening to me? Why do I care? In the midst of our applause, we're all also looking at one another, smiling, sharing our joy and amazement with each other. I'm brought back to every pep rally and homecoming I attended in high school. We are all hoping to be acknowledged by the most popular girl in school. It's fun right now, but we'd scratch each other's eyes out to be able to hang out with her after the big game.

Once Oprah gets us settled down and introduces William Shatner (no shouts to Jesus this time), I am surprised that during the interview she's not always looking at him, but instead at blue cards filled with facts. We never see this part when we're watching TV; it usually appears as if she's deeply engrossed in conversation with her guests. Sometimes when he's answering her questions, she's reading and not making eye contact. Shatner doesn't seem the least bit distracted by this, so I imagine this is the way things are done in their world. I'm eating this up. I can't wait to see the show back in the comfort of my own living room. I love seeing the reality behind the artifice. I guess, in the world of sci-fi geekdom, you could say I'd choose the red pill.

At the end of the show I get to experience a gift giveaway live and in person! We are given a DVD set of the digitally remastered first season of the original *Star Trek* series. Woohoo! Set your phasers to FUN! The crowd goes crazy, even the people who were not brought in specifically for this segment. Even the people who did not raise their hands when we were asked by Oprah's staff if we watched *Star Trek*. I think people are excited simply because Oprah is giving us a present. I try to gauge who will enjoy this gift and who will be auctioning it off on eBay.

Oprah leaves quickly after shooting a promo for *A New Earth* and her online class. I realize it's brilliant that she makes her exit before we're dismissed from our seats. She'd be swamped otherwise. We are told by one of the producers with gracefully arched brows that we'll get our DVDs when we pick up our coats and personal belongings on our way out. She also urges us to visit The Oprah Store once we exit the building. We're instructed about the boutique's exact location, kitty-corner from the studio, lest we miss it.

The mob shuffles from the studio, most of us looking over our shoulders for one last glance at the stage, which is already being adjusted to shoot the next episode. If I could read the mind of the woman dragging her feet in front of me, I think she'd be begging, "Please don't make me go. I want to stay forever."

It's a claustrophobic madhouse on the way out. We pass by a new audience, waiting to claim the seats we've warmed. There's a rumor within the sea of folks leaving the Shatner show that the newbies are here to see past winners from ABC's *Dancing with the Stars*. A woman giggles and says, "I hope Oprah dances! Maybe she'll do the rhuuuuuuumba." We all laugh.

The new crowd is peppy and fun-loving, while my coviewers from the last taping have a panicky edge. Everyone *really* wants their free gift, and there's no lobby for us to refill our purses with our belongings or to put on our coats, hats, and scarves before facing the frigid

Chicago wind. It's similar to the feeling of going through airport security on a busy travel day, with people behind you nudging you forward
before you've retrieved your purse from the X-ray machine or had a
moment to slip on your shoes. Strangers are talking to one another
about how long it's taken them to get tickets to the show (highest claim
I overheard: nine years). Lots of women discuss their sightseeing plans
for the day (there are almost a dozen mentions of the American Girl
Store). Everyone is excited to shop at The Oprah Store, and I hear the
word "cashmere" tossed around more than once.

The morning has run much later than I thought it would, and I
have to go to a lecture at school. I decide that I'll visit the store on my
own at a later date when I can be more relaxed about time. Plus I really
want to get away from the crowd. It's exhausting to be surrounded by
so many bodies, charged up to their eyeballs with frenetic energy. I
imagine Oprah must have scads of people around her for much of the
day. I think I'd find this energizing and draining all at the same time. I
step out into the cold. The sky is brighter now, and I've got a skip in my
step as I walk toward school. I can't wait to show everyone my bright
yellow *Star Trek* DVD set. I covertly turn back toward the television
studio and give it the Vulcan salute as a show of respect. Live long and
prosper, Oprah. Although I think you've got the prosper thing down
pretty well already.

As an artist, writer, and performer, my main goal is to have impact
on those who view or read my work. If I inspire a single conversation
as a result of my writing or performance, I'll be thrilled and honored.
I can't even fathom having the amount of impact Oprah has on her
audience. In all honesty, I think it would terrify me to have such power,
and I wouldn't want to be in her Louboutins for a million bucks. I
don't have enough confidence in myself to lead a flock of women in
every aspect of their lives. I could teach them yoga, some basic knitting
skills, and how to drive a stick shift, but that's about it. But Oprah has
confidence to spare. She might not be an expert at everything, but she
collects authorities who fit cleanly into her world. I've witnessed her
influence grow in intensity and scope over the years but have never seen

her use her power in such a history-making way as she has this year in her support of Barack Obama for Democratic candidate for president of the United States of America.

Before I discuss the presidential primaries, I feel a disclaimer is in order: I do not take my right to vote lightly. I imagine that some folks might think this of me because I placed my vote for the candidate Oprah urged us toward. I was, incidentally, waffling between two candidates before the start of this project. While Obama was one of them, Hillary Clinton was the other. When Living Oprah began, I joked that this project made my decision at the ballot box easier, but inside, I felt quite torn. I knew this would be a true test of my mission in this project: to be an extreme display of what happens when we give our power away to the media, to peer pressure, to outside sources of influence. Dressing in a certain manner, styling my home, cooking my meals, and reading books according to Oprah is one thing, but voting according to her guidance is another creature altogether. Although I felt the point of my project to be vitally important, I was scared and uncomfortable to make it.

I try to ease my inner turmoil by telling myself it's just one vote. It won't *really* count. But this is a load of *S*-shaped poo and I know it. I also frequently remind myself I'd probably vote for Barack Obama anyhow. I know him well as a politician as I paid close attention to his work in Chicago, and have gained great respect for him as my Illinois senator. But there is this gnawing question in the back of my brain: What would I have done if Oprah backed a candidate whom I didn't morally or ethically believe in? Would I have been able to continue this experiment or would I have had to pull the plug? In all honesty, I got incredibly lucky on this one. I was able to fulfill an Oprah suggestion without going against what I believe in. I was able to go to my polling place and vote for the candidate I had the most faith in, while still fulfilling the rules of the project. But I'll always wonder, what if...

I am curious how much the Oprah brand helped Barack Obama win the Democratic candidacy for president. There is always a frenzy created when Winfrey advises her audience to read a book or buy a product. Did she have the same effect on the vote on Super Tuesday?

One study by economists from the University of Maryland says Oprah earned Obama more than a million votes. She also earned herself more power. The fact that people are even speculating that she swayed the election has strengthened the mythology behind her influence. She's a self-perpetuating marketing force. What an amazing phenomenon.

It's no secret: Oprah's influence is deeply effective and widespread. Hers is a household name, and there is no branch of the media in which she does not demand attention and respect. And while she has a crack marketing team, I also believe that we help sustain and build her power the more we talk about it, the more university professors do studies of it, the more comedians joke about it, the more artsy-fartsy types like me do projects about it. We are a vital part of her PR machine. She sustains us with her presence, we sustain her, and the wheel keeps turning.

February 2008 Accounting

Date	Assignment	Cost	Time	Notes
2/1	Read *O* from cover to cover. *(LO)*		3h 0m	Lots of yummy-looking cupcakes, but I've already signed my Best Life Challenge contract. Decent articles, not like many other women's magazines I've read where articles are more like blurbs, with more bells and whistles than text.
2/1	"I'm urging you to do something just for yourself...." Complete "master class" in writing from Wally Lamb. *(MAG)*		0h 10m	This was sort of Writing 101. I will consider his advice as I write my blog, as it is the most public version of my private story I can tell at the moment.
2/1	"Go with your girlfriends and then go have margaritas." (movie *27 Dresses*) *(SHOW)*	30.00	3h 30m	We went on February 15. We all felt the movie kicked feminism back 4 or 5 decades. ($10.50 movie/$19.50 at Agave Bar and Grill)
2/1	Purchase makeup *(WEB)*	42.97	0h 20m	I haven't worn makeup in ages. Trying to follow some how-to's at Oprah.com.
2/5	Vote for Barack Obama. Oprah said "seize the opportunity" and vote for him. "We need Barack Obama." *(POLITICAL ENDORSE-MENT)*		0h 15m	I've seen this replayed on TV a handful of times this year (originally from 12/07 speech in SC).

(cont.)

February 2008 Accounting (*cont.*)

Date	Assignment	Cost	Time	Notes
2/5	Know what to have in the fridge and medicine cabinet if I want to stay young. (Dr Oz's antiaging checklist) *(SHOW)*	64.72	1h 0m	I bought what I didn't already have in the house; lots more supplements than I normally take.
2/6	Scallops in Green Curry Sauce for dinner. *(WEB)*	39.57	0h 45m	Prep was *way* labor intensive but food was *way* yummy. It's approximately $25 more than we'd usually pay for the groceries to make dinner. I bought scallops on sale. That's bad, right?
2/8	Sign up for Suze Orman's MyFico program. *(WEB/ SHOW)*	49.95	0h 10m	Yeah! I have decent credit! I always assume the worst when I don't have all the info about my finances. I am still scared of my own money.
2/13	Download free copy of *Women and Money* by Suze Orman. *(SHOW)*		5h 5m	Empowering. Sort of like finances made simple for the uneducated in money. That's me, all right. (5 minutes to download, approx. 300 minutes to read)
2/14	"Does Your Underwear Need an Overhaul?" Use advice in article to revamp my underwear drawer. *(MAG)*	58.39	0h 30m	I just ordered new stuff online at a discount site. I had some *awful* old, ginormous, stretched-out undies. Soon I will I have some that fit. Sweet!
2/18	Go to see *Horton Hears a Who*. *(SHOW)*	8.50	1h 28m	Um. Blah. Even the 4-year-old daughter of my friend Dara was unimpressed.

2/19	Stop drinking diet soda. *(SHOW)*		0h 0m	Not really a big deal for me anymore, although I used to live on the stuff.
2/19	I sat in the audience of the *Oprah* taping featuring guest William Shatner (the Shat). *(WEB)*		2h 0m	After the taping, we were told to go to The Oprah Store. I will do this on another day as I had to go to a school event.
2/20	10 things every woman needs to have in her closet. *(SHOW)*	354.53	10h 55m	Breakdown: $45.96 trench; $19.00 white T-neck; $19.00 black T-neck; $59.50 white jeans ($13.95 S/H for T-necks and jeans); $33.51 tunics; $7.00 leopard-print flats; $66.65 white denim jacket (inc. SH); $49.99 dark-wash jeans (Michael Kors at Marshalls; Oprah *loves* MK pants); $9.99 black skirt; $9.99 oversized bag (best bargain item I found!); $19.99 black dress
2/21	Intentional Dialogue Exercise. *(WEB)*		0h 20m	Had an argument with husband, so searched for solution on Oprah.com with search term "communication." We thought this was pretty goofy, but laughing about it chilled us out.
2/21	Read *A New Earth*. *(SHOW/ BC)*		0h 55m	No surprises here. I do like Tolle's tone, though.
2/22	Watch *Raisin in the Sun* with my family and a bowl of popcorn. *(SHOW)*	0.25	3h 0m	I'm biased. I preferred the original – who can top S. Poitier? Popcorn was delicious, though. (25¢ for popcorn)

(cont.)

February 2008 Accounting (*cont.*)

Date	Assignment	Cost	Time	Notes
2/25	Get a Walkvest (weighted vest). *(SHOW)*		0h 0m	This was on show with Valerie Bertinelli, who used the vest to lose weight. A student read this post and gave me his weighted vest so I don't have to buy one! *Awesome!*
2/27	"I do want you to start thinking about, as I have started thinking about, how much you consume. I mean, like every time you throw away a paper towel. Every time you are, you know, wasteful with food in your house...just think about how much you really need." *(SHOW)*		0h 0m	If anything, this is helping me save money. I've been much better about wasting paper towels and napkins. Also, taking shorter showers. Trying not to waste food. **(O)**
2/28	"Get a lift when you come in the front door." *(MAG)*		0h 0m	I think of something to be grateful for every time I come in the front door. Plus I've placed photos in our entryway that always make me smile. I also get to see my happy cat when I enter, which makes me happy. **(O)**

2/28	"I want you to savor every meal." (MAG)		0h 0m	This is *great*! I am usually a vacuum cleaner of an eater. I have begun eating much more mindfully. Sometimes I have to remind myself midmeal, but I *really* enjoy this. Addendum: Sometimes I want to rush and feel resentful I have to savor my food. How embarrassing! **(O)**
2/28	"I want you to pay attention to how happy women get that way." (MAG)		0h 0m	I've been observing women so much since this project began anyhow. This has been really interesting. **(O)**
2/28	Take *A Course in Miracles*. (SHOW/WEB)		0h 0m	This is a daily lesson provided on Oprah.com. Will start formally on 3/1/08. **(O)**
2/29	Watch *Oprah's Big Give* (with my family) and make it a party, including homemade pizzas, salad, and a special give-a-tini (virgin!) created by celeb chef Jamie Oliver. (SHOW)	20.43	2h 0m	Wasn't wild about the reality show. I'm rooting for Brandi—she has scoliosis like me! Oprah told us to watch every episode. Will do. ($20.43 for groceries I didn't have in the house)
2/29	"Remember, it's not just about money. It's about what you can do for somebody else. Rally your friends, your family, neighbors, and pull off your own big give. Be creative." (SHOW)		5h 25m	I'm organizing a book drive. I've decided on the organization I'll be donating to. I'm excited! I love books. (250 minutes organization and drop-off, 60 minutes research, 15 minutes letter writing)

(cont.)

February 2008 Accounting (*cont.*)

Date	Assignment	Cost	Time	Notes
Through-out Month	Watch every episode of *Oprah*. *(LO)*		21h 0m	21 episodes
Through-out Month	Do Best Life Challenge exercise. *(BLC)*		5h 20m	I go above and beyond the required BLC minutes but use it to stay consistent. (80 minutes a week for 4 weeks)
MONTHLY TOTAL		669.31	67h 8m	
YEAR-TO-DATE TOTAL		1,376.32	165h 54m	

ONGOING PROJECTS
- "Reinvigorate your appearance with some great advice on how not to look old…"
- "Rethink your eating habits with some absolutely delicious and utterly original meals…"
- Use cloth or reusable bags at grocery store. No more plastic.
- Change lightbulbs to energy-efficient bulbs.
- "I think in terms of investment, it's the best thing you can ever give yourself is to have beautiful surroundings."
- "I would just say to anybody, whatever secret you're holding, live your own truth."
- Sharon Salzberg meditation
- Make your rooms personal.
- Best Life Challenge exercise and diet guidance

Accounting Abbreviations: LO = Living Oprah Project Task, *SHOW = The Oprah Winfrey Show*, WEB = Oprah.com, *MAG = O, The Oprah Magazine*, BC = Oprah's Book Club, BLC = Best Life Challenge, **(O)** = ongoing project

MARCH:

If the leopard-print shoe fits...

Time spent this month: *62 hours, 12 minutes*
Dollars spent this month: *$262.69*
Jim's least favorite activity: *The Evaluate Your Marriage exercise*
Jim's most favorite activity: *Eating Art Smith's Ground Turkey
    Shepherd's Pie*
Words that stuck: *"The best part of all of this is thinking of you when
    watching Oprah and thinking 'Oh, man, poor girl has a lot of
    shopping to do.'"— Comment made by Margaret Hicks on Living
    Oprah blog*

I'VE BEEN shopping my butt off.

I felt confident back on February 20 when I watched a style segment and heard from Oprah's lips, "Here are the ten things every woman needs to have." I was certain if the items on the list were must-haves, then I *must have* most of them already. Nope. Turns out I've been dressing in the Dark Ages. Luckily, Oprah and one of her style experts have offered fashion advice to civilize me. Although I've been attempting to acquire the required clothing, I've not been having the best of luck. I'm not good at scavenger hunts, but the grand prize of this shopping spree is a transformation into Oprah's image of a well-dressed woman, so I'm trying really hard.

Here's my list.

Must-Have Clothing:

- ❏ Trenchcoat (I don't have one, but have always found it romantic to look like a Cold War spy, so I'm excited.)
- ❏ Turtlenecks: one black, one white (I don't have either; need to get.)
- ☑ Black trousers (I have a pair that needs to be tailored.)
- ❏ Tunic top (I don't think I have one but I'll look. One question: What's a tunic top?)
- ❏ White jeans (Why? To wear to the Guns N' Roses concert in 1987?)
- ❏ Dark jeans (I thought I was covered here but was informed I had only a medium wash, so back to the drawing board.)
- ❏ Black dress (Had two; neither fit.)
- ❏ White denim jacket (Huh? I rewind the VCR tape to make sure I heard correctly. Is Oprah in a hair band? I wonder if she'll want me to sing a power ballad on the hood of a Camaro next.)
- ❏ Black skirt (Again, I thought I was all set. Then Jim sees me trying it on and tells me it's way too big, and it is against tailoring and clutter rules to own something that doesn't fit me. He's right. I'll either have to get it altered or get a new skirt. I'll try to do whichever is cheaper.)
- ☑ Cashmere sweater (Thank you, Marshalls, for your great deals.)

Must-Have Accessories:

- ❏ Flats (Leopard print was recommended. I laugh so hard, I cry.)
- ❏ An oversized bag (Don't have. Got rid of these last year since it's not great for my back to carry a lot of weight on my shoulder. Just a thought: If I was allowed to wear cargo pants, I might not need such a big bag. I'd have pockets.)

Here's the funny thing. Until I started writing this book, I never realized they snuck two extra items onto the list. I just shopped for what I was told I needed without counting.

I started my fruitless excursion into retailatopia at the end of

February and it feels never-ending. Shopping in actual stores, not online, falls somewhere on my discomfort scale between being put on hold by the cable company and a bikini wax. Because of my lack of desire to shop (sorry, misogynist comedians, not all women love to spend money on clothes), I know much of this year will be a challenge for me. I have friends who think this will be the fun part of the project. Due to their exuberance, I try to convince myself that buying new clothes can't be that painful. The trouble is I have a pretty long history of feeling guilty when I spend money on myself. It seems like there are always better, more practical ways to spend my hard-earned dollars than on clothing. But this is Living Oprah, not Living Okrant, so I tell myself to suck it up. I eat a healthy, hearty breakfast, and armed with the list of *12* things I need to have in my closet, I hit the sidewalks with my debit card burrowing for safety within the confines of my wallet.

When I finally find some clothing that is in my size and price range, and Oprah-appropriate, or *Oprappriate*, as I start calling it, I head to the dressing room with my fingers crossed. One thing I did not expect was the reaction I had to seeing myself in the mirror while wearing these white jeans, white denim jacket, bright red tunic top, and black oversized bag. I grimace at my reflection: I look like an inside-out Santa and can't peel the clothing off fast enough. I've seen it on makeover shows, the moment where the recently transformed guest cries out in shock, "That doesn't even look like me!" I always thought that sounded a bit overly dramatic, but now I can say I've had the exact same experience. I feel much like I do at the initial fitting for costumes for a play. Nothing fits quite right at first, and I am faced with wearing the projection of how a designer interpreted my character rather than seeing the reflection of what I imagined would be perfect for my role. If I'm ever going to get comfortable in these Oprah-advised clothes, these clothes that everyone is supposed to be wearing, these clothes that make me feel like less of an individual, I need to make a major mental adjustment. But it isn't going to happen in this moment, with price tags dangling from my armpit. I return an armful of ill-fitting clothing to the dressing room attendant, feeling guilty that I've doubled her workload for the day.

I accept that this will be a process, but I have my doubts I'll ever

get used to leopard-print flats. I feel so lucky I didn't have to waste…
er, I mean *spend* too much money on them as I found them in the
clearance section of a major brand-name discount store. Oprah's guest,
stylist Lloyd Boston, said, "When you do leopard, because it goes with
nothing, it goes with everything." It was said in such an authoritative
tone, with Oprah in total agreement, I believed it to be true. But today,
as I slide them on my feet, I feel more like an ass than a wildcat. Who
makes up these rules? Who gets to decide what's beautiful? In subsequent days, I see that the flats indeed look cute on other women, but
I still feel like an impostor. This assignment is way out of my comfort
zone.

While I shop, I can't shake the feeling that I am being watched.
Judged. I think a lot of this sensation stems from a television phenomenon I've witnessed on *Oprah*, as well as other TV shows in the past
decade or so. It has become totally acceptable to cross boundaries and
personal space to ambush people we feel are in need of makeovers,
makeunders, new kitchens, new financial plans, and new housekeeping tactics. This is one of my biggest fears. If I was walking down a
sidewalk in Chicago and was suddenly faced with the lens of a camera and a perfectly dressed, made up, coiffed TV personality spun me
around so everyone in America could see the flat "ass pancake" created
by my ill-fitting jeans, I might melt into a puddle of humiliation on the
concrete.

But do I avert my eyes when I see this sort of thing done on a talk
show? Do I start a letter-writing campaign to end reality television? No
way. I hate to love it. I held firm to my moral ground for many years,
refusing to partake of this type of exploitive entertainment. Somewhere
down the line, though, when I was working from home as a freelance
graphic designer, I "accidentally" began watching a reality show called
*Starting Over** on my lunch break. All hell broke loose and I got hooked
like any other junkie. Because it starred actual people in a dramatic
daily format usually reserved for soap operas, the line between human

---

* Starring life coach Rhonda Britten, a guest on a 2007 *Oprah* about "Resilient Sprits."

being and fictional character became fuzzy. I felt a little gross when the end credits rolled, but I still tuned in and talked about the people on the show as if I knew them. This was like peeking into the window of my neighbors' home, spying on their drama, but even better because it was edited for time and I didn't have to change out of my jammies. I even got online and lurked on message boards where fans discussed the show. I wondered if I was learning from my voyeurism or merely being entertained from a seat of removed superiority.

These days, you can't throw a rock at the television without hitting an ambush makeover show. I call these reality-based programs my guilty pleasures, as if there is something intrinsically and embarrassingly wrong about my choice to view them. It feels sinful to derive entertainment from others' struggles. Sure, most of the shows have happy endings, but they wouldn't be nearly as interesting without the human trauma and drama to kick off the plot. And hey, everyone else watches reality television, so why shouldn't I? I hear Mom's voice in my head when I begged her to let me shave my legs in the fifth grade because everyone else was doing it. "If everyone else jumped off a bridge, would you?" No, Mom, but if everyone else watches an *Oprah* episode about a woman whose hoarding disorder has caused her family so much mortification that she's being ambushed on the show, will I tune in? You bet your silky, hairless legs I will.

If anyone can help the hoarder lady, surely it must be Oprah. Oprah's clutter expert, Peter Walsh, is sent to the rescue (I can't imagine Oprah stepping into that before picture of a home), and the horrified but willing homeowner surrenders to televised guidance.

Oprah seems particularly enamored with the ambush makeover formula, and I've seen many of them on her show. Here's what I've learned from watching: Before a person can be healed, she must be surprised, sometimes embarrassed, and in extreme cases, shamed—brought to her knees publicly. After the TV-viewing audience is given a chance to gasp or laugh, then the truly entertaining healing can begin. I try to remember that there is something to be learned from every situation, and it's my choice how to react to these infotainment shows. Oprah frequently reminds her guests and audience that her tell-all shows are not pulp entertainment, they are for our education. I do take her warning to heart but think that if this is something we must constantly be reminded about, maybe a different format is in order.

In an attempt to keep my project as transparent as possible, I blogged several months ago that when I took a clutter quiz on Oprah's website, I came up with the result "Uh-oh. Looks like you're a hard-core hoarder." I was pissed. I would have been in complete agreement if it said, "Uh-oh. You are really messy" or "Girl, try a *filing cabinet* for all those papers." Sure, I have a couple doors closed in my home when guests come over; sure, half the socks in my drawer don't have a partner. But really, a *hoarder*? Isn't hoarding a psychological problem that should be diagnosed by a specialist rather than an online quiz? Feel free to imagine even more self-righteous angry remarks here. Luckily, like a golden retriever, I am unable to hold a grudge and I forget all about the test results for a while until seeing today's show. To me, this woman is hard-core. I'm totally soft-core. But still, here is an opportunity that I believe Oprah would want me to take: to compare my issues to those of her extreme guests. To see the similarities, rather than get caught up in the differences. To view the hoarder lady less as entertainment and more as a catalyst to change my own life for the better. And in this way, I am able to validate my project as something Oprah herself would likely respect. Living Oprah is hard-core.

Later, after I slip into the only white jeans I could muster the courage to purchase, I photograph myself, and upload the unattractive picture to my blog. I think I look ridiculous but decide not to delete the image. There's nothing original about embarrassing myself publicly. It's done every day on television. For some really weird reason, this gives me comfort. It's not a question of why I'm willing to pour my guts out on line. The question is: Why haven't I done this earlier? Viva la humiliation!

Where's my makeover?

March 22, 2008
When I was a kid, fitting in was a battle. I didn't look anything like my classmates, with my big head of frizzed-out hair, my style of dress

inspired by Madonna and Michael Jackson, and my over-the-top theat-
ricality. While I wanted to be part of the crowd, I couldn't bring myself
to try to fit in in any more than a halfhearted way. Frankly, I don't
think I even understood how to make it happen, but I might have gone
whole hog had I figured out how to look and act trendy. Eventually, I
just embraced my taste and my priorities and felt proud to march to the
beat of my own drummer. With much hubris, I began to think that I
could remain unaffected by the social pressures faced by other women.
Ah, denial. It ain't just a river in Egypt.

On the topic of conformity, one of the most frequent pieces of criticism I hear is that Oprah's audience members are automatons who
dress alike, read the same stuff, regurgitate quotes by Dr. Oz and
Suze Orman, and defer to Oprah as the alpha gal in their pack. I've
heard more than one "woe is me" from male friends regarding the way
their female partners fall into line according to Oprah's dictates. The
word "Stepford" has been applied frequently, and I've enjoyed countless impressions these men have done of Oprah's "Favorite Things"
audience members. And while I believe there is truth to their theory
that many of the women we see in Oprah's audience seem to fit into a
very specific type, can't we say the same thing of Jerry Springer's talk
show? Or Garrison Keillor's Lake Wobegon listeners? There is a certain
amount of contentment to be drawn from surrounding ourselves with
people who have points of view similar to our own. And while I'd like
to think I'm a free spirit, the down and dirty truth is I know I find
comfort in certain moments of conformity, too. For instance...

During March's endless clothing debacle, I am in the Gap to find
the dark-wash jeans that Oprah believes every woman should have in
her closet. While I walk into the store with trepidation, I am soon
thrilled to see how great a pair of mass-produced, mass-marketed jeans
looks on me. Of course, part of this is because, a decade ago, I was too
heavy to fit into Gap clothes, so that's a victory unto itself. My point is,
as I stand barefoot in the store in front of a full-length mirror, I realize
I am wearing the same outfit as the mannequin in the front window.
No lie. Before I am able to experience horror over this, a salesperson
looks up from her supernaturally deft T-shirt folding and assures me I
look fantastic. Of course, she's dressed almost exactly like the headless

mannequin and I are. And I'm surprised that I don't want to run for my life. Instead, I feel like part of the club. I assume it's a sensation similar to what some kids who wear uniforms to school experience. No need to try so hard to express my individuality or worry if I'm being judged for fashion faux pas. I now look like the rest of the women who have a closet filled with must-haves. How easy is that? But much of the direction I'm taking from the show this year is making me feel like less of an individual and this upsets me. There is an inner battle taking place inside this wannabe nonconformist who doesn't want to admit that being Oprah's poster girl is the least bit agreeable.

While the pressure of making the wrong choice is lifted from my shoulders, following a leader and constantly trying to live up to the standards of others takes a lot of time. The jury is still out on whether it's worth it. On one hand, from the outside, things in my life are probably looking better: I'm dressing in a more stylish and trendy manner (according to Oprah and her style experts), I've slimmed down a bit from the regularity of my Best Life Challenge exercise, the readership on my blog is growing steadily (I've had a shocking 13,675 visits to my site), and I'm getting a bit of press about Living Oprah. But inside I'm feeling tired and stressed. Living life in this manner is like an endless run on a woman-sized gerbil wheel. I have a feeling I'll never catch up, I'm never going to be enough. The weight of knowing that I have 291 days left of this experiment and the seeming impossibility of it leaves me feeling destined to fail. It's just too much. I now understand why some of us look like we're caught in a time warp of fashion. At some point, we just throw in the towel and place our priorities elsewhere.

March 26, 2008

Knowing that so many of us give up and allow ourselves to get buried under the lives we've created, Oprah focuses much of her show on helping us pull our heads out of the sand and get clarity in all aspects of our lives. This reality check extends from our health to our finances to our spiritual lives to our homes, and beyond. Of all the experts on her show, I'm particularly fond of Peter Walsh, the master of clutter, although I am chagrined that we've evolved into a culture that needs clutter specialists. We've got no money these days, we have no time, but we sure have stuff. It's coming out of our closets, it's bursting from our drawers and making us into crazy people.

Walsh and Winfrey push the point that our homes are an outward display of our states of mind. I waffle on whether I think the two are entirely comparable, but as a yoga teacher who firmly believes in the mind-body connection, I'll remain open about the possibility of a mind-stuff connection. Of course, I do see a certain irony in the fact that when I have finished cleaning out my closet according to the advice given by Walsh, I have to fill it back up with the 12 things we "need" to have in our closets. It reminds me of when I was in my early 20s and would go on those detox-cleanse things to fast out my toxins in 30 days. I'd celebrate the end of the month by eating a pizza and smoking a pack of cigarettes. Or two. This is just a classier version of my old behavior.

Oprah thinks we might all benefit from Walsh's expertise and tells us to acquire his most recent book. Boy, have I learned a lesson. If I want something that Oprah suggests, I should buy it immediately or risk facing back order. This morning I waited several hours too long before getting online to order, and what do you know, it was out of stock at my regular Internet bookstore. The book was released last year, but when Oprah gave it her seal of approval today, it flew off the virtual shelves. From now on, I'll sit with my cursor poised over "buy now" if Oprah gives any hint that she'll send us out to make a purchase.

I keep hearing people joke about Oprah receiving a cut of the profits a product that she's endorsed on her show earns. I highly doubt this is true. While some of my more cynical friends and readers might disagree strongly, I think Oprah's advice is given in good faith. But I was recently struck with a thought that if we all followed her guidance to a T and every suggestion she offered actually worked, there'd be little reason for shows like hers to exist. Her empire is built on teachings that help us live our "best lives." But if we were living those lives, there would be no demand for the gazillion women's magazines on the shelves or the countless self-help-based talk shows. If we fulfilled her hope for us to spend our time building our relationships, focusing on our passions, and unplugging from the constant stream of electronic distractions, as she's urged us many times, we might never turn on her show again. There would be no need. Most of the sources that encourage us to improve are also expecting us to fail. Even the January issue of *O* had a cover story called "If You've Gained Back Every Pound." The editors projected our diet failures and were ready to offer us a helping hand.

The future of self-help and women's magazines depends on their audiences' constant state of dissatisfaction with themselves. Yes, these publications can probably be found in every room of my home, but I've come to believe many of us have been convinced we are fundamentally broken by the same media that offer us succor. If American women are truly reflected in magazine cover stories and talk show topics, then we are some major sad sacks. We are definitely not thin enough, talented enough between the sheets, we don't know how to raise our kids, and we'll never find or keep a man. We're a mess.

I'm struggling with this when it comes to (what else?) my weight. As I've mentioned, I used to be quite heavy. I wasn't going to get a photo spread in the pages of *Ripley's Believe It or Not*, but I was an unhealthy and out-of-shape 206 pounds when I stepped on the scale at a nutritionist's office in a size 18-20 dress in 1998. While I lost weight some time ago, my fat is like a phantom limb. I still wonder if I'll fit comfortably into an airline seat, and when I see a petite woman standing on a crowded bus, I worry I might crush her with my butt on my way to the exit. And the way I react to any magazine promising a bikini body in four weeks? I buy that thing faster than you can say "Holy crap, that woman just crushed a petite person with her butt."

While I'd like to see a magazine all about body acceptance and stories that insist I'm all right as I am, I don't know if I'm evolved enough to subscribe to it yet ... but I believe I have the capacity to grow. If there weren't talk shows that teach us how to keep our husbands from cheating, or how to ensure our children won't hate us, maybe we could stop living in fear and paranoia. If we stopped seeing shows that ambush women on the street to poke fun at their mom jeans and dated makeup, maybe we wouldn't feel so much pressure to always be our "best." Maybe the very word "best" feels like an impossibly distant

finish line to cross, and "happy" or "satisfying" is a better life to aspire
to and learn how to maintain.

I believe that the reality is most of us are fine and dandy as we are.
And what could possibly be better than living our entire lives feeling
fine? It's healthy to desire growth and change, of course, but not to the
detriment of our own self-acceptance. I aspire to shed the fear that I'm
incomplete, but it's easier said than done. Besides, right now, it's taking
all my energy just to fit in.

March 2008 Accounting

Date	Assignment	Cost	Time	Notes
3/1	Read *O* from cover to cover. *(LO)*		3h 30m	This issue is (mostly) dedicated to how to be happy. If only it was as easy as finding the answers in a magazine, I think most American women would be floating on cloud 9!
3/1	Try compassion meditation. *(MAG)*		0h 20m	I had a hard time focusing. I think it's a good meditation, I'm just distracted. Maybe I'll try it again when I don't have so much on my plate I can't (or won't) step away from.
3/1	Go to Oprah boutique. *(SHOW)*	29.38	1h 0m	Was told by Oprah producers to do this after seeing the show live in Feb. I spent $15 on a mug and $11.95 (plus tax) for South African rooibos tea that Oprah had created especially for her store. I drink many cups of tea per day and thought I'd integrate Oprah into my daily ritual. More employees than shoppers at the store.
3/2	Go to Oprah.com to learn more about the red cup program discussed by Drew Barrymore. *(SHOW)*		0h 10m	I think DB is so fascinating. She's become quite a powerhouse. I'm forwarding info about this program to folks I know.
3/3	Do *A New Earth Workbook* homework. *(BC)*		0h 30m	This is going to be a long process.

3/5	Watch *A New Earth* online class, chapter 1. *(SHOW/BC)*		1h 30m	I had to download this. I kept getting booted on the actual night of the class.
3/7	Watch *Across the Universe* with friends. *(SHOW)*		2h 13m	At least the music was great, but I prefer to hear the real thing, rather than covers.
3/9	Watch the *Big Give*. *(SHOW)*		1h 0m	Yawn. Sorry, but yawn. This could have been terrific, though—a good idea made entirely forgettable.
3/10	Read *ANE*, chapter 2. *(BC)*		0h 30m	
3/10	Do *ANE* workbook homework. *(BC)*		0h 30m	
3/11	Download and watch *ANE*. *(BC)*		1h 30m	I wish the live version was more reliable. I like the idea of watching along with lots of other people.
3/12	"You need a crisp white shirt. You must have." *(SHOW)*	69.50	0h 15m	I originally ordered one thru Old Navy for $16.99, but it arrived with black pinstripes. Oh, the horror, the horror! When I tried to exchange it, they were out of stock. In a knee-jerk show of spending, I bought Oprah's favored crisp white shirt from Brooks Brothers. I'm guilty and a little sick over it. Don't want to tell my husband about it. I did find it at an outlet in New Hampshire (no tax!) for $69.50 (down from $89.50). I'm mortified I got sucked into this. I'm a yoga teacher! Why do I need this shirt?

(cont.)

March 2008 Accounting (*cont.*)

Date	Assignment	Cost	Time	Notes
3/12	"Keep the girls up!" said during a discussion about getting fit for a bra. *(SHOW)*	49.68	0h 20m	My usual sports bras keep the "girls" together, not up. I'll hit the outlets and see what I can find. Bras are so expensive.
3/13	Shop for a bathing suit. *(WEB)*	78.00	1h 10m	I did this online with Oprah.com advice. I hate bathing suit shopping. Purchased a two-piece for the first time since I was in water wings, though. I'm not doing all this BLC exercise for nothing.
3/15	Declutter. *(WEB)*		1h 30m	According to Peter Walsh on Oprah.com. *Love this!* **(O)**
3/16	Watch the *Big Give*. *(SHOW)*		1h 0m	
3/16	Read *ANE*, chapter 3. *(BC)*		0h 40m	Ego. Can't live with it, can't figure out how to live without it.
3/17	Do *ANE* workbook homework. *(BC)*		0h 20m	
3/18	Download and watch *ANE. (BC)*		1h 30m	
3/19	"Try an awakening exercise!" *(WEB)*		0h 10m	I feel inundated by *ANE*.
3/19	Make Art Smith's Ground Turkey Shepherd's Pie recipe. *(WEB)*	19.84	0h 40m	This was delish. Jim loooved it. It is one of the cheaper entrees on the site.
3/23	Watch the *Big Give*. *(SHOW)*		1h 0m	
3/25	Read *ANE*, chapter 4. *(BC)*		0h 45m	About role-playing. Lots of this chapter resonated with me.

3/25	Do *ANE* homework. *(BC)*		0h 35m	
3/25	Download and watch *ANE* web class. *(BC)*		1h 30m	
3/25	Download and listen to *ANE* theme song. *(BC)*		0h 4m	4 minutes of my life I'll never get back
3/26	Do *ANE* exercise. *(BC)*		0h 5m	Stress "meditation" by Eckhart Tolle—it worked well. I will *totally* do this again. **(O)**
3/27	Order *It's All Too Much* by Peter Walsh. *(SHOW)*	16.29	0h 15m	Shopped around for cheapest copy.
3/28	Take Evaluate Your Marriage test. *(WEB)*		1h 15m	I thought I should really put Oprah's approved relationship advice to the test and do this exercise. It was rudimentary but inspired deep conversation (much to Jim's chagrin).
3/30	Watch the *Big Give. (SHOW)*		1h 0m	
Throughout Month	Take *A Course in Miracles. (WEB/ SHOW)*		7h 45m	Approx. 15 minutes for 31 days
Throughout Month	Watch every episode of *Oprah.* *(LO)*		21h 0m	21 shows
Throughout Month	Do Best Life Challenge exercise *(BLC)*		6h 40m	80 minutes a week for 5 weeks
MONTHLY TOTAL		262.69	62h 12m	
YEAR-TO-DATE TOTAL		1,639.01	228h 6m	

ONGOING PROJECTS
 – "Reinvigorate your appearance with some great advice on how not to look old…"
 – "Rethink your eating habits with some absolutely delicious and utterly original meals…"

(cont.)

- Use cloth and reusable bags at grocery store. No more plastic.
- Change lightbulbs to energy-efficient bulbs.
- "I think in terms of investment, it's the best thing you can give ever yourself is to have beautiful surroundings."
- "I would just say to anybody, whatever secret you're holding, live your own truth."
- Sharon Salzberg meditation
- Make your rooms personal.
- Best Life Challenge exercise and diet guidance
- "I do want you to start thinking about, as I have started thinking about, how much you consume. I mean, like every time you throw away a paper towel. Every time you are, you know, wasteful with food in your house...just think about how much you really need."
- "Get a lift when you come in the front door."
- "I want you to savor every meal."
- "I want you to pay attention to how happy women get that way."
- *A Course in Miracles*

Accounting Abbreviations: *LO* = Living Oprah Project Task, *SHOW* = *The Oprah Winfrey Show*, *WEB* = Oprah.com, *MAG* = *O, The Oprah Magazine*, *BC* = Oprah's Book Club, *BLC* = Best Life Challenge, **(O)** = ongoing project

APRIL:

Clarity, enlightenment, and highlighters... OH MY!

Time spent this month: *400 hours, 12 minutes*
Dollars spent this month: *$276.77*
If I never see a slice of bread again, it will be too soon: *Oprah supported Dr. Oz's advice to us to eat a piece of whole grain bread with olive oil every day before dinner for two weeks.*
Words that stuck: *"Do you ever worry, though, that Oprah can only get people to do things they already want to do, like diet and buy stuff?"—Comment made by Duncan on Living Oprah blog*

I'M FEELING like a zombie lately. I am having trouble sleeping and can barely drag myself through the day. While I've experienced insomnia on and off over the years, I'm disappointed about this recurrence, as I was having a good run of solid sleep. In the past month, however, I can fall asleep without trouble, but I wake up a few hours later and am unable to drift off again. It'd be easy to blame this on the chainsaw with whom I share a bed, but it's really not Jim's fault that I am doomed to stare at the shadows on my ceiling for most of the night. From Oprah's show, I've learned that the probable reason I fall asleep the moment my head hits the pillow is I'm exhausted. Not surprising. Living up to someone else's ideal is running me ragged, and I've only finished a quarter of the project.

The question is, why can't I sleep through the night? Sometimes it's anxiety that wakes me up and other times a recurring nightmare interrupts my slumber. At least once a week, I dream I am frenetically rearranging the furniture in my apartment because nothing fits quite right. It's not my actual home but some subconscious version of it that is comically small and contains an inordinate amount of oversized furniture. Remember the huge rocking chair Lily Tomlin used to sit in when she played Edith Ann? That's how big the furniture is in my tiny dream apartment. I'm sweating, moving it all on my own, my back is aching, and every time I think I have it laid out properly, I realize there is no room for the sofa. When I move things around to make space for the sofa, there's no room for the bookcase, and so on and so forth, ad nauseam. This causes me to panic. Nearly at the end of my rope, as I am about to give up in tears, I realize everything has fallen into place on its own. I'm not certain how this has happened, but I'm flooded with relief until it dawns on me that I am asleep and I'm going to awaken at any moment. I tell myself I must remember exactly how I've put together my furniture so I can re-create it when I'm awake because it will make me tremendously and eternally happy. But when I do wake up, usually around 3 AM, I can't recall where anything is supposed to go. In that floaty moment between being asleep and fully awake, I am mournful about the loss of potentially infinite joy. It's a feeling I can't shake as I spend the rest of the night tossing and turning until our alarm goes off and Jim jumps up to start his day. When I try to explain the nightmare to him, he doesn't seem overly impressed. Maybe it's because I've told him the story too many times to count, or maybe it's because I'm telling him through the bathroom door when he'd rather be left alone. It's been really frustrating. For both of us.

Initially, I thought I was having these dreams because of Oprah's surplus of shows about home decoration. But one morning I flop on the couch with my laptop and do a little research on the Internet. I discover that rearranging furniture in a dream can mean I am in the midst of juggling all my priorities or that I'm desperately trying to please others. These two interpretations seem entirely plausible. I am constantly reorganizing my life in order to fulfill the "must" list created by Oprah in the past several months. But in regard to the latter interpretation, I am trying to figure out just who I am trying to please with such fervor that it's infecting my dream life. High on the list are my blog readers, for sure. I'm up to 19,577 visits on my site (OMG!) and have become committed to this group of strangers who constantly support and challenge me. I actually spend more time with them each week than I am able to devote to my own friends. I feel a huge amount of responsibility to start interesting and meaningful discourse, to entertain, and to moderate conversations when necessary. My blog readers keep me on my toes.

I'm also trying to live up to the expectations of a relentless and merciless judge. And no, I'm not talking about Oprah. I'm referring to myself. I'd never be this unyielding with any other person, but I won't give myself an inch when it comes to my LO work each and every day. Like the U.S. Postal Service credo, neither snow nor rain, nor exhaustion, nor my incomplete MFA thesis will hinder me from accomplishing my goal. Oddly enough, the only party I am not concerned about pleasing is Oprah. This is probably because I'm not doing this for her. I'm doing it for myself, and I'm doing it for an audience curious to learn what my year will bring.

I make myself another cup of green tea to keep my eyes open and read my e-mail. One of the questions I am asked most frequently is whether Winfrey has gotten in contact with me and, if so, what she thinks of my project. While I'm flattered anyone thinks enough of my experiment to imagine it would be even the weakest of blips on her radar, I have to disappoint those who make this inquiry. I tell them I haven't heard from her and doubt I'm in Oprah's Fave Five. I am inconsequential in her world, but I am still grappling to live by her rules.

The main source of my discomfort is a deepening frustration over the programming on the show. It must be a really rough job to puzzle a show together day after day, month after month, year after year. But the messages Oprah tries to impart get muddied due to contradiction. Some biggies that stand out to me: in January, I signed my Best Life Challenge contract, and Oprah and Bob Greene were a two-person pep rally for healthy diet and weight loss. No emotional eating, they said, and focus on nutrition. The very next morning, I watched Oprah eating a sinful-looking ice cream concoction from Cold Stone Creamery. My mouth watered over her luscious mixture of pumpkin ice cream, pecans, graham crackers, and caramel. As I popped a baby carrot into my mouth, I felt a little cheated.

It's also uncomfortable to enjoy a celebrity lovefest on *Oprah* after I've spent an hour completing my reading assignment for *A New Earth*. Oprah's Book Club selection focuses on separating ourselves from our ego and learning to connect with people on an authentic level rather than a superficial one. I don't see how a segment on the show glamorizing Mariah Carey's lingerie closet supports the work Oprah's asked us to do. I am beginning to wonder if her show follows a different rule book than the one she's handing out to us.

Another case in point: This month Oprah is asking us to think about our consumption, our wastefulness, the way we treat the planet. Several shows are dedicated to this topic, especially as Earth Day falls in April. But smack in the middle of a couple pro-planet episodes, a ginormous, gas-guzzling SUV is given away as a gift to a man originally seen on Oprah's prime-time television series *Oprah's Big Give*. Whether he keeps the car or sells it, is it really necessary to put another huge car on the road? It doesn't support Oprah's central message to be kind to the earth. How about her private jet? Is it a hybrid? I wish she'd be more transparent and mention her own excesses while she challenges her audiences to live simply. But maybe do-as-I-say, not-as-I-do is completely acceptible because Oprah inspires millions to treat the planet with more respect. Maybe I should focus more on the message and less on the messenger. I'm still very conflicted about this.

Some of my readers don't have a problem with Oprah's contradictory programming and think I'm nitpicking, while others have sworn off her show because of it. It might not be a mortal sin to preach decluttering one day and urge consumerism the next, but I find the inconsistency distracting. I try to cut Winfrey some slack — it's impossible to make everyone happy. I appreciate how hard she tries to fulfill her viewers' desire for programming and still stay true to her objectives, but it dilutes the show for me.

Maybe my expectations are too high, but in my mind, "With great power comes great responsibility."* If Oprah was merely an entertainer,

---

* Uncle Ben from the movie *Spider-man*, 2002. I told you I was a geek.

I wouldn't be so eager for her to rein in the horses, hone her message, and trim the fat off the show. But she is so much more than that.

This is why, wide awake in the predawn hours, listening to Jim's spot-on impersonation of a speedboat, I'm trying to decide: What exactly is *The Oprah Winfrey Show*? Is it flat-out spectacle and entertainment? I don't think it's that simple. Is it a guide for living? Is it one hour a day we can spend in the presence of our favorite gal pal? Is it a place we can tune in to join a community of common thinkers? Or is it a glossy show we can use as background noise as we get ready for work, feed the kids, and do our laundry? Maybe all of the above and more. Until this project, I thought of the show as a sort of aural wallpaper, the sound of it following me throughout my apartment as I ate breakfast, fed the cat, and searched for my house keys. When certain words jumped out at me, like "Oprah's favorite" or "can't live without" or "you'll never believe," I'd hurry back into the living room and pay closer attention. This is how I learned about the Bra Revolution in 2005 and the magic of Spanx in 2007. While I usually lean toward sports bras and granny underwear (poor Jim!), I ran out and bought items seen on these episodes. Let's just say my T&A have never looked better.

The more I think about it, the deeper question for me becomes, Is Oprah Winfrey *The Oprah Winfrey Show*? Pretty profound. Right up there with what's the sound of one hand clapping. If we tune in on a regular basis to be showered by Oprah's knowledge and lifestyle advice, we also hear about gadgets she cannot live without and learn that panini makers are "the thing to have." The line between Oprah's philosophy and Oprah's power as a marketing force becomes blurred. I believe in the separation of church and state, and this year has also convinced me that self-help and spiritual guidance should be autonomous from advertising and consumerism as well. The combination of the two doesn't sit right with me.

What's a gal to do when Oprah's advice for attaining my "best life" is all twisted up in her excitement about exorbitant, to-die-for Christian Louboutin shoes? Whether or not this is her intention, her delight hints that material goods can bring us happiness. Of course, Oprah will always remind us that we can't be defined by our things, but she sure looks like she's having a great time with them. Certainly the annual "Favorite Things" episode, when her audience is driven to a wild frenzy over free cupcakes and crystal watches, doesn't discourage anyone from worshipping consumerism. In fact, it looks more like a cautionary tale about how greed makes us appear bananas on national television. I can't imagine the perception other nations must have of us after watching one of these episodes. They probably have the same feeling I get from reality TV: slightly grossed out but unable to look away. That being said, I would happily exchange the prehistoric fridge in my apartment with one of those sharp stainless steel refrigerators with an embedded LCD TV from last year's Favorites list.* Those were super cool.

Of course, there is no sassy fridge in my near future, but I do have to buy a fire pit. It's the newest item on my list of must-haves to be purchased from Oprah's favorite hardware store. Yes, Oprah has a favorite hardware store. Where else do you think she buys hammers? I'm actually a little bit happy about this purchase. I couldn't have asked for a better way to display that one-size-fits-all advice is never one size fits all. But my smug satisfaction about having to buy this unwieldy hunk of iron ends as soon as I get it home. It's so big we can't bring it through our narrow doorways without turning it sideways. We don't even have a backyard that will allow the enjoyment of combustibles, so the ginormous pit gets pushed onto our messy enclosed back porch. The happiest member in the household is the cat, who loves to play and sleep curled up in the big iron bowl.

Incidentally, in an economy where few of us are making home improvements, the store's main competitor has seen a major dip in customer traffic, while Oprah's favorite hardware store keeps its corporate head above water. I don't believe in coincidences, especially when it comes to Oprah and lumber.

Oprah wants us to be honest in all our relationships, so I'm starting with you. I want to admit I've officially flipped out. How do I know

---

* Oprah.com says these appliances cost approximately $3,799.

this for sure? Did I take a sanity quiz on her website that yielded a result of, "Oh, no, you're crazy like a fox!"? No, this is self-diagnosed mental illness, based on the fact that I'm starting to use language such as "Oprah told me to buy a fire pit." And "Oprah thinks I should recycle." Friends will roll their eyes and point out that Oprah didn't actually tell *me* to start thinking about the impact I make on the planet, she told her entire audience. I assure them I know this and try to cover my discomfort with a little forced laughter that makes us all uneasy.

Since starting my Living Oprah blog, I hear from people all the time who say they love Winfrey. They use that actual word: "love." I thought that was totally wackadoodle. How could they possibly love someone they've never met? And while I can't profess adoration, in just three and a half short months of watching Oprah's show every single day (plus twenty or so years of seeing it intermittently), let's say I have formed a strong connection to her. In fact, it's no exaggeration to say my relationship with Oprah is currently more complicated than with any other woman in my life. I must sound like a nutball. I can't define what is happening to me. The best I can come up with is that I've developed a weird mutation of the Stockholm syndrome. Like Patty Hearst, who ended up relating to her captors in the Symbionese Liberation Army, I'm forming a (one-sided) bond with the talk show host to whom I've given all my power this year. If I start calling myself Tania, dial 911.

Enlightenment, watch out, here I come. The *A New Earth: Awakening to Your Life's Purpose* webinar is in full swing. Each week, homework in hand, I watch my downloaded podcast of the 90-minute class. It was intended to be a live, interactive Internet class, but last month when I tried to log on with the rest of the eager spiritual beavers, there were technical difficulties and I was bounced. After a couple weeks of website problems, Oprah decreed we could download the weekly, ten-part course from iTunes. Oprah fails so rarely that when her site can't handle all the registered enlightenment seekers, it becomes big news, as if no other company's website or software has ever crashed before. If Microsoft can't keep new operating systems from flopping, how can Oprah be held responsible for her technical difficulties? I'm always fascinated by people who get such a thrill whenever Oprah's weaknesses become public. This seems to be another symptom of our celebrity-worshipping culture. We root for the underdog until she becomes an overdog, and then we wait on the edge of our seat for her to crash and burn. Clearly we all need to awaken to the real meaning of life. It's a shame Oprah's website keeps crashing or we could all log on and get educated.

I think it's our culture's nature to desire a glimpse of frailty in those who appear to be superhuman. To quote a David Cassidy album title, *The Higher They Climb the Harder They Fall.* (This reference is not as random as it seems. Cassidy was a guest on Oprah's couch in February.) It's a toughie for me. I admire her self-worth and dignity but squirm when these qualities come across as arrogance. She writes a monthly column in her magazine called "What I Know for Sure." I'll be honest, I've never been fond of this title. Implying one knows something for sure insinuates there's nothing left to learn on that topic. I was always taught the only sure things in life are death and taxes. I alternate between being so impressed by Oprah's confidence and feeling turned off by it. I wish she'd change the name of her column to "What I Know for Now." It's just more realistic.

She is absolutely unwavering in her support of her latest Book Club pick, and her webinar is proof of her commitment. For those of you who aren't aware of the online class, here's the scoop. Eckhart Tolle, the book's author, does a lovely job in simplifying and communicating his message, while Oprah acts as coteacher, translator, mediator, and cheerleader. Viewers can ask questions via e-mail and live Internet video. I can tell she's very excited about this material. Her energy is contagious. My main concern is when language is used that insinuates if readers don't appreciate the teachings, or if the philosophy doesn't resonate with them, it's because they are not ready to receive it. It comes across as condescending and elitist to many of my readers who don't agree with the author's ideology or simply dislike the book. Although I'm comfortable with the book, absorbing what works for me and disregarding the rest, I can completely empathize with their discomfort.

While I cringe at the exclusivity that has upset those uninterested in *A New Earth*, I have to say I've gotten a couple useful tidbits out of the book and the supporting materials provided by Oprah. I have done an exercise Tolle's given us several times already. To release ourselves from negativity, he tells us to close our eyes and imagine ourselves as transparent. From Oprah.com:

> Feel yourself becoming transparent, without the solidity of a material body. Now allow whatever you are reacting negatively to—the noise of the car alarm, the dog barking, the traffic jam—to pass right through you. It is no longer hitting a solid "wall" inside you.

I find this especially effective while standing in line at the grocery store when the cashier is as slow as molasses, the woman in front of me isn't taking the keys away from her toddler who keeps slamming them against the candy display, and someone behind me keeps hitting me in the Achilles tendons with her cart. It just takes closing my eyes, a few slow breaths, some visualization, and I find myself calmer and more relaxed. I don't recommend it while operating heavy machinery, though, so turn off that thresher if you're going to give it a whirl.

I whined about this Book Club pick at first, but I've grown to appreciate it. I could do without the ten-week online class, but there are times when I'm genuinely delighted by Tolle's wisdom. *A New Earth* feels a bit like Buddhism Light: half the carbs and none of the dogma. I think it's ironic that the message I receive from his writing (our true essence is so much more than the definitions we've created for ourselves: we are not our jobs, our appearance, our stuff, our station in life, and so forth) is being taught on a talk show that frequently celebrates these things. Still, his message is a good one for me to hear.

The more I think about it, the more I believe it's brave that Oprah chose it for her Book Club. This culture we live in rejoices in our things, our money, our education, our career, anything that differentiates between the haves and the have-nots. Tolle's book reminds us that these social constructs are just illusions we use to separate ourselves from our own truths and from one another. I've heard that picking it for her club lost Oprah a substantial number of audience members, but in selecting it, she was true to herself. The philosophy within its pages is vitally important to her. She wanted to share it with us and was open to the consequences. I admire this about her and think it sets a good example for women to be fearless in the face of judgment. She's built this queendom, for better or for worse, and she's made herself at home in it. Those of us who want to stay are welcome, and those who want to move to greener pastures know where the drawbridge is.

April 2008 Accounting

Date	Assignment	Cost	Time	Notes
4/1	Read *O* from cover to cover. *(LO)*		3h 20m	As I'm broke heading into the end of grad school, I was really struck with how many products on the pages of this magazine are totally out of my grasp. I found the magazine's items both lovely and slightly depressing. I don't mind not owning things, I'd just prefer to avoid the window shopping.
4/1	"With the arrival of spring, I hope you, too, will reconnect with nature." *(MAG)*		2h 0m	P. 55 letter from Oprah. I went on a few walks, specifically trying to take in my natural surroundings. I found it very peaceful… but very hard to schedule. **(O)**
4/1	Read *ANE*, chapter 5. *(BC)*		0h 35m	This chapter really resonated with me.
4/1	Do *ANE* homework. *(BC)*		0h 30m	
4/1	Download and watch *ANE* online class. *(BC)*		1h 30m	
4/1	Eat a piece of whole grain bread with olive oil every day before dinner for 2 weeks. *(SHOW)*	5.79	0h 42m	We had olive oil in the house, so I didn't have to buy that. I did not like doing this *at all*. I don't need nutrition dumbed down—I get it. For the first week, I made homemade bread. Oddly, there is no whole grain bread recipe on Oprah.com that I can find. Second week I got lazy and bought it. (3 minutes per slice/14 days)

(cont.)

April 2008 Accounting (*cont.*)

Date	Assignment	Cost	Time	Notes
4/5	Outrageous Oreo Crunch Brownies. *(WEB)*	32.48	1h 10m	Everyone loved these brownies. I sent some to work with Jim, and his coworkers enjoyed them. For this price, I'm relieved! On Peapod.com "Pillsbury Thick 'n Fudgy Brownie Mix Chocolate Chunk" costs $1.99.
4/6	Watch the *Big Give*. (SHOW)		1h 0m	
4/7	Go to Oprah.com and read the rest of Oprah's conversation with *Big Give* contestant Rachael. *(SHOW)*		0h 10m	This contestant got everyone's hackles up. Oprah did a good job with her. Spicy conversation!
4/7	Buy several packs of Pampers (the One Pack, One Vaccine program) and put them in "a pretty box." *(SHOW)*	47.11	0h 15m	Wow, pooping babies are expensive. Bought pretty boxes. Possibly too pretty for diapers. Donated these.
4/8	Read *ANE*, chapter 6. *(BC)*		0h 25m	
4/8	Do *ANE* homework. *(BC)*		0h 20m	
4/8	Call and watch this *Oprah* episode with "best friend." *(SHOW)*		0h 5m	I'm not counting this as an hour since I would have watched anyhow. I just counted the phone call. Show was about Martina Navratilova and Coach Vivian Stringer. Awesome women.

4/8	Download and watch *ANE* online class. *(BC)*		1h 30m	
4/9	Buy *Standing Tall: A Memoir of Tragedy and Triumph* by Coach Stringer and give it to a young woman in your life. *(SHOW)*	20.46	0h 10m	Sent this to my cousin Taryn because she plays college basketball. Go, T!
4/13	Watch the *Big Give*. *(SHOW)*		1h 0m	
4/14	Read *ANE*, chapter 7. *(BC)*		0h 40m	
4/14	Do *ANE* homework. *(BC)*		0h 25m	
4/15	Download *ANE* webinar and watch. *(BC)*		1h 30m	
4/16	Tape the show… "This show is going to liberate women everywhere." *(SHOW)*	2.99	0h 0m	I guess I'm counting the amount I spent on the tape, since it's an assignment.
4/17	"This is a show I want you to start thinking about for you and your family… to try to live with less… how much do you really need?" *(SHOW)*		0h 0m	

(cont.)

April 2008 Accounting (*cont.*)

Date	Assignment	Cost	Time	Notes
4/17	Check out the "Your Family's 'Live with Less' Challenge." *(SHOW)*		336h 0m	This was optional if we wanted to create some change in our lives. My husband and I always talk about wanting to get better at this, so we decided to do it. We did the project every moment we were awake, so I subtracted 8 hours a day while we were sleeping. A big lifestyle change that had a larger effect than I thought it would. (16 hours a day for 21 days)
4/17	"Don't waste another second of your life on a job that you hate. Free yourself." *(SHOW)*		0h 0m	I love my job, luckily. What if I had to quit a job in this economy?
4/20	Watch the *Big Give*. *(SHOW)*		1h 0m	
4/21	Use neti pot. *(WEB)*		0h 5m	I am sick. Dr. Oz's suggestion on Oprah.com was to use the neti. I had one buried in my linen dresser. Dug it out and used it.
4/21	Read *ANE*, chapter 8. *(BC)*		1h 0m	Heavy, dude.
4/21	Do *ANE* homework. *(BC)*		0h 30m	
4/22	Download *ANE* webinar and watch. *(BC)*		1h 30m	

4/22	Own a copy of *Planet Earth*. *(SHOW)*	34.99	1h 0m	Cheapest copy I could find.
4/22	"Become part of this new and exciting global consciousness. You can begin by doing just one or two things differently starting today. Start with plastic bottles and paper bags." *(SHOW)*	41.90	0h 30m	We love our Siggs. ($19.95 for Jim and $21.95 for me)
4/25	Put a little tray on a table in the entry of my home. *(SHOW)*	16.00	0h 30m	Cute. Cute. Cute. I love my tray.
4/25	Buy a Lowe's fire pit. *(SHOW)*	65.05	2h 0m	Got it on sale! Lowe's is far away from my home. My friend Grace drove. Thx, G!
4/28	Read chapter 9, *ANE. (BC)*		0h 35m	
4/28	Do *ANE* homework. *(BC)*		0h 30m	
4/29	Make donation to Angel's Gate veterinary facility. *(SHOW)*	10.00	0h 5m	It's all I've got. I love animals, wish I could give more right now.
4/29	Download *ANE* webinar and watch. *(BC)*		1h 30m	I see a light at the end of the tunnel.
Through-out Month	Watch every episode of *Oprah*. *(LO)*		22h 0m	22 shows

(cont.)

April 2008 Accounting (*cont.*)

Date	Assignment	Cost	Time	Notes
Throughout Month	Do Best Life Challenge exercise. *(BLC)*		6h 40m	80 minutes a week for 5 weeks
Throughout Month	Take *A Course in Miracles. (WEB/SHOW)*		7h 30m	approx. 15 minutes a day for 30 days
MONTHLY TOTAL		276.77	400h 12m	
YEAR-TO-DATE TOTAL		1,915.78	628h 18m	

ONGOING PROJECTS
- "Reinvigorate your appearance with some great advice on how not to look old…"
- "Rethink your eating habits with some absolutely delicious and utterly original meals…"
- Use cloth and reusable bags at grocery store. No more plastic.
- Change lightbulbs to energy-efficient bulbs.
- "I think in terms of investment, it's the best thing you can ever give yourself is to have beautiful surroundings."
- "I would just say to anybody, whatever secret you're holding, live your own truth."
- Sharon Salzberg meditation
- Make your rooms personal.
- Best Life Challenge exercise and diet guidance
- "I do want you to start thinking about, as I have started thinking about, how much you consume. I mean, like every time you throw away a paper towel. Every time you are, you know, wasteful with food in your house…just think about how much you really need."
- "Get a lift when you come in the front door."
- "I want you to savor every meal."
- "I want you to pay attention to how happy women get that way."
- *A Course in Miracles*
- Declutter home/life.
- *A New Earth* meditation

Accounting Abbreviations: *LO* = Living Oprah Project Task, *SHOW* = *The Oprah Winfrey Show*, *WEB* = Oprah.com, *MAG* = *O, The Oprah Magazine*, *BC* = Oprah's Book Club, *BLC* = Best Life Challenge, **(O)** = ongoing project

MAY:

I'd kill for a burger and a latte right about now

Time spent this month: *140 hours, 23 minutes*
Dollars spent this month: *$417.64*
Advice that made my dad roll his eyes: *Oprah's suggestion to watch her show on past life regression with "an open mind."*
Most surreal moment of the month: *Seeing myself as a character in a syndicated comic strip called "Blog Jam" by Greg Williams. My hair even looks frizzy in a cartoon. As Charlie Brown would say, *SIGH*.*
Poll result: *Do you think Oprah is more content than the average woman?*
Yes (43%)
Probably the same (27%)
No (29%)

APRIL SHOWERS bring May's rash of celebrity interviews. These shows are light and fluffy, like televised meringue. They might not be groundbreaking or full of useful information, but most feel like a breather for me, and the 60 minutes fly by.

Oprah appears laid-back with her famous guests. The delineation of status is not quite as pronounced as it is with her average Jane and Joe visitors, and absent is my sense that she might be talking down to people or feel the necessity to act as their guide or teacher. The more famous the guest, the more level the playing field. This, in turn, makes me feel more relaxed when I watch the show. Of course, whether her guests are famous or not, they are appropriately deferential to their hostess, and many female celebrities arrive wearing the telltale red-soled shoes of Oprah's favorite footwear designer. Today, on May 1, three-quarters of the principal cast members of *Sex and the City* wear their Louboutins to visit the set. Including Oprah's, there are eight red-soled shoes on the stage, and a quick calculation lets me estimate that these women are walking around on over a month's worth of my salary.

No matter how huge the celebrity is who sits on her couch, no one sasses Winfrey or challenges her in any substantial manner. Everyone compliments her copiously, and most people mention at least once how amazing it is to be on her show. It's her world; she is always treated with respect and honored as an institution. It reminds me of the protocol that is required when one meets the Queen of England. Or so I'm told. The Q of E and I don't hang out as much as we used to.

Oprah has created a cult of personality for herself, and even if her ratings falter, her status does not. To the outside eye, she has seemingly impervious prestige. "Queen of Talk" might be an honorific, but she's a reigning member of the media monarchy. This in itself is an admirable feat for someone who didn't arrive in the world of show business through nepotism, endless connections, or with her pockets already overflowing with dough. She earned every rung she climbed on the ladder. Harpo is her Camelot, and many of us who live and work outside the walls of her company wonder what mysteries lurk there. I imagine many experts, such as Dr. Oz, Suze Orman, and Nate Berkus, to be her Knights of the O Table. Their mission? To guide Oprah's audience to find the elusive Best Life grail. This is no democracy. When appearing on her show, writing for her magazine, or recording a piece for her satellite radio station, they do not veer from Oprah's mission. And while they might be the experts, Oprah is their leader and the catalyst of much of their fame and visibility.

They are authorities in their own fields and famous in their own right, but their influence cannot hold a candle to Oprah's. No one in the world can understand the experience of wielding her power. There are other wealthy folks out there, other giants of industry, other entertainers, other philanthropists, other highly loved and respected celebrities, other self-help gurus, other political pundits, but no one I am aware of has all of these facets (and more) rolled up in one. She's like a burrito with the works. That's when it dawns on me: Oprah is peerless. If she so chooses, she can hobnob with every aspect of our culture's so-called elite, with movers and shakers. And there is no question that she has friends. But she doesn't have anyone else in her position with whom she can commiserate over a plate of potato skins. Whom can she ask, "What do you do when Marie Osmond's company makes a creepy baby doll in your image? Doesn't it freak you out when the doll's eyes follow you around the room?" Her words would echo off the walls because there's no one quite on a par with Oprah. Yes, yes, yes, we are all unique and special like snowflakes, and while I don't think Oprah is any more important than we are, she is literally without a peer.

The extraordinary niche she's created for herself has left her in a position where it's absolutely impossible to find an equal. I can't fathom this, and it kills any desire I might have to walk in her shoes. On the surface, it all looks very sexy and cool to live in her world, but in reality, I think I prefer the simplicity of my life.

Oprah recently said, "I don't get excited about a lot of things." I replayed this a couple times on my VCR because it was such a foreign thought to me. Oprah has had a huge range of experiences: ups and downs, wealth and poverty, discrimination and total adoration. How can she keep her sense of wonder alive when there is very little left to amaze her? That night in bed, I'm still thinking about her statement.

I roll over to face Jim. "Oprah says she doesn't get too excited about much. I was thinking about it. I think I get excited about everything."

Jim thinks for a moment. "Um, yeah, you do. It's exhausting."

"For me or you?" I ask.

He laughs, but won't answer.

Maybe it's her lack of excitement that compels her to keep building her empire. Thrills aren't experienced as regularly for her as they are for most of us, so perhaps she needs to create her own. She strikes me as a woman who would become bored out of her gourd if she stopped growing and moving forward. Oprah generates her own excitement.

*   *   *

Today I learn Oprah doesn't believe in having a television in the bedroom. I'm nervous about sharing this tidbit with my husband. I'm worried he'll turn to stone and crack into a million pieces when I tell him
that he'll need to bid farewell to the small TV on his side of the bed.
Last December, when we decided to give this project the green light,
we never suspected the toll it would have on him. But now I'm really
concerned he's starting to feel that his role in my life is taking a backseat to my commitment to Living Oprah. This is not remotely true in
my heart—words are not enough to represent the depth of my feelings
for him—but in interpreting my behavior this year, I can see why he
might come to the conclusion that he's less important to me than my
experiment. Maybe I'm just paranoid. I know he understands because
he's an artist as well, but I think he's uneasy.

Tonight, I approach him while he's scooping the cat's litter. I ask
him how he's doing with everything so far this year.

He doesn't turn around but answers, "Fine."

I was right.

He's not happy.

I'm going to be squeaky-clean inside and out. Oprah is plunging into a
21-day vegan cleanse and has invited us to join her. The idea of doing
something *with* Oprah rather than performing something decreed by
her is interesting, and I look forward to hearing how she manages this
period of deprivation. I'm excited to give it a try, but nervous about it
at the same time. Over a decade ago, when I was at my heaviest, I was
a vegan. I am such a talented eater that I got fat on tofu and organic
spinach. I also have memories of doing many ultralow calorie cleanses
to kick-start weight loss. I'd lose a ton of weight in a short period of
time (I once dropped 30 pounds in 30 days) and gain a ton and a half
back (you do the math). Because of those experiences, I've shied away
from any program with "cleanse" in the title.

I am relieved when the creator of this particular program describes
it to us. It's going to be tough but not unhealthy and is more about
conscientiousness than low-calorie fasting. We're to give up all animal
products, sugar, alcohol, gluten, and caffeine for 21 days. A headache

starts to creep up on me as I begin to yearn in a very deep way for my much-beloved cup of green tea. I actually just finished a mug of sencha, so the pain and the craving are totally psychological. It's hard to break a daily habit even when I know it could do me some good. I won't lie, though. My mental timer has started counting down to the finish line. I have 20 days, 23 hours, and 51 minutes to go. This will be a breeze.

Oprah commits to blogging about her experience. I'm excited to hear what she will create in her kitchen. Although I have heard her discuss cooking in the past, I really can't imagine her getting down and dirty, making her own vegan cheese. Maybe she'll acquire some live culture to make her own soy yogurt. Or not. I start to think about what I will need to survive and make a mental shopping list. I'm glad I have a relatively omnivorous husband or I'd have to figure out what to do with a fridge full of newly forbidden food. I don't bother asking Jim if he'd like to join me on this one. In fact, I feel the need to tiptoe around the subject of Living Oprah these days. I don't want to test the limits of his patience, especially as it's only May and he's still mourning the loss of his TV.

As the cleanse moves forward, I'm able to redouble my efforts to "savor every meal." This was one of my ongoing assignments from January and it's been an eye-opener. My usual habit, to put it as delicately as possible, is to eat my food like an industrial vacuum sucks clogs out of pipes. This suggestion has definitely slowed me down, and I've been making even more meals from scratch. And I could be crazy, but meals eaten while sitting at a table seem to taste better than those eaten standing up in the kitchen.

This program is also shedding light on my eating habits; specifically, the ruts that I fall into and the way I make food choices to fill an emotional need. I may eat healthy meals, but I create them based on what might make me feel better, more comfortable. In many ways, this 21-day program is allowing me to find a deeper level to the commitment I made when I signed my Best Life Challenge contract. I appreciate it when different pieces of Oprah's advice fit together rather than conflict.

Reading Oprah's account of her 21-day cleanse experience, I'm envious for the first two weeks that she has a personal chef. Of course, if I had her resources (according to MSN Money, she "makes $523.21 every minute, even when she's asleep"), I'd hire someone to soak my beans as well. She even has this professional vegan chef FedEx her food when she travels to Vegas. I would love to have restaurant-quality food delivered to my door each day. If I have one more broccoli and tempeh stir-fry, I might weep soy-sauce tears. And while I bemoan the extra planning, shopping, and preparation all my meals require, I think it's been an invaluable part of the experience. Every bite I've put in my mouth during this program has been taken conscientiously, beginning with the moment I placed an item on my shopping list. While I frequently feel as if I'm on a different cleanse than Oprah, due to the more hands-on role I have the time to take with my food, I can relate to some of the thoughts she shares on her blog. In reading them, I'm able to see some of my own habits mirrored back at me.

Oprah clearly wants to fill an emotional void by eating and drinking. She speaks very vulnerably at one point about the frustration of not being able to turn to soda and junk food and how she misses the comfort of an alcoholic beverage. I get a little teary reading her frustration as it brings up so many feelings for me and I become aware that, although I am not actively overeating, those waters run deep and the tendency is probably always going to be with me. There is also a relief in reading about Oprah's vulnerability. This is the Winfrey I used to enjoy wholeheartedly. The one I could relate to.

Oprah doesn't allow herself to budge a bit on the rules of the cleanse, even though the program's creator told us all to do our best and simply "lean into" the adjustments we're making. Oprah even gives her blessing to her staff to enjoy a glass of wine but won't relax the guidelines for herself. This is me in a nutshell. I find myself tensing up as I read. I relate not only to her behavior around food but also to her relentless expectations for herself.

I suppose I should be grateful, as I usually struggle to find a connection across the Oprah-Okrant divide. I think almost all of us can empathize with the desire to use outside sources to numb our feelings at some point in our lives. Food, drink, exercise, sex, shopping, television, the Internet, or simply emotionally shutting down: These are ruts we all can find ourselves in, no matter what our station in life. Maybe

Oprah's honesty will inspire others to find their own path to healing. What a powerful tool she has in her hands, and what a responsibility to her audience.

This might be a little stream of consciousness, but I'm going to lay something on the line I have been scared to say up to this point. Here goes. I think Oprah devalues women by focusing so much on our bodies. Before anyone grabs pitchforks and torches to storm my front door, I should say that Oprah isn't alone. I've been guilty of focusing on other women's bodies, too, but Oprah's the one with a top-rated talk show seen by millions around the world. I realize that might be subversive and unpopular, and I imagine my editor's red pencil hovering ominously above this page even as I type. Hear me out, please. I am going to make a disclaimer before I delve into this because I'm frightened of being stoned to death in the town square: I believe Oprah's ultimate intention is to empower women and girls. She does a great deal to positively reinforce our choices to take care of ourselves, to start businesses, to raise families, to take exciting risks, and to grow.

However.

She spends an inordinate amount of time asking other women how they lost weight, how they got their muscular arms, how they lost weight, how they got their abs, and how they lost weight. Sometimes the show will air long segments about an actress or singer's exercise routine that overshadows her new album, book, or movie. So this next message is for Oprah, and I'd appreciate it if no one else would read it....

Oprah, I am begging you to break this cycle. I know it's what we're all used to seeing on TV and that their perfect-seeming bodies are why many of us admire celebs. Still, I think it demeans women to think the first thing we need to know about other gals is their waist size. You, more than any other individual I can think of, have the power to kick off a change in the status quo. Sure, your audience might go through some withdrawal. We might wonder why you're not asking identical twin actresses what they eat for breakfast, or telling a popular country singer to pull up her shirt so we can see her abs. But I think in the end we'll respect you for the change you've made, for teaching us through your example how to honor one another in a deeper way.

You can empower women by subverting the typical gender stereotype. Please consider my request. It doesn't have to be a sudden change in your style. You can just "lean into" it.

Now, if you'll excuse me, I'm going to change my name and go into hiding.

May 16, 2008.
Shhhh...listen carefully. If you're very quiet, you can hear the echoes of screaming triggered by the surprise announcement that today's audience is being treated to Oprah's "Favorite Things" for summer. Have you ever thrown a handful of feed to chickens who have been in their coop all night? If so, you've experienced their high-pitched, eardrum-piercing noise, frenetic energy, and swift, slightly frightening movement. I am really hesitant to compare women to barnyard foul, but I can think of no more apt way to describe the sound, energy, and motion of this crowd. Except, of course, chickens don't cry. These women cry, and then they cry some more. I freeze in terror, watching them cluck and peck and jump and weep for almost a full minute and a half, and I shudder to think what I might end up adding to my to-do list by the end of the hour.

During the show, I learn Oprah thinks that everyone should try the turkey burger served at Donald Trump's private resort in Florida. I've never heard of Mar-a-Lago in Palm Beach before. Teaching yoga might seem like a glamorous world filled with champagne, caviar, racing cars, and custom yachts, but I'm going to have to burst your bubble. I think the last hotel I stayed in was a Holiday Inn Express. I go online to learn more about Oprah's vacation destination and discover that the website allows only members to access specifics about the property. I pretend I don't even care about that dumb old private resort anyhow and shut down my browser.

Trump permits his chef to bestow upon us his secret recipe for the Oprah-recommended turkey burgers. In return for his generosity in sharing these cooking instructions, I would like to give Donald Trump my own highly prized recipe for turkey burgers.

INGREDIENTS:
Lean ground turkey (whatever is on sale tastes best)
Salt
Pepper

INSTRUCTIONS:
1. Mix all ingredients.
2. Make husband form patties because raw ground meat grosses you out.
3. Cook patties anyplace except over fire pit or you might burn the cat sleeping in it.
4. Overcook patties because you are afraid of salmonella, based, among other things, on Oprah's 2004 show entitled "Is Your House Making You Sick?"
5. Eat patties between whatever bread-ish product you have in cabinet.
6. Tell husband you cooked, so he should clean.

Voilà!
Oprah's favorite turkey burgers cost me more than $50 to make and are waaaay more labor intensive than my schedule usually allows. Also, they have ingredients I've never heard of before. For example: Major Grey's chutney. My goodness, who was this Major Grey and how on earth did he come up with such delicious but hard-to-find relish? I really loved this burger. Oprah was right. It was awesome. I probably won't ever make them again because of time and money, but they were super yummy. Jim actually said they transcended turkey burgers. But as much as we enjoyed them, we both agreed we'd rather order these in a restaurant than cook them at home.

I'm relatively unscathed by this year's "Favorite Things" for summer episode as there aren't many assignments on which I'll need to spend. It's a relief and a bit anticlimactic at the same time. Oprah's guests include Heidi Klum, who teaches us how to shop for a bathing suit. Proving money and fame can't buy self-esteem or physical acceptance, Oprah says, "Now, anybody who knows me also knows I am not putting on a bathing suit. If you ever see a picture of me in a bathing suit, it's a fake. Mm-mm. No-ho-ho. Nowhere, no time."

Also, we learn about Oprah's favorite cosmetics, her "O-ward winners," as they are called. She doesn't appear to have seen these items before, as her best friend and *O*'s editor at large, Gayle King, walks us through mascara and nail polish and the like. Oprah introduces an adorable rolling travel duffel and I hold my breath in anticipation, hoping she tells us it's a must-have. She doesn't. The show rolls on and the only other thing I'm told to do is to "treat yourself to a weekend getaway." I immediately start the calculations in my head and can't think of a way we can afford a trip right now. Even a local one. I teach on the weekends and don't get vacation pay, so whatever days I take off, I lose in salary. I decide I'll tack on a weekend to a business trip this summer. I can stay at my mom and dad's house in New England. Sadly, this time around, Jim will have to stay at home because of finances.

The last item Oprah gives away is a copy of *A New Earth*, which leaves me puzzled. The philosophy behind the book doesn't seem to relate to the indulgences seen on this episode. It's like rewarding couch potatoes for becoming more active by giving them premium cable and a gift certificate for pizza delivery.

This has been a fun month in many ways, but I feel I am becoming very isolated. With all the hours and energy it takes to follow someone else's ideals of beauty, spirituality, and happiness, I'm drifting away from my friends, speaking less to my family, and having very little time for my husband. On a personal level, this is really upsetting. But as far as the project is concerned, it's not such a bad thing. Perhaps it won't feel like I'm swimming upstream all the time if I can allow my priorities to take a back burner to Oprah's.

Luckily, Oprah has created some social time for my girlfriends and me, sending us to see chick flicks and setting time aside to go for drinks afterward. This isn't what I'd normally do with my friends. I'm less of an event person and more of a hang out and drink tea while chatting the afternoon away with a good friend kind of girl. So, while I am happy to see them, I still miss having a more personal experience with the gals, without the construct of a girls' night out.

Whenever my family calls, the conversation is preceded by their statement, "I know you don't have a lot of time, but..." I must be giving off energy that says I'm up to my eyeballs in work, and hope nobody needs anything too time-consuming from me. My family and I are incredibly close, so I feel a great deal of guilt about this. I turn to Oprah.com for guidance on how to manage these emotions, and my search turns up a couple ways to overcome them and forgive myself. These exercises only make me feel guiltier as I suspect I am using them to rationalize my absenteeism.

And Jim? Ah, Jim... I vaguely remember him. He's the tall drink of water I live with. How understanding can one man be? I've been measuring our relationship with the Oprah stick, using evaluations from her website to test the strength of our marriage, following relationship advice offered by her experts, and asking Jim to be more patient with me than required by our vows. The worst moment comes every morning when *Oprah* begins. I start watching it like a hawk so I don't miss a word (or I'll have to rewatch the show several times), and I can tell Jim really wants to connect before he leaves for work. Instead, he gives me a quick kiss and looks at me sadly from the door for a moment before shutting it behind him.

Ohhhh boy... I better go do my guilt exercises again. They seem to have worn off.

May 17, 2008

I am moments away from graduating with my MFA. Imagine the "Hallelujah Chorus" sung by angels here. Of course, there will be no rest for the weary. My thesis might be complete, but my work this year is far from over. When I devised LO, I thought it'd be a light project that would give me something simple to focus on between finishing my master's degree and beginning whatever I chose to do afterward. While I hoped I'd gather enough interesting information to write and perform a one-woman show about my year, I had my doubts. I never guessed how it would snowball into an all-consuming project.

Every time I am tempted to throw in the towel and put an end to Living Oprah, I remember a workshop I attended at school early this year. We were discussing the work we were planning for the future. I'd just introduced my project to a crowd of people: students, faculty at the school, and other professionals in the art world. While my colleagues were generally very positive and excited by my plan, there was one nay-sayer, an adjunct faculty member, who shrugged it off. He said it was impossible to do and insinuated that Living Oprah couldn't be completed successfully. He came up with several ways in which I could fail. While positive reinforcement would have been appreciated, his negativity lit a fire under my butt. Whenever I get overwhelmed and wonder if I can continue, I think of him and know there's no way I'll ever back down. I'm going to finish out this year, come hell or high water.

Cue the angels, please.

May 2008 Accounting

Date	Assignment	Cost	Time	Notes
5/1	Read *O* from cover to cover. *(LO)*		4h 0m	Oy! Big magazine this month. Lots of spiritual guidance, lots of products, lots of advice, lots of advertising. However, I think it's important to note that at least there weren't any ads within the main spirituality section.
5/1	On seeing the *Sex and the City* movie: "This is an event and we owe it to ourselves, America, to make this an event for girlfriends to remember.... Go for drinks. Have a designated driver. Make a night of it!" *(SHOW)*	23.00	4h 0m	Girl time was lovely. ($8 for movie, $15 for the night out—I'm a cheap date)
5/2	Get clear skin. *(WEB)*		5h 0m	I'm following instructions but am working against lack of sleep and stress. I did this for 30 days. Skin looked pretty much the same afterward. (10 minutes a day)
5/4	Read *ANE,* chapter 10. *(BC)*		0h 45m	
5/5	Do *ANE* homework. *(BC)*		0h 20m	
5/6	Download and watch *ANE* webinar. *(BC)*		1h 30m	

(cont.)

May 2008 Accounting (*cont.*)

Date	Assignment	Cost	Time	Notes
5/6	Buy Barbara Walters's book *Audition*. *(SHOW)*	29.95	0h 15m	This book weighs 800 pounds. I could use it to do my Best Life Challenge exercise.
5/7	Dance in my living room to Tina-Cher show. *(SHOW)*		0h 10m	Does this count as BLC exercise? Oh, what the hell, I'm counting it.
5/7	No more TV in bedroom (Oprah doesn't believe in them). *(SHOW)*		0h 10m	Took some convincing—the sad thing is, now Jim comes to bed much later after he watches TV in the living room. Bedroom is quieter, but I miss his presence.
5/8	Love Cher. (Oprah shouted that we do.) *(SHOW)*		0h 0m	I thought about what I like about Cher. Was actually able to whip up affection. Love? I tried. When Oprah tells us how to feel, it can be hard to generate the emotion.
5/12	"Get up on your feet!" to do the cha-cha slide with 9-year old Quincy Eaton. *(SHOW)*		0h 3m	My cat fled the room in fear.
5/13	Watch show on past life regression with "an open mind." *(SHOW)*		0h 0m	I don't know. I think some people have an open mind to certain things and others don't. It's not so simple as telling them to change.

5/16	Make and eat Mar-a-Lago (Donald Trump's private resort) Turkey Burgers ("I definitely want you to have it too"). *(SHOW)*	56.24	1h 15m	Delicious! Thank goodness for leftovers. This was *way* too expensive for one meal. Here's the breakdown of what I had to buy: Major Grey chutney $4.19, celery $3.22, pears $2.64, lemon $0.82, chipotle Tabasco sauce $1.69, hamburger roll $2.99, organic turkey $28, apples $4.12, canola oil $4.59, raisins $3.09, parsley $0.89.
5/16	"Treat yourself to a weekend getaway." *(SHOW)*	231.00	48h 0m	I work on the weekends, so while it didn't cost me any extra to go on my "getaway" (I just tacked 2 days onto a biz trip), it cost me in lost income ($231 is what I would have made teaching my classes).
5/20	Join Oprah on the 21-Day cleanse "if you're interested." *(SHOW)*	73.50	39h 45m	Grocery shopping 60 minutes each week/3 weeks; meals (eating, prep, storage) 105 minutes each day. Only counting food costs above and beyond my usual shopping list.

(cont.)

May 2008 Accounting (*cont.*)

Date	Assignment	Cost	Time	Notes
5/23	"When you think that you're going to get in a car and drive, I want you to think about this mother holding her daughter's head on the side of the highway. That's the thought I want to come to your mind before you go to get in the car after having even one drink." *(SHOW)*		0h 0m	Traumatizing. I don't really drive, but can't shake the image. **(O)**
5/31	Purchase *O* magazine. *(LO)*	3.95	0h 5m	My June issue hasn't shown up. Needed to buy this at the drugstore.
Through-out Month	Watch every episode of *Oprah*. *(LO)*		22h 0m	22 shows
Through-out Month	Do Best Life Challenge exercise. *(BLC)*		5h 20m	80 minutes a week for 4 weeks
Through-out Month	Take *A Course in Miracles*. *(WEB/SHOW)*		7h 45m	approx. 15 minutes a day for 31 days
MONTHLY TOTAL		417.64	140h 23m	
YEAR-TO-DATE TOTAL		2,333.42	768h 41m	

ONGOING PROJECTS
- "Reinvigorate your appearance with some great advice on how not to look old…"
- "Rethink your eating habits with some absolutely delicious and utterly original meals…"
- Use cloth and reusable bags at grocery store. No more plastic.
- Change lightbulbs to energy-efficient bulbs.
- "I think in terms of investment, it's the best thing you can ever give yourself is to have beautiful surroundings."

- "I would just say to anybody, whatever secret you're holding, live your own truth."
- Sharon Salzberg meditation
- Make your rooms personal.
- Best Life Challenge exercise and diet guidance
- "I do want you to start thinking about, as I have started thinking about, how much you consume. I mean, like every time you throw away a paper towel. Every time you are, you know, wasteful with food in your house...just think about how much you really need."
- "Get a lift when you come in the front door."
- "I want you to savor every meal."
- "I want you to pay attention to how happy women get that way."
- *A Course in Miracles*
- Declutter home/life.
- *A New Earth* meditation
- "With the arrival of spring, I hope you, too, will reconnect with nature."

Accounting Abbreviations: *LO* = Living Oprah Project Task, *SHOW* = *The Oprah Winfrey Show*, *WEB* = Oprah.com, *MAG* = *O, The Oprah Magazine*, *BC* = Oprah's Book Club, *BLC* = Best Life Challenge, **(O)** = ongoing project

JUNE:

Living with less while dreaming of more

Time spent this month: *46 hours, 10 minutes*
Dollars spent this month: *$321.77*
Advice bound to fail: *"I think everybody should have a little garden, no matter where you live." My thumb is so black, I could kill silk flowers. I'm a danger to flora. The florist even delivered dead bouquets for my wedding. They looked like props for a Tim Burton movie. I think flowers wilt at the mere mention of my name. Maybe I'll have better luck with an herb garden.*
Words that stuck: *"Maybe we're giving her an impossible role to fill. Can any woman really be an idol AND a relatable peer?"— Comment made by Lawren Ashley Smith on Living Oprah blog*

J IM AND I are searching for a new apartment this month. Our current building was bought by a new landlord and our $1,000-a-month rent, which is already as high as we're able to pay, is going up several hundred dollars. We've spoken at length about what to do, what sacrifices we might be able to make to avoid the dreaded task of moving. The reality is, we don't want to give up our dinners out or movie dates just to remain in a home we don't even own. Also, although relocating is at the bottom of our list of preferred summer activities, we want to make certain we live in a place we can afford no matter what this year brings. This project is being funded by our own bank account, after all. What if Oprah tells us we have to fly first class to Tahiti and spend a week lolling on the beach? That could get very expensive. And frankly, the idea of living in fresh new surroundings makes us happy to think about.

After weeks of searching, the only place we find that meets our specifications and falls within our price range is much smaller than our present treasured apartment. It's a bright space, just a few blocks away from our old address, but it's itty-bitty. And you know what that means—more decluttering! Less space means less stuff. This is major growth. Before this project began, less space meant it was harder for me to close my closet doors.

In order to reduce the possibility of conflict, Jim and I have been using the Peter Walsh book Oprah suggested back in March to help us organize and pack for our move. It's less likely to cause an argument if I point to a passage in Walsh's book than if I nag my husband to throw or give any of his neglected belongings away. But let's get real. How many Dungeons and Dragons manuals does one grown man need? It's been going very well. We have a shared tendency to get sentimental and hold on to lots of things, but we're learning this year, through lessons gleaned from the show, how to honor what truly means a lot to us and release the detritus that clutters our home. I've even tossed away all the matchless socks in my drawer. Oprah says she thinks our homes should "rise up to meet us." I don't know exactly what that means, but I do know that our apartment wasn't going to do any rising when it was so heavily bogged down with stuff.

As I tape up my umpteenth box of the day, it dawns on me that at some point this afternoon I accidentally packed the Walsh book. I wish I were going for a laugh here, but I'm not. It's nowhere to be seen. I'm annoyed with myself, but I'm not willing to cut open boxes to find it. My fingers are crossed that we learned enough to get us through the remainder of the packing work. Although, between you and me, I'm pretty sure that when my back was turned, Jim packed his dusty LPs, thinking I didn't notice. And while I am in no way anti-vinyl, we haven't owned a record player for the past five years.

The most difficult part of the packing for me is getting rid of books I no longer read or need. We've got several cases full and I'm poring lovingly over each one, a bit melancholy, knowing that Oprah wouldn't give me the thumbs-up on keeping and cramming every book into our small new living room. I place them in piles, according to which friend or family member will be receiving each title, which books we'll donate, and which we'll keep. As much as I'll miss the bulk and comfort of having so many of them, I do get excited, knowing I still have unread books awaiting me once I catch up on my Living Oprah assignments. It's my reward.

The books that have sat dormant on my shelves since the inception of this project are more a tool for me to practice my dusting skills than anything else. Still, as we pack to move to our new apartment, I get a little thrill each time I place one in its appropriate box, imagining myself kicking off my leopard-print flats, sitting on Chicago's lakefront, sipping a cool drink and losing myself in the story of fabulous characters.

My fantasy is cut short when an e-mail arrives in my in-box from Oprah's Book Club that lists "The Five Books Everyone Needs to Read Once." I click open the e-mail with the same anticipation and trepidation a prospective student would have upon receiving an envelope from her dream university. I suppose my reaction could be compared to seeing I've been wait-listed, and I sadly pack away the remainder of the books I had chosen to read this summer. The good news is, there are three books on Oprah's inventory that I've already read: *Lolita* by Vladimir Nabokov, *Things Fall Apart* by Chinua Achebe, and *Waiting for Godot* by Samuel Beckett. Since the e-mail clearly uses the word "once," revisiting them isn't necessary. The other two are not books I'd ever place on my own "must" list, but they get placed at the bottom of my ever-growing catalog of to-do's, regardless. One is *Four Quartets* by T. S. Eliot and the other is *The Wisdom of the Desert: Sayings from the Desert Fathers of the Fourth Century*, translated by Thomas Merton.

When I place my order for these books, I wonder what qualities they have that inspired Oprah to sign off on them as the "must reads" for our lifetime. There isn't an explanation of the selection process, only an indication that these readings "will blow open your understanding of the world."

That's heavy.

June 9, 2008
I am knee-deep in *Oprah* reruns. It's depressing. When I wake up in the morning, I feel ho-hum knowing I'll be turning on a repeat of a past show. I'm amazed, but in all honesty, as this project has drawn on, I've come to feel a little zip of excitement when I think I might see something new. I watch promos for future episodes with anticipation; will I be surprised with a fresh *Oprah*? Nope-rah. Sadly, we've just entered the warm months and I know the drill: It's going to be a stultifying summer of reruns for me. There's so much languorous sighing as I sink into my couch at 9 AM every morning, my neighbor probably thinks I'm rehearsing for a Tennessee Williams play.

I blame my discomfort on side effects of the television habit that I suffer bravely, alongside others who share my chronic disease. TV creates in us an addiction for fresh, original entertainment every time we pick up the remote. We, in turn, demand to be continually surprised and excited. If a network doesn't step up to the plate and fulfill our craving by serving us something new, we turn the channel. As much as I might want to flip to something else during Oprah's rerun season or, dare I say it, turn off the TV, I can't. I'm still following her advice, even if it did have a previous airing.

So far this year, I've watched 114 episodes of *Oprah*, and even the new episodes are starting to feel like reruns. Without intending to sound cynical, I have to say I don't think there's much brand-new information for women out here in the land of TV watching, magazine reading, Web surfing, and radio listening. I'm not opposed to any of these mediums. In fact, short of getting down on one knee and proposing to it, I can honestly say I love television. But while it might be sexier and hipper than me, it's not smarter (or so I like to think). I understand that in order to create magnetic entertainment, half the battle is creating a great show and the other half is effectively advertising it. Not necessarily in those proportions.

If there is a finite viewer pool to draw from, what's a show to do? Well, in the case of Oprah's program, the star herself is the best advertising spokeswoman anyone could wish for. She is convincing and trustworthy. When she does her own show promotions, many of us are quite likely to listen to what she's saying. Still, there are lots of other talk shows bombarding us with their marketing. What's to stop me from straying from my relationship with Oprah to fool around with Maury? The easy answer is every time I see even a couple minutes of Maury's show, I feel like I've contracted an STD.

It's the words that are written for Oprah to say during her promos that really seal the deal and suck us in. "Exclusive!" "Original!" "Never before seen!" As I've said, I think we are convinced by a number of sources that we are in a constant state of disrepair. Because of this, many of us are entirely willing to watch something packaged as new, even if we suspect we've heard the information before.

This year, many of the shows touted as pristine feel secondhand. Even *Oprah* show exclusives, like her conversation with a pregnant man and the first time cameras were allowed into a polygamist sect's compound, are old hat. I've seen sensational stories on television before. I know when to gasp and when to cry and when to talk back to the TV in anger. I've become a bit jaded by the hours of TV drama I've seen, I suppose, and very little comes as a surprise anymore. But I keep tuning in to get that "high." Before the project began, I was still able to find delight when I hit the power button on the old Samsung, but in these short months, my capacity to enjoy repetitive infotainment has dwindled. While boredom settles over me as I watch, I am reminded of the summer of 1994.

After graduating from college, I worked a couple jobs so I could afford to move from New Hampshire to Chicago. For a short time, I babysat two young sisters who demanded to watch a video about a purple dinosaur so often I almost lost my mind. I'd annoy my friends by unconsciously singing its cloying theme song everywhere we went. I used to marvel that kids could watch the same thing so often and still remain entertained by it. However, I mirrored their behavior by spacing out in front of my own formulaic soap operas, followed by an hour of *Oprah*. Winfrey's theme song at the time, "I'm Every Woman," ran in a constant loop in my brain for about two years straight. Cut to me, 14 years later, zoning out in front of a franchised prime-time cop show. Its comfortable, well-worn formula is so familiar and unwavering that it teeters on meditation for me. Later that night, I find myself humming its theme music as I brush my teeth. And that's just on Wednesdays.

We stay safe by watching the same shows every week, and television producers stay safe by churning them out. You know how some fish will swim around and around and around in their fishbowls without ever stopping, and they don't seem to know they keep passing the same little scuba diver figurine over and over and over again? It's easier to swim with the current rather than against it, and I suppose eventually one even forgets that there are other directions in which to swim. Those little fish are an apt metaphor for how I watch television. I just hope that before her tenure as a talk show host comes to an end, Winfrey will transfer me to a more interesting fish tank.

In the five months of doing this project, I have come to realize I owe it to myself to turn off the white noise that these repetitive shows create and enjoy some silence or, dare I say it, my own thoughts. Becoming willing to kick my TV habit in the middle of a project that requires me to watch TV every day is not the best timing, I realize. I'm worried that feeding my addiction this year might make it more difficult to let it go when the clock strikes midnight on December 31. Will I be conditioned to click on *Oprah* even when the project is complete? People ask me this all the time, and I don't know what to tell them. In the meantime, I'll try not to vilify television, or, in the words of Gollum from *The Lord of the Rings*, "my Precious."

June 27, 2008
"Make your own vision board. I'm going to make one."

Woohoo! Something to break up the summer monotony—a new assignment during rerun season. Oprah has made it our mission to create this visual interpretation and reminder of our goals. I've heard of this exercise before and know it's used as a tool to keep one's eyes on one's prize. When the wildly successful self-help book and subsequent movie *The Secret* were released, I knew several women who bought into the idea of the law of attraction and made their own boards, filling them with pictures of dream homes, dream men, and dream vacations.

They'd hang this physical representation of their objectives in a location where they'd be certain to see it every day. I lazily considered making one but, in my limited understanding of the device, thought it was just a variation on a Christmas list and felt a little uninspired to spend so much time focused on material items.

When I was in junior high school, however, I made collages from photos, words, and other objects I considered profound and inspiring. I cut them out from sources like *National Geographic*, *Seventeen*, and *TV Guide* and taped them to a large piece of poster board. I vaguely remember images of Prince, Kirk Cameron, a Tony Award, the Milky Way (galaxy, not candy bar), and the lyrics to Michael Jackson's "Beat It" filling every inch of space. I hung the board in my room, on the back of the door so I could stare at it as I lay in bed. During my early weeks as a freshman in high school, it was driven home to me that I was not cool. Chances were pretty good that everything I owned was not cool, and I tore down the display before it could embarrass me in front of potential cool friends. I would give anything to have it back. It'd be like a time capsule of myself, and I'd be proud to hang it on the bedroom door now.

This is my chance to make up for the mistake I made back in 1986 when I tried to project a concocted image of myself to others rather than stick to my own collage-making guns. I put the word out to some friends and to my husband's coworkers that I'd love their unwanted magazines. And even as I send out the e-mail, I imagine Oprah and Peter Walsh shaking their heads at me in disappointment. I promise I won't let periodicals pile up and will recycle them as soon as I create my vision board in my new home.

It just dawned on me that I should do my best to explain the law of attraction. Oprah has done several shows about this topic, and I recently viewed an episode called "The Secret Behind *The Secret*." *The Secret* is the aforementioned self-help book and DVD that became a household word in 2006. And by household, I'm referring to my own. So for those of you who do not live in my apartment, who might not peruse the personal growth section of the bookstore, who do not watch *Oprah*, or perhaps lived aboard the International Space Station in 2006 and are missing a year of your pop culture knowledge, allow me to supply a rough and dirty definition of this phenomenon.

The idea is that our thoughts manifest themselves as things. Every time we think something, we're sending energy out into the universe, and similar energy returns to us. So if we're projecting positive thoughts, we attract positivity into our lives. The movie suggests that this might take the form of a new bike, a better job, a new home, scads of money, better health, a relationship, or even respect from those around us.

On the flip side of *The Secret*, our negative thinking has an equal response from the universe. Negativity begets negativity: Getting stuck in traffic, trudging through unfulfilling jobs, being dragged down by disease, and other nastiness are all caused by our pessimistic energy. While I believe we make our own luck, I am convinced there are outside influences at play. If I'm wrong, then every tragedy that has befallen mankind occurred because of our own stinkin' thinkin'. Perhaps I'm not open-minded or evolved enough, but I just can't get my mind around this.

Maybe I'm taking this all a bit personally. I saw the video of *The Secret* for the first time after Oprah promoted it early in 2007. My friend Grace lent me her copy, and while I dug much of it, when it came to the topic of health and disease, my feathers became ruffled. I felt I was being blamed for my own genetics, as if twisted thinking brought on my scoliosis. I became offended and felt the movie implied that if I had a more positive outlook on life, my spine would straighten and I'd live forever pain-free riding my pet unicorn through a field of rainbows.

Lucky for me, Oprah succeeds in delving deeper into the law of attraction, where *The Secret* fell short. As she is a huge proponent of the principle of attraction in all aspects of our lives, she does several shows on the topic with multiple experts to help explain the philosophy. While *The Secret* focused so much on the acquisition of material wealth, I'm relieved that Oprah's emphasis isn't entirely on that component. She's not advising us all to make a wish list of things we dream of owning.

Everyone brought on the show to discuss the law of attraction is a cheerleader for the cause. I'd love to hear more than one perspective on this issue but have learned not to expect one. Debate isn't a feature frequently seen on Oprah's show.

According to my blog readers, many people feel excluded or turned off by Oprah's focus on this philosophy. I hear from people who say they stopped watching the show, after years of dedication to it, because of the spiritual path Oprah has promoted. Speaking as someone who, in early childhood, felt excluded by my peers due to my own religion, I can empathize with their feelings. It really stinks to have the most influential woman on television (or the most popular kid in school, in my case) omit you from her circle because your beliefs do not correspond with her own. Still, we all have the power to physically turn off the television if we're spiritually turned off by Oprah.

I do worry about the possibility that some viewers' health could be compromised by the areas in which they are applying the law of attraction as seen on *Oprah*. In a recent rerun, even Winfrey seemed concerned by the effect her powerful message had on her audience. She spoke with a woman who was so gung ho since learning about *The Secret* from watching an episode of *Oprah* that she was forgoing conventional medical advice about her cancer treatment. She'd decided to heal herself using the law of attraction. Oprah wanted us to make certain we were receiving good medical care in addition to using the law of attraction to heal ourselves. It was the first and, I believe, only time this year I heard her suggest there are other laws in the universe, and that attraction is just one tool we might utilize. I find myself more amenable to her suggestions when they are flexible, inclusive, and open to debate than when they are delivered as edicts. Unless of course she proclaims I should go to Tahiti. I have no moral qualms on this subject whatsoever.

My goodness, it's been such a busy month, I never told you that Jim and I are currently living with less. That's right, I've bitten Oprah's hook and decided to try an optional program she's offered. It's called the "Your Family's 'Live With Less' Challenge." Oprah is on a crusade to get us to stop being so wasteful. I initially blanched at the thought of a woman who owns a private jet, several homes, and gazillion-dollar shoes (that are so painful, she admits, "I have to tell you, no exaggeration, I complain about it every day") telling me that *I'm* part of the consumption problem. But you know what? I don't necessarily think she's wrong. At the beginning of the year, as a result of a show about recycling and being kind to the earth, I bought aluminum reusable bottles and added to our collection of reusable shopping bags so we wouldn't be adding to landfills with plastic bags and bottles. Luckily, we already had a jump on this project. Here's Oprah's letter, laying out the program to her audience:

Dear Family,

Thanks for agreeing to live with less for a week. Your challenge starts now!

This week, you will be eating at home every meal. No more eating out, no more takeout. And you have to eat your leftovers. If you throw food in the trash, you've got to 'fess up.

For one week, you're going to give up the bottled water habit. Get a water filter — time to get to know your tap.

No more disposable plates, cups, napkins or paper towels. Try cloth — you might like it!-

For entertainment, you'll have to rely on each other. For one week, I'm asking you to give up your iPods and video games, and your computers only get turned on for homework. TV is limited to one hour per night — one TV only.

That thermostat is going way down ... to 69 degrees. If you get cold, put on a sweater.

Give your washing machine a break — try to wash only clothes that are TRULY dirty.

When you leave a room, lights out. Ditto for fans. When you're done using an appliance, unplug it. Don't forget your computer and cell phone chargers too.

Showers are going to be shorter — eight minutes max. Use a kitchen timer to help you keep track.

Want to go shopping? Head to your closets. That's your
wardrobe for the week. The mall is off-limits.

Your final challenge—no buying anything other than food for
seven days.

Good luck,
Oprah

There's no indication that Oprah's tried her own suggestions, so
I can't be certain if she completed the weeklong program, but I've found
it enlightening so far. Jim and I definitely have more time together,
unencumbered by noise. And even though we're supposed to do the
wash only if things are TRULY dirty, we're creating more laundry by
using many more towels and rags, since we can't use paper products. It
makes me wonder what has more impact on the planet: using recycled
paper towels and napkins or using water, biodegradable soap, and electricity to do laundry. It's confusing. I want to be a good earthling, but
it's hard to do everything right without wondering if I'm going about it
the wrong way. Normally, I'd research the topic and make an informed
decision on how to proceed, but this year I'm so busy it's all I can do
to follow the leader without stopping to dig deeper into the truth. It
makes me reflect upon how many times, before the project, I might
have reflexively followed advice seen on TV without stopping to ask for
a second opinion.

I like to have my iPod on at the gym, and I miss it. It lessens the
pain of my Best Life Challenge exercise to have "Eye of the Tiger"
blasting in my ears as I near the end of my workout. I can't even watch
the television hanging on the wall in front of my treadmill because
I am allowed only an hour of it each night. Instead, I find myself staring at the timer, which makes my exercise interminable.

As the weeklong challenge draws to an end, I feel similar to the way
I did when my 21-day cleanse ended. Voracious. I definitely learned
good lessons from deprivation, but it's these crash courses that make
my behavior even more extreme when they're over. No wonder so many
of us are doomed to fail at these projects, whether they are centered

on health, weight loss, or lifestyle changes, when there is no follow-up information on how to transition from the extreme back to "normal." Most self-help is focused on the radical change part of the plan rather than on the maintenance of it. Now, if you'll excuse me, I need to get off my high horse. They don't allow animals into the restaurant where I'm about to dine, and this wasteful consumer is eating out tonight.

One of Oprah's greatest skills is that of a motivator. Sometimes she does this with her own oration, but more frequently she inspires her audience by acting as a catalyst for her guests' inspirational stories. Oprah is able to draw to her show a wide array of guests we might not see gathered by any other single outlet. From entrepreneurs to criminals behind bars to movie stars, she books them all. Sitting on Oprah's couch garners a guest insta-respect, insta-profits, or an insta-platform upon which to share one's brand with millions of eager viewers. And yet it's the guests who have little to gain who interest me the most this year. It is while viewing one of these episodes that I become more inspired than I've ever been by a talk show.

That's right, I can absolutely say without irony that an *Oprah* episode changed my life. Was I expecting any of the shows this season to hit me in such a profound way? Not really. Could I have learned about the people I saw on today's show through sources other than Oprah? Certainly. But I didn't. I saw them on Winfrey's stage.

All my judgment over repetitive shows and reruns drains out of my body and I'm actually feeling a little naked. I find myself reconsidering if it really matters how much crap we need to wade through in order to hear one bit of inspiration we've never before received. Could it be that all my wasted time in front of the television set is worth it, hearing one thing that changes my life for the better? Maybe forever?

I'm speaking, of course, about Oprah's episode focused on the *Sex and the City* movie.

No, I'm totally joking. I just needed to lighten up for a moment.

I'm actually referring to a show about two people with incurable cancer, Dr. Randy Pausch and Kris Carr. It is their concentrated energy and their ability to live each and every day with the fullest expression of themselves that is so impressive. I am deeply touched by their stories.

They seem more vital and excited by life than most people with healthy bodies I know. Carr says her cancer has been her "teacher," and I well up with tears.

As someone with a painful, chronic physical problem and as a human being who can be knocked to the ground by life's hard times, that message shakes me to my core. It is as if suddenly a weight that I didn't even know I was lugging around is removed from my shoulders (and, people with spinal problems, you know what a relief that is). I start to think about how my pain can be my guide, rather than an enemy. Instead of feeling like my health is presenting me with one obstacle after the next and that I might not have the strength to persevere, my mind floods with the possibilities of how I can adapt my thinking. I'm so overwhelmed with emotion that I can't write about the show on my blog right away, and instead need to get some fresh air.

Oprah is the curator of her "Best Life" gallery, and I have finally stumbled upon a piece that makes me understand why she has so many devout followers. In hearing a message that changes my life for the better, I'm more excited about the prospect of turning on the show the next day and possibly getting another nugget.

June 2008 Accounting

Date	Assignment	Cost	Time	Notes
6/1	Read *O* from cover to cover. *(LO)*		4h 0m	
6/1	"Stop defining yourself by what you see or think you see when you look in the mirror." *(MAG)*		0h 0m	Goal stated by Oprah in her "Here We Go!" letter (p. 35). **(0)**
6/2	"Join us for our all-new Soul Series." *(SHOW)*		1h 30m	More Tolle. Downloaded on iTunes.
6/11	"I think everybody should have a little garden, no matter where you live." *(SHOW)*	37.50	1h 0m	Gotta turn my black thumbs *green* ($28.95 for herb starter kit, $8.55 for SH, no tax). I had to do this twice since the first time was a flop. Second time is sad, but I see sprouting....
6/11	"You need a garden tote." *(SHOW)*		0h 0m	Although she was indicating a specific one, she didn't specifically tell us to get a brand/model, so I'm recycling an old tote I have for the purpose of this assignment.
6/11	"You need an ergonomic tool set." *(SHOW)*	50.40	0h 15m	Purchased set online. ($39.99 for tools, SH $6.57, tax $3.84)
6/11	"You need a BloemBox tiny little tin.". *(SHOW)*	10.90	0h 5m	Purchased online. ($5.95 for tiny tin, SH $4.95)
6/11	"You need the *Inspired* book from Jamie Durie." *(SHOW)*	20.30	0h 20m	Looked for lower price, couldn't find one. Pretty book.

6/11	"And you also need a $150 gift card from Lowe's..." (this was to go into the Summer in a Box garden basket she gave out to her audience). *(SHOW)*	150.00	0h 5m	Ordered online. I'm sure this will come in handy at some point, or I'll give it as a gift or donation.
6/11	"By the end of this hour...I hope you will agree: It's high time to reach out, extend yourself, and meet your neighbors. Do something nice for them." *(SHOW)*	14.68	1h 0m	We were moving out of our old place so were able to write a card to our old neighbor. Still need to do something for our new ones. Stopped by new neighbor's apartment... met some of his family. Update: We did create Halloween bags for our neighbors with little greetings in them. (old neighbor: card and candy $6.68; new neighbors: $8)
6/12	"Everybody think about this: On the way to work or on the way to do whatever you do during the day...how many negative things....the negative tape that's playing in your head all day long about yourself. *I can't do that, I shouldn't do that, I'm too fat, oh, look at my thighs...."* *(SHOW)*		0h 45m	Did this on walk to work. **(O)**

(cont.)

June 2008 Accounting (*cont.*)

Date	Assignment	Cost	Time	Notes
6/16	"So if you have a brother or sister, call them or send an e-mail just to let them know you're thinking about them today." *(SHOW)*		0h 5m	I zapped Elisabeth an e-mail. This show was on National Sibling Day. Love you, sistah!
6/25	"I think we should be open like Horton." *(SHOW)*		0h 0m	I commit to remain as open to all possibilities as possible even without concrete proof (at least for this year!). **(O)**
6/26	Read "the five books everyone needs to read once." *(BC)*	25.51	2h 15m	*Lolita* (READ IT ALREADY!) by Vladimir Nabokov *Waiting for Godot* (READ IT!) by Samuel Beckett *Things Fall Apart* (READ IT!) by Chinua Achebe *Four Quartets* (GOING ON THE LIST) by T. S. Eliot *The Wisdom of the Desert: Sayings from the Desert Fathers of the Fourth Century* (ALSO GOING ON THE LIST) translated by Thomas Merton Two books: $20.53; SH $4.98 (75 minutes *Four Quartets*; 60 minutes so far on *The Wisdom of the Desert*)

6/27	"Make your own Vision Board." (SHOW)	12.48	1h 0m	I was surprised at how much I enjoyed creating it. But even though I placed in it my living room I forget to look at it. (Corkboard $10.49, pins $1.99. Friends gave me magazines.) I will update this board as needed! (O)
Through-out Month	Watch every episode of Oprah. (LO)		21h 0m	21 shows
Through-out Month	Do Best Life Challenge exercise. (BLC)		5h 20m	80 minutes a week for 4 weeks
Through-out Month	Take A Course in Miracles. (WEB/ SHOW)		7h 30m	approx. 15 min/30 days
MONTHLY TOTAL		321.77	46h 10m	
YEAR-TO-DATE TOTAL		2,655.19	814h 51m	

ONGOING PROJECTS

- "Reinvigorate your appearance with some great advice on how not to look old…"
- "Rethink your eating habits with some absolutely delicious and utterly original meals.…"
- Use cloth and reusable bags at grocery store. No more plastic.
- Change lightbulbs to energy-efficient bulbs.
- "I think in terms of investment, it's the best thing you can ever give yourself is to have beautiful surroundings."
- "I would just say to anybody, whatever secret you're holding, live your own truth."
- Sharon Salzberg meditation
- Make your rooms personal.
- Best Life Challenge exercise and diet guidance
- "I do want you to start thinking about, as I have started thinking about, how much you consume. I mean, like every time you throw away a paper towel. Every time you are, you know, wasteful with food in your house… just think about how much you really need."
- "Get a lift when you come in the front door."
- "I want you to savor every meal."
- "I want you to pay attention to how happy women get that way."
- A Course in Miracles
- Declutter home/life.
- A New Earth meditation

(cont.)

- "With the arrival of spring, I hope you, too, will reconnect with nature."
- "When you think that you're going to get in a car and drive, I want you to think about this mother holding her daughter's head on the side of the highway. That's the thought I want to come to your mind before you go to get in the car after having even one drink."

Accounting Abbreviations: *LO* = Living Oprah Project Task, *SHOW* = *The Oprah Winfrey Show*, *WEB* = Oprah.com, *MAG* = *O, The Oprah Magazine*, *BC* = Oprah's Book Club, *BLC* = Best Life Challenge, **(O)** = ongoing project

JULY:

Name that blogger

Time spent this month: *58 hours, 57 minutes*
Dollars spent this month: *$113.39*
Oh, is THAT all?: *"Learn to accept all people."*
Words that stuck: *"I think O's audience have stuck with her *because**
she's their shepherd. . . . Everyone is looking to someone or something
for leadership, guidance, protection, and nourishment, so whether
we find that in God or Oprah or Obama or Drudge, it's a need that
must be met."—Comment made by Dawn-Michelle Springer on
LivingOprah.com

I AM sitting aboard a Chicago El train with Jim. We're on our way downtown to do some errands. I have yet to buy the requisite over-sized handbag mentioned by Oprah back in January, and I'm hoping to find some sales. He's been elbowing me for the past few stops as he's spotted people with the *Chicago Reader*, a popular free weekly news-paper, open to a story about my Living Oprah experiment. I'm in a cold sweat, trying to use my powers of telepathy to determine whether these folks think I'm nuts or if they're intrigued by my project. Just as I assumed, I'm not remotely telepathic and I give up the fruitless mind reading.

I push my sunglasses higher up on my nose. Somehow, they feel like armor against the possibility of horrified glances thrown in my direction. I keep reminding myself that the journalist who wrote the article honored my anonymity and that it's probably a sign of a warped, inflated ego to assume anyone knows who I am. I am definitely excited by the attention that the project has been given, and it's on the cover, no less. Still, I'm finding myself uncomfortable.

This is Oprah's city, too, after all. Thousands of people pick up their copies of the *Reader* religiously every Thursday, and someone on her staff is certain to mention that there is a goofball in Chicago doing everything Winfrey says for a year. I briefly wonder if I'm doing anything that would prompt her to try to shut my project down. I'm not using her likeness, and while I am quoting her on my blog, I'm careful to do so in a precise manner. I suppose I don't have anything to worry about from Winfrey's camp, but I'm concerned some of her überfans might think I'm taking Oprah's name in vain. As I witnessed during the taping of the show, her fans can be extremely emotional, and I worry they might hunt me for sport and eat me for dinner.

Jim points out that I'm breathing funny. I force myself to stop my brain from spinning and try to chill out. I'm a yoga teacher, shouldn't I have a State of Well-Being Switch?

We notice a woman pick up an abandoned copy of the *Reader*. She checks out the cover and opens the paper to the article. Jim's errant elbow finds my ribs again.

"I see her." I wish my sunglasses were larger, maybe the size of dinner plates.

She glances at the article for about ten seconds, sighs audibly, and then throws the paper on the floor. Jim inhales sharply. This is the first time I've ever been litter, and I feel guilty about losing control of my carbon footprint. As we stand up to exit at our stop, I look back at the paper lying on the floor of the car, my photo peering up the dresses of the ladies who are standing aboard the train. My heart feels a little heavy as it dawns on me that people are bound to step on my face.

The next morning, things have returned to normal. I'm more relaxed and my head's back in the game. I'm flopped on the couch, eating a bowl of oatmeal with antioxidant-laden blueberries (Oprah loves 'em), watching an episode about children of sperm donors. The show is interesting not only because of its sympathetic guests but because its subject matter harkens back to old-school sensational talk show topics. But while lesser talk show hosts might make a spectacle of their guests, Oprah handles them with respect and sophistication.

We have several copies of the *Chicago Reader* lying on the floor. I haven't brought myself to read the whole article yet. In truth, the papers make me a little nervous, Oprah's eyes on the cover seeming to bore into me. I can almost hear her voice demanding answers. "Why, Robyn? Why, when I do so much good in the world, would you do this critique? Doesn't my good work outweigh the bad? Does it really matter if I use the word 'vajayjay' instead of proper anatomical terms for the female anatomy? What are you trying to say with this experiment, you big fraud?" I nudge the papers under the coffee table and the cat bats at them. To my project to-do list, I add "look up 'conquering self-doubt' on Oprah.com."

While I'm trying with all my strength to focus on this morning's show, I am distracted and know I'll have to watch this one several times to be certain I haven't missed a single word. Then I start to giggle as I think of the Oprah-approved baked goods I've sent to Jim's coworkers today. You might recall I attempted a recipe on New Year's Day, culled from Oprah.com, based on Jessica Seinfeld's cookbook. The result: tasty blueberry treats with a layer of conspicuous green slime that many of my friends politely avoided or, after taking an obligatory bite, wrapped the remainder in a napkin. Not to be deterred by a less than successful first outing into the exciting world of hiding vegetables in baked goods, I decided to create a recipe Oprah appeared to adore on her show. Who doesn't love chocolate chip cookies? Oprah seemed amazed, while eating one, that garbanzo beans were hiding amid the chocolate chunks and cookie goodness. "That's shocking," she said. "That is shocking, there's a chickpea in there." And she repeated once more for good measure, "That is shocking." Impressive.

As someone who enjoys healthy food, I'm always looking for new ways to convince my husband to put down the slice of pizza and pick up something more nutritious. This can be an uphill battle, so I'm not above trickery. In fact, I'm so tickled by the idea of feeding these goodies to Jim that I had to laugh as I created my shopping list yesterday. I snickered last night as I walked the aisles of the grocery store, dropping ingredients in my cart. I tittered on the bus trip home, bags brimming with chocolate and legumes. And when I actually baked the cookies... you get the idea. I had a pretty amusing evening.

Jim, who might be tempted to eat a tennis shoe if it had chocolate on it, was not too impressed with the cookies. I couldn't even convince him to have more than one. Still, he was totally excited about the prospect of inflicting... er, I mean... *sharing* them with his coworkers. He packed up every single cookie, without saving himself a single one, and brought them to the office this morning. I am so eager to learn about the results, I keep clicking refresh on my e-mail to hear the verdict.

Instead, I am surprised by a new interview request. As much as I want to open the e-mail instantly to find out who it's from, I remember I need to continue savoring every bite of my meal, and although it goes against my driving curiosity, I close my laptop and breathe as I eat. Food is so much more enjoyable when I take time to taste it.

I'm glad I finished breakfast before opening the e-mail or else oats and blueberries would certainly have fallen out of my mouth as my jaw dropped open. The inquiry was sent by a producer from *All Things Considered* on National Public Radio. I have been listening to this show for as long as I can remember. It's kept me company in the afternoon at many desk jobs in the past. This e-mail is the equivalent of Ted Turner calling my dad and asking him to play first base for the Atlanta Braves. It's big. It's such a big deal for me, I call my mother before I answer the e-mail. After some shared hooting and hollering, I calm down and pretend to be a normal human being as I get back to the producer. We set up an interview for the following week.

I am unable to compartmentalize Living Oprah from my everyday life. It's all-consuming. However, I am generally able to put this year's press into a different space in my mind, and keep focused on the matter at hand. I tuck it into the "denial" lobe of my brain, which is highly developed. It's what allows me to wear my white denim jacket in public and think I look snazzy.

As a person who is mainly involved in creative endeavors, I struggle to find the resources to market my work and frequently rely on newspaper reviews to attract audience members. The theater and performance population in Chicago is massive and competitive. It's difficult to get the coverage we'd all appreciate. This is a town filled with grassroots PR efforts and guerrilla marketing. Yet, because I imagined no one but my mom would be interested in my blog, I didn't actively seek out any public attention beyond my daily online journal. I didn't even bother to write a press release for it. Other bloggers have e-mailed me asking for advice on how to spread the word about their websites. I wish I had more knowledge to share, besides suggesting they write with regularity and hone the focus of their blog. Frankly, I consider myself incredibly lucky, not crafty or clever when it comes to marketing.

I tell my friend Nicky on a brisk walk to Whole Foods, "I can't believe this is happening. I'm shocked by all the press about Living Oprah."

Nicky stops short and says, "I don't think the press is *about* your project, it's happening as a *result* of it."

I look at Nicky totally confused. She patiently points out that I'm following all of Oprah's advice and receiving more media attention for my work than I have in the fifteen years I've been in the arts. She has me wondering—is Oprah's advice actually working for me? It's definitely changing my life, but is it for the better? I start to get a headache. It feels like a really strong man has his palms on either side of my skull and is pressing as hard as his beefy arms will allow. It's just too much for me to process. I had intended to be more dispassionate and scientific about this year. I wanted to stay neutral, but the nature of Oprah's advice and my own personality aren't allowing me to do this. It's nearly impossible to perform the project and analyze it at the same time. I need more distance to understand the ramifications.

I start to look forward to the end of December. I was worried this moment might come, but like Dick Clark in warp speed, I begin my countdown to the New Year. Of course, it's July, so the ball isn't so much dropping as it is crawling.

July 16, 2008
I'm standing on a crowded bus, heading to the WBEZ studios for my *All Things Considered* interview. I have such a big grin on my face my cheeks hurt. I'm excited but have the worst dry mouth I've

ever experienced. I'm worried I might make an ass out of myself on a national level. I transfer from one bus to the next on my route and feel like I'll never arrive. Public transportation seems to be moving in slow motion, but the clock's hands are in fast forward. We're taping in about 45 minutes. The interview will be done remotely: I'll be in a studio in Chicago and the host, Michele Norris, will be in Washington, D.C.

My cell phone vibrates, indicating I've missed a phone call from the *ATC* producer. I can barely understand his message on this loud bus, and I decide it's best to hop off and walk the rest of the way. He's got bad news for me that sends me reeling. He tells me that the show will not do anonymous interviews. I'm confused. I'm not trying to conceal any information from NPR (I've already given him my name and other personal information), I simply want to keep my identity private from the listening audience. He apologizes. I insist it's an integral part of the project and I really don't want to divulge my name. Nothing can be done, it's the show's policy. He tries to convince me to do the interview anyhow, saying that more good could come out of it than bad. I'm getting upset and nervous. I've bent over backward this year to keep my name secret.

I begin to get angry that this wasn't discussed with me before I agreed to do the interview. Anonymity has kept me feeling safe enough to be vulnerable and unfiltered on my blog. I want Oprah to be the Big Personality this year, while I allow my own identity to get lost in the sea of her audience. I try to wheel and deal with the producer in order to maintain my privacy, but to no avail. He really can't budge, and I understand it's not his decision to make. I ask if he can give me a moment and I'll call him back. He is patient with me and nicely says I can have some time.

I'm hyper now. I start to build a scattered pro-con list in my mind. I feel the clock ticking and make some frantic phone calls to Jim, my mom, my friend Grace, the producer of the show, my mom again, Jim, Grace, my newly acquired literary agent (who probably thinks I'm nuts), my mom. I can feel myself going so far over my cell phone minutes that I wonder if stock in US Cellular is shooting through the roof. I'm pacing back and forth in front of the building's entrance, the valets watching the crazy lady gesticulating madly and huffing and puffing like a rhino.

I feel ambushed by the show. And I feel like a bad person that I'm angry at public radio, the most innocuous of all media. During my chats with the producer in the past minutes, he's been very persuasive. This would give my project a new platform, and who knows if I'll ever receive such an amazing opportunity again. If I'm attempting to make any sort of statement by doing this, why am I so frightened to take the plunge? While I usually bemoan the difficulty and competition of being a creative type, maybe I've gotten comfortable and accepted that I shouldn't expect a wider audience for my work. I also wonder if I'm afraid of the new level of accountability this could bring.

I'm ridiculous. We're at war, the economy is crumbling, the polar ice caps are melting, and I'm making a big deal about whether or not I should show my face on the radio. I force myself to consider WWOD? What would Oprah do?

I tell myself that before she could create the program of her dreams, Oprah had to step into prevailing talk show protocol and master those rules. Only when she created a foothold for herself was she able to bring about evolution of the existing format. So while my anonymity may be important to me, I might need to be flexible to cultivate my project. I'm not entirely convinced it's the right thing to do, but I decide to step *waaaay* outside my comfort zone and do the interview.

But then I think about the time, early in her career, a local news show wanted Oprah to change her name to a less distinctive, easier to remember moniker than her own: Suzie. She told the news director no. The Baltimore audience would just have to learn to accept an anchor by the name of Oprah Winfrey. Now that's integrity. It might have been easier to bend to the will of the people writing her paycheck, but she knew that giving up her identity to keep a job was not the right decision. Clearly, this worked out well for Oprah. I should stick to my guns, too, and decide not to do the interview.

But my project is about the effect that the media has on women. Why would I turn down the opportunity to see my project from the inside and allow myself to be directly impacted by the press? Why am

I so afraid? I shudder at the thought: Everyone will know my name. The line between my personal life and my public blog persona will be permanently blurred. Just like it is for Oprah. Okay, okay, it's a microscopic version of what Oprah experiences. Still, I have speculated about how Oprah finesses the divide between her public and private life. Maybe I should take advantage of this opportunity to open myself up to the same analysis.

I stop short. I made myself a deal when I began this project to be receptive to whatever resulted from it. Oprah preaches that we should be true to our personal intention, so I'm going to stick to mine. My world has been so safe this year, as I've allowed someone else to make all my choices for me. It's time for me to suck it up and take a risk. So why am I still pacing around, driving myself crazy? My mother, on the other end of the phone call, wonders the same thing. I dial the producer's phone number and get ready to go on the air.

July 19, 2008

Luckily, I have breathing room built into my year. A couple days after my NPR interview I get out of Dodge for some work-related travel. True, yoga teachers don't usually go on business trips. You generally don't see us running through the airport to catch a connecting flight, swinging yoga mat–shaped briefcases over our heads and yelling, "Hold the plane! Hold the plane! Namaste! OMMMMMM!" Yet here I am, traveling to New England for some additional yoga teacher training. Plus, the great news is, I'm taking Oprah's suggested "weekend getaway" at my parents' home before the workshop begins. I wish Jim could have traveled with me, but it wasn't in the budget. I miss him. Hanging with the folks is great, though, and while shopping with my mom, I find a couple tunic tops for the summer months. I can finally replace those winter tunics in my closet's must-have section. (Besides, one of my friends informed me what I was calling a tunic was, in reality, just a really big shirt.)

When Sunday rolls around, I arrive at Kripalu, a yoga and healthful living retreat in Massachusetts. I'm here to learn how to better assist my yoga students with scoliosis. One of the reasons I became a yoga teacher was to help people avoid or manage back pain. This program allows me to specialize in an area about which I am passionate. I'm excited but am still balancing how I can get the most out of this experience without taking a vacation from the project.

There is no television here at the retreat. Anywhere. Jim is taping every episode of *Oprah* I miss, so I'll have to watch those when I get back to Chicago. Still, I commit to blogging every day and maintaining Oprah's lifestyle suggestions even when I'm far away from home. I kick this off immediately by choosing to take all my meals in the silent dining room, where I am able to savor my food in quiet comfort. The only sound is a mountain breeze whooshing through the window, and muffled chattering and the clattering of silverware from the main dining hall.

There is a warm feeling in this place of peace, generosity, acceptance, simplicity, and a focus on health. These are many of the qualities Oprah teaches us on a daily basis, but there are so many conflicting messages on her show that I am frequently filled with too much turmoil to enjoy these lessons entirely. Being in this place is so different. No one gives a hoot if I'm dressed like a schlumpadinka, no one's trying to conquer the world. The emphasis here is on *being* rather than *doing*. And the mirrors here are tiny. I can't imagine anyone hunting down a full-length reflection to see if her yoga pants make her butt look fat.

There is clarity here that I haven't experienced all year, and my initial thought is it's because I'm not striving to make myself, my home, or my world rise up to someone else's definition of beauty. Instead, I'm asked to find and appreciate the beauty in everything about and around me without judgment. It's more relaxing when I'm not worried about measuring up and I'm not feeling as confined by the fear that I'm doing things in a manner Oprah might pooh-pooh. I'm not saying I want to live in an environment like this full-time. I'd miss the fall lineup of television shows, and that would blow my peace of mind immediately. I am saying I'm having my doubts about finding true happiness as a result of Living Oprah.

I really do miss the blog community, though. I didn't bring my laptop with me and I'm regretting it. I have a smart phone with a tiny keyboard, however. I've been writing out my blog posts longhand, and then I thumb them into my phone. I send them to my mother, who corrects them and puts them online. As Sly and the Family Stone sang, "It's a Family Affair." I am lucky that my mom's a high school teacher and has the summer off to help me out. I'm not sure how I'd make this happen otherwise. I'm on the phone with her frequently: before yoga class, after yoga class, on breaks. My program is an intensive one. It's physically, mentally, and emotionally pretty draining, and Mom's taking a huge amount of pressure off of me by acting as my online eyes and ears. She's reading me people's comments when I can't get Internet access through my phone, and acting as my gal Friday. I don't even have to provide her with dental insurance.

Because I'm not watching the show every day, I have time to collect myself and evaluate the project so far and how it's changed for me. I started out the year in a much more lighthearted way. I began as a blank slate and had boundless energy, optimism, and curiosity. Now I'm feeling overwhelmed and am experiencing more extreme reactions toward each episode. I feel a twinge of fear when I turn on *Oprah* every morning, as if I'll hear something else I'm doing wrong or missing in life that I wasn't even aware of. I'm having a little childish resentment toward Oprah and often feel she's pressuring me to live in a world that doesn't mesh with my own priorities. I'm not having much fun right now.

It's interesting because as my readership grows with each new radio, Web, or newspaper story about me (I'm up to 53,730 visits), I feel as if I'm expected to be lighthearted and amusing. They're the organ grinders, I'm the dancing monkey. Still, I'm attempting to be the most authentic and honest primate I can be, even if it means being a killjoy and talking about the glaring differences between Oprah's idealized world and my own. I notice many interviewers are nudging me toward deriding Oprah or are expecting me to mock her.

One radio host keeps asking me, "What do you hate about Oprah?"

I tell him, "Nothing."

He says, "Just tell me one thing you can't stand about her."

I tell him, "Nothing."

He says, "Just one thing. One thing you absolutely hate about her."

I look at the clock.

Here at Kripalu, I pass a framed poster of the Dalai Lama in the stairwell on my way to my room. Underneath his photo is a quote that hits me in the gut: "Through compassion, you find that all human beings are just like you."

I have an epiphany, or what Oprah calls an "Aha! moment." During times of internal conflict, seeing differences is always easier than finding common ground. I notice myself falling into that rut and decide to take advantage of the positivity of this sanctuary and spend my quiet time considering how Oprah and I might be alike. At first it's difficult, and the only thing that jumps to mind is our common struggle with weight, but then, as the days pass, I find a new similarity each time I thumb a new blog entry into my phone.

Day One: Neither Oprah nor I can be all things to all people. I've been receiving requests from companies to endorse their products on my blog. One person actually thought I'd make a good spokesperson for cleaning products. Hilarious. Clearly they hadn't read my blog entry admitting that Oprah's website diagnosed me as a hardcore hoarder or that, more than once, I've worn a bathing suit top as a bra because I ran out of laundry. If my tiny project and the small amount of media attention I've received is an indication that being in the public eye makes you a target for this type of request, then I have to imagine Oprah is literally bombarded by such inquiries every day.

I've also been receiving requests to support people's pet causes on my website or promote their worthwhile events. At first, I can't understand why. I'm really no one special, just a yoga teacher with a blog. Then I figure it out: They are less interested in me than they are in taking advantage of my frequently read website. Instead of feeling used, I have a driving desire to help everyone. But I won't advertise on my blog, and I guiltily turn down requests to promote other causes on the website. While I do what I can monetarily, my shallow pockets keep me from being an effective philanthropist. I wish I could be of more assistance.

As much as Oprah does to promote positive change in the world, she's frequently blamed for not doing enough. I've received e-mail from people very upset that she does not publicly or actively support their specific organizations. Others feel slighted and distressed when she raises millions for philanthropic causes other than their own. I've read messages from readers upset she built a school in Africa; they wish she had allocated her funds to American schools. How on earth is Oprah expected to be all things to all people? She runs a billion-dollar corporation and already has thousands of people depending on her. I can't be, and all I do is write and teach people how to do downward-facing dog.

Day Two: We both love inspirational quotes. Many of Oprah's bulk e-mails are graced with some of her favorites, and she frequently shares quotes she loves on her show. She's acquainted us with one of her favorites from *A New Earth*: "Life will give you whatever experience is most helpful for the evolution of your consciousness." I'll admit, that's a pretty good one. Still, it's a far cry from my all-time favorite: "Nobody puts Baby in the corner."*

Words are powerful, life changing, and life affirming. Clearly, Oprah and I both appreciate statements that stop us in our tracks and inspire us.

Day Three: Oprah and I forget to have fun. She seemed shocked in a recent episode that most of her audience made certain they stopped to have fun every single day. It's an important step in achieving a healthy and harmonious life according to her guest Kathy Freston, author of *Quantum Wellness* and creator of the 21-day vegan cleanse. Oprah reflected on how much she works, and it appeared to me that she rarely has time to inject fun into her daily life. This spurred me to contemplate my own habit of filling every waking moment with activity, responsibilities, new projects, obligations, and plans for the future. At the beginning of the year, Oprah mentioned in her magazine that we all need to take a breather. I think I might need to go back and read that issue.

---

* Patrick Swayze as Johnny Castle. *Dirty Dancing*, 1987.

Day Four: We talk A LOT about our friends. We think they're talented, smart, caring, and fabulous. We're amazed and inspired by them. Oprah gushes about Gayle King, John Travolta, and Maya Angelou. I can go on and on for days about Scott, Grace, and Jefferson. Don't envy us. I'm sure you have notable friends of your own. In addition to her megafamous buddies, Oprah also has a talent for making her audience feel as if they're in her group of girlfriends. Many of the women I've spoken to feel as if they have a personal bond with her. I'm relieved I'm not the only one who has an imaginary relationship with Oprah.

Day Five: We both require other people's acceptance and support to do our work. Whether I am teaching, performing, or writing, I'd be doing it in a vacuum unless I made other people happy. As a freelance graphic designer, I worked in a home office. I didn't see anyone for the entire day, communicating almost exclusively via e-mail. My poor husband would come home from his own job and I'd start chattering a mile a minute, like a squirrel on crack. As much as I enjoy my alone time, I do thrive by working around other people. My current work is mainly about making other people feel good or entertaining them. Sometimes I get lucky and manage both those things. If I don't constantly challenge myself to improve as a teacher or keep taking risks as an artist, no one is going to show up and I'm going to be doing sun salutations alone in a room or end up using an unread script as a pot holder.

While Oprah no longer has to bend over backward to maintain her audience like I do (that's a little yoga teacher humor), she must constantly please, fulfill, and meet the expectations of a wide variety of people in order to stay in business. We both must strike a balance between keeping people satisfied and staying true to our own vision. Sometimes there are compromises to be made. For me, it might be to adjust a couple lines in a play to make a producer happy. For Oprah, it might be promoting an ice cream company the day after her Best Life Challenge episode. Our success is dependent on the acceptance of our audiences or the people whom we teach.

These five ways Oprah and I are alike might seem like a stretch, but I'm not trying to be silly or tongue-in-cheek. At this moment, they are a bit of a lifeline to me. These commonalities, even if I'm just imagining them, are keeping me from feeling alienated from her and by her. Plus, it's nice to know I can find some similarities with an incredibly bright, successful leader. It's like a game of Six Degrees of Separation, except using personality traits instead of tenuous personal connections.

July 30, 2008
How do you know if you're having an out-of-body experience?

I feel as if I'm watching myself in a surreal scene: I am sitting cross-legged on the floor, creating my vision board, knocking another item off Oprah's advice list. I'm also being interviewed by a journalist from the *New York Times* and there is a photographer snapping pictures of my adventure in self-reflective arts and crafts. They've been in my apartment for several hours, watching me like hawks. They watch me watch *Oprah*. They watch me eat. They watch me blog. Right now they're watching me cut out pictures of healthy spines, a beach paradise, and the city of Paris from magazines. I'm growing a little paranoid. Now that my anonymity is broken, I have something else in common with Oprah: The public interpretation of my project, my intelligence, and my motives is entirely out of my control. Everything I say can be chopped up, shuffled, and tossed like a salad. I had more control over my project when everything was simpler. Just me, my TV, and my blog.

I try to relax and breathe. I really do believe I can trust these people in my apartment. They seem to understand what I'm attempting. But maybe I'm just naive. I try to convince myself that no one reads the *New York Times*, but even I have limits on my denial-o-meter. I'm feeling very vulnerable right now and wish I had more control over the moment. This is not a position I relish.

I cut out the words "security" and "peaceful" from a magazine and place them prominently on my vision board.

July 2008 Accounting

Date	Assignment	Cost	Time	Notes
7/1	Read *O* from cover to cover. *(LO)*		3h 30m	This one wasn't really a standout for me, although I liked Martha Beck's article quite a bit. I imagine I'll think about it when regret seeps into my life.
7/10	"Alexis Stewart talks candidly about trying to get pregnant on her radio show *Whatever*, on Martha Stewart Living Radio. Tune in to follow her progress there." *(SHOW)*		4h 0m	I can't find this anywhere. Is she still talking about this topic? The show was a rerun. Still looking…still listening. **(O)**
7/10	Bake cookies that Oprah loved from Jessica Seinfeld's *Deceptively Delicious*. *(SHOW/WEB)*	14.45	0h 30m	Hilarious! www.livingoprah.com/2008/07/deception.htm
7/18	"I want the world to see this movie because we need it. We need it." (re: *Akeela and the Bee*) *(SHOW)*		1h 52m	Cute!
7/21	"Anytime you are forced to have sex against your will, it's rape. Even if it's your husband. And if you need help, you call the National Domestic Violence Hotline." *(SHOW)*		0h 0m	I hope this resonates with all women who need help.

(cont.)

July 2008 Accounting (*cont.*)

Date	Assignment	Cost	Time	Notes
7/22	Take the YOU: Staying Young Aging Quiz. *(SHOW)*		5h 0m	I scored an 80 to 89 percent. I know how I can improve and I want to! **(O)**
7/24	Learn to accept all people. *(SHOW)*		0h 0m	Working on it. This has made me a lot less angry during election season. **(O)**
7/25	Read *Eat, Pray, Love* in 2 weeks. *(SHOW)*	15.00	5h 0m	Wow. I want to take that trip. I've always wanted to travel to India, especially. I wish I could leave tomorrow.
7/28	"…the Miraval Spa in Arizona. If you ever get the chance in life, that's where you want to go." *(SHOW)*		0h 0m	I can't imagine I'll ever get the chance—yoga teachers can't usually afford to go to spas, unless we work at them! **(O)**
7/29	Dye hair roots with Perfect 10 hair color. *(MAG)*	83.94	1h 40m	I touch up my roots approximately every 4 weeks. ($13.99 per box × 6)
Through-out Month	Watch every episode of *Oprah*. *(LO)*		23h 0m	23 shows
Through-out Month	Do Best Life Challenge exercise. *(BLC)*		6h 40m	80 minutes a week for 5 weeks
Through-out Month	Take *A Course in Miracles*. *(WEB/ SHOW)*		7h 45m	approx. 15 minutes a day for 31 days
MONTHLY TOTAL		113.39	58h 57m	
YEAR-TO-DATE TOTAL		2,768.58	873h 48m	

ONGOING PROJECTS
 – "Reinvigorate your appearance with some great advice on how not to look old…"
 – "Rethink your eating habits with some absolutely delicious and utterly original meals…"

- Use cloth and reusable bags at grocery store. No more plastic.
- Change lightbulbs to energy-efficient bulbs.
- "I think in terms of investment, it's the best thing you can ever give yourself is to have beautiful surroundings."
- "I would just say to anybody, whatever secret you're holding, live your own truth."
- Sharon Salzberg meditation
- Make your rooms personal.
- Best Life Challenge exercise and diet guidance
- "I do want you to start thinking about, as I have started thinking about, how much you consume. I mean, like every time you throw away a paper towel. Every time you are, you know, wasteful with food in your house...just think about how much you really need."
- "Get a lift when you come in the front door."
- "I want you to savor every meal."
- "I want you to pay attention to how happy women get that way."
- *A Course in Miracles*
- Declutter home/life.
- *A New Earth* meditation
- "With the arrival of spring, I hope you, too, will reconnect with nature."
- "When you think that you're going to get in a car and drive, I want you to think about this mother holding her daughter's head on the side of the highway. That's the thought I want to come to your mind before you go to get in the car after having even one drink."
- "Stop defining yourself by what you see—or think you see—when you look in the mirror."
- "Everybody think about this: On the way to work or on the way to do whatever you do during the day...how many negative things...The negative tape that's playing in your head all day long about yourself. *I can't do that, I shouldn't do that, I'm too fat, oh, look at my thighs...*"
- "I think we should be open like Horton."

Accounting Abbreviations: *LO* = Living Oprah Project Task, *SHOW* = *The Oprah Winfrey Show*, *WEB* = Oprah.com, *MAG* = *O, The Oprah Magazine*, *BC* = Oprah's Book Club, *BLC* = Best Life Challenge, **(O)** = ongoing project

AUGUST:

America gets a report card

Time spent this month: 65 *hours,* 25 *minutes*
Dollars spent this month: $282.74
Most adorable and cuddly suggestion: To adopt a pet from a reputable shelter (inspired by the show as well as advice on Oprah.com). Welcome to our new kitty, Selmarie! I could just eat her up.
Words that stuck: "I've noticed, no matter how long someone may have been doing their thing, they haven't truly been discovered until Oprah says so." — Comment made by Samantha Marquis on Living Oprah blog

O PRAH BURNS up the TV screen with a rapid-fire week about what is wrong with our country. From schools to health care, she leaves no stone unturned. To borrow a phrase, she's mad as hell, and she's not going to take it anymore. She doesn't think we should, either. It's as if this series of reruns has been specifically designed to impress upon us that we are one broken nation. The commenters on my blog are fired up, and as my cell phone vibrates to notify me when I get a new note, it sounds like I've got a beehive in my purse. Inspired by Oprah's political shows and her involvement in this year's presidential campaign, many people have been speculating that she will end up running for or be appointed to public office, but I disagree. At this point in her career, I can't imagine why she'd involve herself in the red tape of government when her own platform is already incredibly powerful. She doesn't create policy, but she definitely impacts it. She rouses us to vote a certain way or call upon our elected representatives to generate the change she believes will make our country a better place. Just ask Pennsylvania's state senators who were bombarded with letters from Oprah's audience to vote for H.B. 2525 (otherwise known as Pennsylvania's Dog Law) to prevent inhumane treatment of canines. Oprah asked her viewers to use the form letter on her website to contact their senators. The vote will be in October, and I'm pretty sure I know which way the tide will turn.

While I don't disagree with her shows about America's broken systems per se, I wonder if there's an ulterior motive to the timing of this programming. We're up to our eyeballs in the presidential campaign, and these shows are a not-so-subtle reminder that the US of A is in trouble and is in need of positive change. I don't think there's any coincidence Oprah's candidate is running on this platform. These gloomy episodes are painful to watch, and I will admit if I weren't doing this project, I'd turn off the television. Luckily, I signed my Best Life Challenge contract or I might feel the urge to turn to food for emotional comfort right about now.

I tell myself I'm just doing research as I check out Oprah's former personal chef's recipes on her website. Art Smith isn't putting any chickpeas in his desserts, that's for sure. If I had a drug of choice, it might be his Hummingbird Cake. Salivating, I force myself to turn off the computer and go for a bike ride.

On the topic of avoiding emotional eating, the Best Life contract troubles me. Oprah really likes having us put things in writing in order to prove our commitment. When I ask my readers to let me know if they are still following their contract, my usually full in-box is devoid of incoming e-mail. I look up the word "contract" on Oprah's website and the search comes up with countless entries. There's even a scanned copy of the 2002 contract that Oprah wrote and signed to commit to a six-week program of healthy eating and exercise. Bob Greene signed it as her witness. That's pretty formal. I've created contracts with myself in the past and swore I'd exercise more, eat better, save money, stop procrastinating. They never panned out for me. Maybe I should have had them notarized or something. When I inevitably failed at whatever pledge I made, I really hated myself for it. After I dealt several such blows to my self-esteem, I decided I'd never sign one again.

Until this year, of course. I was not too happy when I had to commit to the Best Life contract in January. Based on past experiences, I was worried it might derail me. Luckily, I'm hanging tough. I am trying to make the successful completion of Living Oprah my goal, rather than fixing or changing my body.

My fidelity to this specific food- and exercise-related component of the project has had physical ramifications. I started working with a personal trainer and I've gotten a bit slimmer and definitely more muscular. Now when I wear my white jeans and white denim jacket, I don't feel like I'm promoting the baby beluga whale exhibit down at the aquarium.

I'm far more confident about my body. I feel strong and can honestly say I *usually* like what I see when I look in the mirror...which my husband gingerly tells me I'm doing all the time now. I laugh this off, but truthfully, I'm quite embarrassed. He's right. There were pre-LO days when I don't think I even looked in the mirror once before I left for work. It wasn't lack of self-esteem that drove this ignorance of my appearance, it simply wasn't a high priority for me. Now the way I look when I leave the house has a definitive impact on how I feel.

I can't say exactly when my appearance obsession began this year, but if I had a nickel for every time I checked my appearance in a reflection, I might have enough money to join an exclusive members-only resort in Florida. At the very least, I could afford to make those turkey burgers again. I miss them. I've caught the cat staring at me as I strain to look at my butt in an outfit and end up walking in circles as I look over my own shoulder like a dog chasing its tail. Vanity 1, Dignity 0.

Most of my friends think I look great, and I get lots of positive comments on my body, but my husband isn't quite sure my changed physique is worth my moments of narcissism. Plus, he points out, it takes a lot longer for me to get ready to leave the house in the morning. He insists I'm always asking him if an outfit makes me look heavy or older than my 35 years. I hear the frustration in his voice but also feel he just doesn't understand. To placate him, I show him my muscular arms.

"Look!" I tell him enthusiastically. "They don't waddle when I wave good-bye anymore!"

I yank my short sleeve over my shoulder so he can clearly see my whole arm, and I wave at him several different ways, with varying speed and vigor. I beam with pride. He stares at me in silence.

"Stop saying that."

Oprah states this unequivocally, and I feel like she's speaking to most of the women I know, including me. Maria Shriver is visiting the show, and the discussion centers around how many of us reduce our own value by the language we choose to define ourselves. It's been pointed out that we use words like "just," as in "I'm *just* a yoga teacher." We give ourselves demotions in importance before anyone else can. I've been noticing this when I reconnect with female friends whom I haven't seen since high school or college. If I ask what they're doing in life these days, they usually answer, "I'm *just* a stay-at-home mom" or "I *just* work in an office." It's as if they're apologizing for their existence, telling me they know how much of a failure they are, before I can judge them. And I answer back, "I'm *just* writing a blog."

I think it's great that Oprah's telling us to cut it out. I wonder if she can relate to us at all, however, when and why we feel like we need to use this type of language. Saying, "I'm *just* Oprah" doesn't really have the same resonance. She's usually a good example. For instance, she's chosen not to raise children, but she never doubts her decision publicly. She doesn't openly bemoan her paths not taken. There's no reason for us to do so, either, simply because we've chosen different priorities from one another.

The very first day I put this on my Oprah to-do list, I catch myself almost falling into that old self-derision trap a few times. I nearly did it once in reference to my writing, once in reference to my age, and once regarding the fact that I don't have kids. This is going to be a toughie—the emotional assignments usually are. I have to ask myself whom I'm trying to please and whom I think I need to impress. Years ago, I was advised that if I'm constantly judging myself and I'm worrying about the judgment of others, then I should also look to see if I'm placing judgments on other women. These actions tend to go hand in hand. They perpetuate each other.

As I watch the show with Oprah and Shriver, I start to get

uncomfortable as I consider my involvement in this cycle of criticism and judgment. We all talk about how much pressure we put on ourselves. I do, Oprah does, Oprah's guests and audience do. But I think that's just part of the problem. It seems to me that not only do we have incredibly high expectations of ourselves, but many of us also have the same standards for each other. If we are busting our butts to live our best lives, shouldn't everyone else?

Grace and I frequently marvel over a friend of hers who is a prolific and successful writer, an entrepreneur, a mother, a wife, has a beautiful home, works out, and always looks amazing. We talk about how remarkable this woman is whenever we're feeling overwhelmed. I think of another acquaintance who is a stay-at-home mom, taking a break from her career to raise her kids. The last time I saw her, she was wearing mismatched socks and had peanut butter in her hair (from her son's lunch). She wasn't the least bit self-conscious about it. Why doesn't that warrant an "amazing" from my lips? I have a tendency to be more impressed by women who appear to choose their cake recipe, bake it, ice it, and eat it, too. This is a trend in the majority of my peers. We're go-for-it gals who are inspired by others of the same ilk.

Perhaps this is why Oprah tends to impress us so much. She appears to have the ability to keep all her plates spinning, and let's face it, she must have a ton of china. As overwhelmed as I feel on a daily basis, I don't understand why I look up to women who give the impression of working 25 hours a day, eight days a week. I already feel like I'm running at capacity and don't want to take anything else on my shoulders. Yet I look at Oprah and think I should be able to squeeze in just *one* more project. Clearly, I'm confused. But I'm also right where Oprah needs me to be. I am a target audience member. I need to learn to prioritize, to achieve my life's goals, to relax, to strengthen my relationships. No need to look for any other outlet when I can learn all about these things in the one hour of television viewing I consume each morning. The *Oprah* show is one-stop emotional shopping for the modern woman who wants every aspect of her life to feel satisfying and full.

I took a test today on Oprah.com called the Satisfaction with Life Scale. I found it when I saw this on her home page: "How happy are

you? Take the quiz." I was in a pretty good mood and felt game for it.
I went in thinking I'd score relatively high since I think of myself as
quite delighted by life in general. Imagine my disappointment when
the test results conclude I'm only moderately happy. It totally soured
my disposition. I, in turn, created a one question quiz called the "How
Annoyed Am I at Having My Feelings Diagnosed by a Five-Question
Quiz?" I score off the charts on that one.

I do a little more hunting on Oprah.com and find another exam,
The Are You Happy quiz. This one, which originally appeared in her
magazine in 2004, is made up of 24 multiple-choice questions. I score
66, which came with the explanation, "If you scored between 50 and
72, congratulations! Consider yourself a happy person." HA! I knew it.
I *am* happy. Eat that, Satisfaction with Life Scale!

What is it with all the quizzes? They are in magazines, on television, online. I remember taking magazine quizzes with girlfriends as
far back as junior high school. They used to be quite exciting when
I was young. I would thrill at the possibility of learning what type
of boy would make the perfect date or what my future job would be.
There seemed to be a disconnect between my test results and real life,
however. My dream boy must not have gotten the memo as I didn't
get asked out once in high school. And as far as my dream occupa-
tion was concerned, archeologist was a far cry from my job scooping ice cream. I had to contend with puberty before I'd be invited on
any digs.

Nowadays, I put as much faith in these tests as I do in the mood ring
I haven't worn in years. The only difference between them is that the
happiness quiz doesn't turn my finger green. But while I continue out
of habit to take them, they exemplify my trouble with talk show advice
in general: They offer up one-size-fits-all diagnoses to life's complicated
questions. I think human beings are far too nuanced for multiple-
choice questions. At worst, these tests push us even further away from
developing and trusting our own intuition. At best, they waste a bit of
time and provide some diversion from real self-examination. I worry
that I'm beginning to sound bitter, a choleric stick-in-the-mud, rain-
ing on everyone else's magazine quiz parade. I do a little hunting on
Oprah.com for some answers and come upon a test created by Martha

Beck called Are You Screaming on the Inside? When I first try to take it, the website is down, which really annoys me. When it's finally up and running, my results are: "There are times when you act more passively than you want. Learn more about the situations that make you angry to see where you can assert yourself." I run a search on Oprah's site: "Where should I assert myself?" I get twenty pages of results in return. Holy crap, that's a *lot* of asserting.

I'm in mourning. My love affair with Dr. Oz's appearances on *Oprah* has ended. I'm officially sick of seeing the doctor. I know it's a drastic change. It was with much excitement that I anticipated seeing him at the beginning of the year. Now, if I glimpse the slightest hint of surgical scrubs, I get a little stomachache and have to pop a Tums. I still love health-related episodes, but I'm just tired of the man Oprah has dubbed America's Doctor.

I've grown wary of his transition from medical professional into TV star. Television may grant credibility, but it can also taketh away. When Oprah transformed Bob Greene into a celebrity, he jumped on the product endorsement bandwagon, and it made me trust his intentions less. I suppose there is a piece of me that's waiting for Dr. Oz to do the same. It's just a matter of time before I see his name emblazoned on a loaf of whole grain bread or his face silk-screened onto a yoga mat. He will have his own show next year, produced in part by Harpo Productions. He's been under Oprah's tutelage for so long now, it's no surprise he'll carry on the proud tradition of Winfrey spin-offs. As *The Jeffersons* and (my favorite) *Maude* were to *All in the Family*, Dr. Phil, Rachel Ray, and now Dr. Oz are to Oprah. He's had an amazing apprenticeship with Oprah, but I have my doubts if he'll be able to infotain an audience five days a week. Because I believe knowledge is power when it comes to our bodies, I hope he does teach people to become empowered about their health. Just because I don't plan to watch doesn't mean he won't be incredibly popular. I don't tune into Rachel Ray or Dr. Phil, either, and my absence certainly doesn't hurt their ratings. Who knows, with Oprah's support, a little luck, and a great director, Mehmet Oz might be the next Bea Arthur.

*   *   *

Guess whose eyes gleam and whose face breaks into a broad smile as she shouts out, "We love shoes!" Oprah extolls her love of all things soled, and because of her definitive language, now I will as well. At least, I'm trying to develop strong feelings for them. Oprah beams with happiness and I try to catch her footwear fever. Whenever she tells us how we feel and I'm at odds with her emotions, I do my best to whip myself into the appropriate depth of feeling. I've been told that I love Cher, designer outfits, and that I'm certain to love the must-see movies she sends her audience to view. So far, so good. I've had to get a little creative at times, but I've managed to open myself up to whatever Oprah leads me to treasure. Usually it's easy because Winfrey's energy is infectious. No wonder companies pray she'll endorse their products. Every woman I know is an empathetic creature, and most of us are emotional sponges, easily caught up in one another's energy. If Oprah, the most successful self-made woman I can think of, says she loves a panini maker, then her words pack a wallop. Just ask my breasts. They're sitting in Oprah's favorite bra right now.

After I write my blog for the morning, I peruse this month's *O* magazine. It's as if the editorial staff has read my mind. I can't afford to have my gray roots touched up professionally, and my clumsy at-home hair dyeing is leaving something to be desired. My bathroom always looks like the set of *Psycho* after the infamous shower scene. Also, nothing seems to stay on my stubborn grays long enough to fool anyone taller than me. I've caught Jim's eyes flitting away from the part in my hair, as if he hadn't been staring.

While the rules of my project are to follow only the advice I receive directly from Oprah's lips or pen, I'm occasionally tempted to try non-Winfrey suggestions, recipes, and products mentioned in *O*. It's just so darn pretty. And I'm thrilled to see a one-pager on "the best" hair dye this month. There's one fancy-schmancy brand, which I wish I could afford, but given that I have to dye my fast-growing hair every three to four weeks, there's no way I can swing it. It's $30 a box! Come to think of it, I've never heard of an upscale home hair dye kit. Isn't that an oxymoron? The other Oprah-approved dye that I'm going to try is cheaper, at $14 a box (which is still $5 more than my usual product). I hope it works. I'm not emotionally prepared to be a 30-something silver fox.

I go purchase some dye, read the directions, and coat my hair accordingly. Waiting for the timer to ring so I can wash the chemicals off my head, I open *O* magazine.

This month's "What I Know for Sure" column has been my favorite. Oprah takes us on a walk down memory lane and shares with us how she grew her company on instinct and gut feelings. I admire that she built the foundation of her empire on intuition. That's a tool we can all develop. Not many people are brave enough to trust their inner voice to take such bold risks. I greatly respect Oprah for this quality and her willingness to share her experience with her readers.

While her words have the power to inspire, they can also confuse me. I'll admit to you that this happens to me frequently when I tackle some self-help terminology. The words sound beautiful at first but become emptier the more I read them. This month's offering had my brow knitted as I read and reread it. "Each of us represents our own life brand. And using your instinct and feelings as your personal GPS puts you in a position to make the best choices for you." It is lovely-sounding initially, but after I give it further thought in order to implement it in my own life, I am flummoxed by the language and catchphrases. Maybe my inner GPS is low on batteries, because I'm feeling a little lost in Oprah's words. I think this is one of the things I appreciate about her columnist Martha Beck. Her words are imaginative, and I am never discombobulated by her choice of metaphor. But Martha Beck is Martha Beck and Oprah is Oprah. It's like comparing apples to media moguls.

I recall some philosophy from *A New Earth*. Basically, Tolle writes that the essence of a person can never be defined in words. Language is merely a human construct, created to represent the world around us. It can never completely define the truth, because as a facsimile, it is fundamentally limited. This was one of my favorite sections in Tolle's book. It really resonated with me, but it also deflated some of the power that I felt when reading Oprah's GPS metaphor. I wonder how she contends with this in her daily life when much of her industry is powered by words meant to lead us toward our authentic selves. It's a complicated dilemma. I pin the word "clarity" to my vision board and hope for the best.

The timer rings and I jump in the shower to wash the dye out of my hair. I'm really pleased with the results. Oprah's staff was right—this stuff works great. My locks look fabulous. Then I realize I must have accidentally allowed the goop to drip down my face. I now have a matching set of muttonchop sideburns to match my dark brown curls. I look like a cross between Elvis Presley and Wolverine.

This morning, I watch Oprah personally endorse another product, a pink cell phone with three months' worth of coverage. I'll never get used to the insanity that follows one of these announcements, and distracted, my mind starts to wander all over the place. If there are aliens flying around in spacecraft learning everything they can about humankind by watching *Oprah*, they might think the most effective way to distract a woman is through free gifts. I wonder if this is how they might divert our attention when they want to take over the planet, their tinny voices projecting from their ships, "New bubblegum-hued gadgets for all human women!" And then they'd sit back, crossing their multiple pairs of arms smugly, waiting for us all to start screaming and jumping up and down in a blind frenzy so they can invade Earth. Would we be deaf to the destructive explosions around us in our ecstasy over our new toys?

I am appalled by the thought and decide I need to get away from my TV for a while. I pull on my leopard-print shoes and whisper "we love you" to them as I head out for the day.

August 2008 Accounting

Date	Assignment	Cost	Time	Notes
8/1	Read *O* from cover to cover. *(LO)*		3h 30m	I like the "sexy" article. AND the men-centric articles.
8/1	"Stop saying that." (re: using the word "just" to describe ourselves) *(SHOW)*		0h 0m	Great advice. **(O)**
8/4	Purchase *O*. *(LO)*	4.50	0h 5m	Where is my subscription?
8/5	Make sure you get the D3 (500 IU twice a day) / 400 mcg twice a day (folic acid or folate, or folicin, which is sometimes listed as vitamin B9) / either 1 gm of distilled fish oil before lunch and before dinner (Dr. Oz) *(SHOW/WEB)*	38.91	0h 0m	There were more vitamins to take, but these were the ones missing from my daily routine. These were recommended by Dr. Oz for women age 20–40. [$24.61(Omega 3 fish oil), $3.32 (folic acid), $5.99 (vitamin D), $4.99 SH] **(O)**
8/7	"If you wanna know how bad schools really are in the nation, read *The Shame of the Nation.*" *(SHOW)*	10.17	4h 0m	I always get defensive about this topic as my mom is a terrific public school teacher.

(cont.)

August 2008 Accounting (*cont.*)

Date	Assignment	Cost	Time	Notes
8/7	"If you've watched this show today, and you realize that your child is one of the children who is not getting the best that this nation has to offer or if you are concerned about what's happening to other kids in this country, go to StandUp.org." *(SHOW)*		0h 15m	When I first visited Bill and Melinda Gates's Standup website, it wasn't functioning. How ironic.
8/13	Rise and Shine: How to wake up less stressed. *(WEB)*		3h 30m	I liked this! (30 minutes a day for 7 days). Will continue. **(O)**
8/13	Shiatsu *(WEB)*		1h 10m	This was nice...but I'd prefer someone else to do the work. (10 minutes a day for 7 days)
8/14	"So, *Why Did I Get Married?* You and your friends'll be talking about it. Better yet, talk about it with your husband." *(SHOW)*		0h 10m	Talked to Jim about the movie. We're all set. Thanks!
8/19	"Play along" with Oprah's live audience and take Dr. Oz's online health quiz. *(SHOW)*		0h 5m	I did pretty well. I learned about jellyfish stings. Handy.

8/19	"Be sure to check him out on XM156, *Oprah and Friends*, and also on our section of Oprah. com. Keep those questions coming." *(SHOW)*		0h 20m	For some reason, I'm intimidated by satellite radio. **(O)**
8/20	"This Sunday… let this story inspire you. Instead of pitching those coupons, cash them in, go to your grocery store.…The better thing I think you can do is to combine it, get your friends in on it, combine them…go to the grocery store, use the coupons, give the food to your local pantry…do what you can." *(SHOW)*	13.15	1h 0m	Deposit was to the Greater Chicago Food Depository. This made me feel awesome. I can't believe with coupons and other sales, I spent $11.65 on $25 worth of groceries. Too cool. Sadly, the coupons weren't for food I'd eat, necessarily, but still it was relatively nutritious. I did my best not to get junk. I plan to do this even when the year is up. It felt better doing something with my own time and hands rather than just sending in a donation. ($1.50 for newspaper and $11.65 for groceries) (15 minutes clipping / 45 minutes to shop and donate)
8/20	"Go to Oprah. com for more information on the pajama program. And we want new pajamas, too, we don't want your old, discarded pajamas." *(SHOW)*	10.00	0h 5m	Donation to program.

(cont.)

August 2008 Accounting (*cont.*)

Date	Assignment	Cost	Time	Notes
8/20	If we're inspired by John Wood's Room to Read program, we can go to Oprah.com to help. *(SHOW)*	25.00	0h 10m	Decided to give to girls' scholarships in Nepal, a country I care a great deal for. I spent about a month there in 2001.
8/24	Adopt a cat from a shelter. *(SHOW/WEB)*	85.00	4h 0m	Welcome to little Selmarie! We love you already. Followed Oprah.com advice on pet adoption. ($75 adoption fees/$10 required cat carrier)
8/27	Read "Ten Secrets to a Better Love Life." *(WEB)*		9h 30m	Oooh-la-la. **(O)**
8/27	Paint bedroom. ("First of all, you need a good color." — Oprah) *(SHOW)*	76.24	3h 0m	This is meant to help us sleep better. (60 minutes to choose color and shop; 2 hours painting)
8/27	Purchase *O, The Oprah Magazine Cookbook (LO)*	19.77	0h 30m	Will let Jim choose recipes. Going to try to cook recipes with ingredients I already have in the house, so I can stop spending so much money.
Throughout Month	Watch every episode of *Oprah.* *(LO)*		21h 0m	21 shows
Throughout Month	Do Best Life Challenge exercise. *(BLC)*		5h 20m	80 minutes a week for 4 weeks
Throughout Month	Take *A Course in Miracles.* *(WEB/SHOW)*		7h 45m	approx. 15 minutes a day for 31 days
MONTHLY TOTAL		282.74	65h 25m	
YEAR-TO-DATE TOTAL		3,051.32	939h 13m	

ONGOING PROJECTS

- "Reinvigorate your appearance with some great advice on how not to look old..."
- "Rethink your eating habits with some absolutely delicious and utterly original meals..."
- Use cloth and reusable bags at grocery store. No more plastic.
- Change lightbulbs to energy-efficient bulbs.
- "I think in terms of investment, it's the best thing you can ever give yourself is to have beautiful surroundings."
- "I would just say to anybody, whatever secret you're holding, live your own truth."
- Sharon Salzberg meditation
- Make your rooms personal.
- Best Life Challenge exercise and diet guidance
- "I do want you to start thinking about, as I have started thinking about, how much you consume. I mean, like every time you throw away a paper towel. Every time you are, you know, wasteful with food in your house...just think about how much you really need."
- "Get a lift when you come in the front door."
- "I want you to savor every meal."
- "I want you to pay attention to how happy women get that way."
- *A Course in Miracles*
- Declutter home/life.
- *A New Earth* meditation
- "With the arrival of spring, I hope you, too, will reconnect with nature."
- "When you think that you're going to get in a car and drive, I want you to think about this mother holding her daughter's head on the side of the highway. That's the thought I want to come to your mind before you go to get in the car after having even one drink."
- "Stop defining yourself by what you see—or think you see—when you look in the mirror."
- "Everybody think about this: On the way to work or on the way to do whatever you do during the day...how many negative things...the negative tape that's playing in your head all day long about yourself. *I can't do that, I shouldn't do that, I'm too fat, oh look at my thighs...*"
- "I think we should be open like Horton."
- "Alexis Stewart talks candidly about trying to get pregnant on her radio show *Whatever*, on Martha Stewart Living Radio. Tune in to follow her progress there."
- The YOU: Staying Young Aging quiz.
- Learn to accept all people.

Accounting Abbreviations: LO = Living Oprah Project Task, *SHOW* = *The Oprah Winfrey Show*, *WEB* = Oprah.com, *MAG* = O, *The Oprah Magazine*, *BC* = Oprah's Book Club, *BLC* = Best Life Challenge, **(O)** = ongoing project

SEPTEMBER:

Shaky ground

Time spent this month: 70 hours, 45 minutes
Dollars spent this month: $580.28
Oprah quote that made my (single) friend Grace scream: "As long as you have a husband, you can have as many cats as you want."
Just when I got them worn in the way I like: *Change bedroom pillows if we "have the same pillows that you got married with. That is just wrong."*
Words that stuck: *"In the book, please don't kill off Jim, he was one of my favorite characters. ;)"—Comment made by Seb Sharp from Australia on Living Oprah blog*

IN THE ninth month of Living Oprah, I've decided to change my husband's name to Saintly McSainterton. He's either the most patient man on the planet or this project has beaten him down to an emotional pulp. One way or the other, it's worked out great for me. He's put up with changes around the house and tests to our relationship. I thought he'd run screaming when I told him we'd be completing Oprah's Evaluate Your Marriage questionnaire back in March, but he didn't. I thought he'd put up a fight when I told him we'd be removing the TV from our bedroom in May, but aside from a little puppylike whimpering, he acquiesced. I thought he'd panic when I informed him we'd be publicly improving our sex life with the Spice It Up in the Bedroom program. This time I was right. Two out of three is really commendable, though, isn't it?

He was worried (read: terrified) about how I would disclose information online about our sextravaganza, and so, in the best interest of my marriage, I promised to be discreet and vowed not to spill too many erotic beans on my blog. I made no such promises when I signed my contract for this book, however, so let's get dirty, shall we? (Elsewhere in the city of Chicago, Jim gets an inexplicable shiver up his spine that causes him to drop a glass of ice water in his lap. Coincidence? I think not.) Actually, it really only gets PG-13, so you don't need to turn on the Barry White music or pour yourself a glass of wine.

Like many couples swept up in the hustle and bustle of our lives, we tend not to take special time out to connect. The program urges us to make dates. And while at first we think this is pretty dorky, we end up really enjoying ourselves. We alternate responsibility for planning the dates we've penciled in our calendars each Friday night. Right now, we're a bit broke because of the project, grad school, and the general financial wear and tear of the year, so we have to get creative with our planning. It's refreshing. We like each other! I return to the website, feeling quite successful in step one of the miniproject, and I'm excited to move on. Then I realize that, in my haste, I originally read the page wrong. We're not just supposed to have a date night to spend time together, we're supposed to make a date night to actually have sex. Ohhhh! I get it. Well, I didn't, but I will now. And what the heck, we already have Friday nights set aside, so why not continue to use them? What follows is the most boring, perfunctory sex of our marriage. After one of these dates, instead of cuddling, we actually work together to unclog a stubborn bathtub drain. Ah, the romance. We decide to move on to the next step.

Step two is to have sex out of the house. I wonder if all our friends and family reading this book now are a little freaked out by our offers to housesit at the end of 2008. Are you regretting that you took us up on the offer? Don't worry, only a few of you should be concerned. Moving on!

Step three is to redecorate our bedroom. We already decorated à la Nate Berkus, so we don't relish the idea of repeating the project. Also, our bedroom has space for only our queen-sized bed, with about 18

inches between the sides of the mattress and the walls. It's not the easi-
est space to get creative with. Still, we hang a couple framed posters and
get new sheets. We buy jersey sheets, and after our first night sleeping
on them realize we probably didn't make the sexiest choice. When we
crawl into bed, it feels like we're climbing into a Gap T-shirt display,
and we both conk out pretty quickly, swathed in cottony comfort. I put
some scented candles on the windowsill and light them, which sends
Jim into a sneezy, allergic fit. I replace them with a less smelly variety
and buy Jim a box of tissues. With lotion.

The next steps are fun and lead us to explore what each of us wants
in the sack. I always wanted jersey sheets, so I'm already pretty happy.
In all seriousness, the communication is really helpful. I thought we had
been open with each other before, but this peels a few more layers of the
sexy onion. I share fantasies with Jim that I never have before and learn
more about him than ever. It's fun. Exciting. There's a charged energy
in the room whenever we have one of these discussions. After months
of barely having sex because we've been so focused on the project, it's
nice to reconnect. And yes, when I type the word "reconnect," I am
winking and nudging my computer.

We're urged in the next step to try something new and to stop
ignoring any physical sexual problems we might be having. We head to
our neighborhood drugstore and take a romantic stroll down the erotic
aisle, which is perplexingly combined with the foot care section. We
purchase a new product we've seen on TV recently that is supposed to
be sexually stimulating for both men and women. I also pick up some
callus remover while I'm there. I'm embarrassed to tell you what the
sensual product is because my in-laws will be reading this book. Let's
just say it is suggested on Oprah.com and it rhymes with zubricant. We
rush home to give it a go. Unfortunately, Jim doesn't really experience
anything different, but I feel as if someone's set fire to my vajayjay.
After ruling out the need to make an embarrassing trip to the emer-
gency room, we decide we can check that off the list and move on. I
have to stand up for the remainder of the evening.

The next steps advise us to take it slow and not to be worried at
all about what we think is normal. We're not supposed to compare

ourselves to anyone else. I've been a little panicked as of late because Dr. Oz told us that men should have sex four times a week to lengthen their life span. So, if I'm not in the mood, I am basically sending Jim to an early grave. No pressure there.

Frankly, I do compare myself to other people around me when it comes to sex. If the amount of shows Oprah dedicates to sexual dysfunction and confusion are any indication, it's clear that lots of us feel like we can't cut the mustard. I take some comfort in knowing I'm not alone. And yet, all the messages I'm receiving in the movies and on TV definitely give me a skewed sense of what a normal sex life should look like. Jim and I agree to stop pressuring ourselves and decide we are just fine as we are. Moments later, I've gone back to judging myself, but I don't let on to Jim, who seems content for the time being.

The last suggestion to couples is to keep trying. This year has been pretty trying so far, that's for sure. Still, Jim and I always desire to strengthen our relationship, and "keep trying" should be on our to-do list every single day, regardless of whether or not I'm Living Oprah. After just five years of marriage, it's clear that things can get pretty stale if we're not vigilant. We want to be in a continually evolving partnership; it's just that sometimes we forget. I guess it takes the website of an unmarried talk show host to remind us.

I receive my *Oprah's Spirit Newsletter* today via e-mail. I get a lot of bulk O-mail this year: from Bob Greene and the Best Life Challenge to missives advertising the Oprah and Friends satellite radio network. My in-box also fills with Book Club newsletters, Oprah.com Money News, The Oprah Store advertisements, *Oprah* magazine mail, the Angel network, and so on and so forth. I generally unsubscribe from bulk e-mail so fast that you'd think it carried the plague, but I consider Oprah's e-mail to be research and allow it to pour in. It's a little overwhelming. The *Spirit* e-mails tend to focus on such topics as gaining clarity, managing stress, and discovering the meaning and purpose of life. Today's topic is friendship, and I am a little surprised to read that there are "5 Friends Every Woman Should Have." I've never before broken my friends into types, but I am fascinated. I have to find out if my relationships meet Oprah's standards.

I click on the link and am sent to an article on Oprah.com written by Michelle Burford for *O* magazine. The friend categories are:

1. The Uplifter
2. The Travel Buddy
3. The Truth Teller
4. The Girl Who Just Wants to Have Fun
5. The Unlikely Friend

After reading the short text, I discover I am more or less covered in four of the five friend-egories. The companion I seem to be missing is the Girl Who Just Wants to Have Fun.

I rack my brain but can't think of any current friend who would fall into this classification. I never felt lacking in great friends, but maybe the folks at *O* are right and I might be missing out. The e-mail did say that *every* one of us should have these gals in our lives. I decide to reacquaint myself with the only person I can think of who once filled this slot in my mid-twenties.

I drop her an e-mail and receive a note back the next morning filled with exclamation points and animated smiley-face emoticons. My life is much more mellow than when she and I were close, and while I might regret this, I set up a date with her for the following week. In the days leading up to our lunch, I show Jim some old photos of us. She and I are almost always in action in these shots, as if we can barely contain our energy when we're together. I repeat stories of our antics over and over again, and Jim pretends he hasn't heard them a million times before.

I am getting excited to see her now. I've gotten so serious over the course of this year and could use some help lightening up. She reschedules with me twice, and when the big day finally arrives, she calls a few minutes before our meeting time to tell me she's running a bit behind. Thirty minutes later, she rushes in the door, and instantly my irritation at having to wait for her dissipates. We find a table and sit. I'm ready to have fun with a capital *F*.

I used to love hanging out with this friend, although we've drifted apart over the years. I take the initiative and kick off our reminiscing.

I remind her about when we were both single, and during one brutally hot summer, we'd sit in her air-conditioned car with takeout Thai food, singing classic rock songs at the top of our lungs, neither of us able to carry a tune to save our lives. I'm ready to skip lightly together down memory lane. My friend, however, looks exhausted, a bit disheveled, and doesn't take off her gigantic sunglasses even though we're seated inside. After she orders herself a drink, she launches into the latest stories of her life: Her marriage is breaking apart, she can't find meaningful work, and her health hasn't been good. She looks painfully sad. We sit for several hours, catching up, speaking in a more deeply honest way than we ever did in the old days.

I never do tell her that I called her because I thought she would fulfill the Girl Who Just Wants to Have Fun role in my life. In her delicate emotional state, she probably wouldn't appreciate the irony.

Oprah is singular and extraordinary and so are we all, whether we have an unmatched level of power and celebrity or we're one of the countless graduating students vying for the same job as everyone else. I am always surprised when Oprah publishes articles or produces show topics that congeal us into a few standard types. It seems to go against everything she tries to teach us — that we have many commonalities, but we should find and celebrate our individuality. Diversity is what makes us interesting.

While I know Oprah didn't write the article, I still credit her for its existence. After all, the magazine is called *O, The OPRAH Magazine*. Everything printed in it falls under the umbrella of her power. At least I think it does. This is where the line between Oprah the person and Oprah the business gets confusing for me. I think, due to the way her companies are marketed, we're meant to feel that every single word we hear, read, or see comes directly from her lips, her brain, her pen. That is why, when I read articles such as this, I throw my hands in the air and wonder what purpose she felt it served.

I do appreciate that Oprah seeks to make our lives better and to guide us toward a more substantial existence. In many ways, I can relate to her mission. My work, on a more minuscule but in my opinion no less meaningful level, is all about making other people feel good. All I want for my yoga students is better health, to discover the connection between their physical and emotional selves, and to find a deeper sense of well-being. But I'm just a cog in their so-called self-improvement machinery, making suggestions when I can be of assistance and staying out of the way when I can't. I know I will never be all things to all people. On the other hand, Oprah has built a self-help empire that gives the impression she is omniscient. She never professes to be an expert in any one area, but she has amassed an army of experts who allow her to be a guru and who bestow upon her the aura of authority.

This month's magazine boasts an article called "48 Decisions We've Made for You," and I find myself cringing when I read the title. I like Oprah best when she's acting as a guide and moderator, but I get prickly when I feel as if she's telling me she knows best. The items in the aforementioned article are somewhat obvious, nothing that stomps on the toes of my sensibility. And yet it's the choice of language that gets under my skin the most. I don't want anyone else to make my decisions for me! Complacency might make life feel easier, but it undermines self-empowerment and is certainly not a lesson one would garner from studying Oprah's path to success. It's the principle that I find upsetting and will be my biggest obstacle when it comes to the possibility of retaining anything positive and long-lasting from this year.

September 3, 2008
It's a very special day. Today is the first time that my morning deposit is S-shaped. I screech with joy, and Jim rushes into the bathroom to see if I am okay. I slam down the toilet lid, hiding my treasure. I'd like there to be a couple mysteries left in our relationship. I assure him that I'm all right. As he heads down the hall, back to the kitchen, I remind him to sprinkle some wheat germ on his oatmeal. There's no reason I should celebrate alone this morning.

My stomach is in knots. Don't worry, I'm not going to talk about bowel movements again. Spurred on by a show about how to keep our husbands from being unfaithful, I took a test on Oprah's site called Is

He Cheating? I know I promised myself I'd stop taking these, but it doesn't seem possible while Living Oprah is in full swing. I was confident when I took the test because Jim has never given me even the slightest reason to doubt his fidelity. And yet my nemesis, the online quiz, has chipped away at my sense of security. The test results tell me we're "on shaky ground." When I inform Jim about this, he's really steamed but can't figure out where to direct his ire. And while I trust my life partner over Oprah's technology, I have to admit I'm stirred up. I can't even see beyond the results to find any positive lesson at the moment. I am restless and unfocused.

Additionally, this morning's show has made me hopping mad. Misery loves company and I feel validated that my blog readers are also in a tizzy. Oprah's guest, a psychologist selling a book, has taken it upon himself to inform a mostly female audience how we are partly to blame for our cheating spouses in an episode entitled "Affair-Proof Your Marriage." I wonder if he plans on a trip to the Lincoln Park Zoo after the show, where he will poke hungry lions with a short stick. The crowd looks really annoyed. Not even a free download of his book can keep Oprah's audience from self-righteous anger. I'd normally find the lack of excitement over a gift from Oprah absolutely hilarious, but rage dampens my sense of humor. Our hostess has guessed how we'll react. She knows her audience very well. Still, the consummate professional, she helps him clarify his points. She's not going to take a bullet for him, but she is attempting to ease a little tension. She even stands behind some of his suggestions and adds her own flair: "The truth of the matter is, men do need to be made to feel like they're winners. They do need to have themselves built up."

It's probably no surprise that I get a little smug here and think, "Don't *I* need to feel like a winner, Oprah? Shouldn't *that* be my priority, rather than blowing smoke up Jim's——."

Then I take a breath. These assignments are not for me to judge, just to follow. Besides, I'm positive that Jim will see through this bolstering of his ego and ask me to stop.

When he gets home from work, I ask him to open a jar of marinara for me. Because of my Best Life Challenge exercise, I've been lifting weights regularly, and I could give Michelle Obama a run for her money in an arm wrestling match. I don't need a man to pop a top for me. Still, I dutifully ask, calling on all my past acting classes to allow me to maintain the guise of sincerity. When the lid comes off, Jim hands it to me.

"Whoa!" I say, widening my eyes, "I couldn't even budge it. I can't believe you did that."

He flexes his bicep. "That's because I'm badass." He pats me on the tush and heads out of the kitchen.

Hook, line, and sinker.

Throughout the autumn, I compliment him copiously. While we paint our bedroom, because Oprah's advised us to have a sleep-promoting color on our walls, I tell him he's really good with a brush: very precise, no drips. You'd think the guy had just painted the ceiling of the Sistine Chapel, he is grinning so much. I make sure I tell him how funny he is, how creative, how smart. I thank him for going to work in the morning, and I pat him on the back when he's finished his day. I really do appreciate all he does, but I've never made it a priority to tell him at every opportunity. While I can't help but feel as if I'm coddling a child, Jim has never seemed happier. I came home from teaching today to discover a vase filled with my favorite orange and hot pink gerbera daisies on the table. He brought them home "just because."

I'll admit, this is working out pretty well. And because I can't leave it alone, I tell him that as much as he feels like a million bucks every time I compliment him, I would also like to hear the same appreciation. He eagerly agrees and gives it a go. All the bolstering doesn't do quite as much for me, I find. Perhaps it's because I asked him for it (and had to remind him a few times) or maybe just because his mind is wired to absorb compliments differently than mine. Still, all in all, a very successful lesson from Oprah, and it didn't cost me a cent.

Today I learned that Oprah has the power to stop time. She only has to utter these words, "And for you at home, if you haven't seen Céline in concert: you *must*." Jim (or should I say, my big, strong husband) is running late for work when he hears Oprah's commandment. I howl and wonder if I've done something karmically to earn this fate. Once the initial shock subsides a bit and the hands on the clock begin to move again, Jim says to me in a little, teenie voice, "Please don't make me go." I look into his eyes and know I cannot inflict this upon him. He's earned a get-out-of-jail-free card this year.

Oh, I should probably mention that I am not a fan of Céline Dion's. She might be a kind and altruistic woman, but I would rather do the vegan cleanse for the remainder of the year than go to this concert. I love French-speaking Canada. I spent a lot of time there as a kid and even honeymooned there in 2003. However, I've never developed a taste for their most popular export. The woman sure can belt out a tune, but to my savage ears, all those ballads sound exactly the same. Plus, she's notorious for holding incredibly long concerts, and I can't sit still for more than an hour. I'm actually sweating.

Jim beats a hasty retreat to work and forgets his lunch on the kitchen table. I quickly call my friend Jefferson and rope him into being my date for the show. He has stipulated that he'll only go if I do not censor him in any way at the concert. I'm frightened of what this might mean but am even more terrified to attend the show on my own. I throw caution to the wind, agree to his demands, and quickly buy our tickets before he can change his mind. This is one of the most unwelcome assignments to date, and I don't receive the least bit of sympathy from my friends. They think this is hilarious and really rub it in, as they know how I feel about the Québecois crooner. *Merde!*

Oprah states, with firm conviction, that she is campaigning for Barack Obama as a private citizen. She can say this all she wants, but Oprah, standing on any stage, with a microphone in her hand, is not a private citizen. Sure, she's not endorsing him on her show, but if she publicly tells people to vote, then a little bit of that magic which inspires people to go out and buy fire pits and crisp white shirts is evoked. As consumers, millions are under her spell. Is her charm just as potent to voters? I'd like to think we will all make our own decisions, regardless of what famous person endorses which candidate. But I might just be

fooling myself. If so many viewers allow Oprah to guide them spiritually, then why not politically, as well? I'm completely torn by this use of
her power. Barack Obama is, without a doubt, my favored candidate.
I want him to win. But I feel uncomfortable at the thought that an
Oprah endorsement (or one by any famous personality) is what will
win voters over, rather than their faith in the man and his promise as a
leader. I want to believe that our touch-screen fingers are guided by our
personal beliefs, not as an extension of our Winfrey fan club member-
ship. When she spoke of Mr. Obama to Larry King back in 2007, she
said, "I think that my value to him, my support of him, is probably
worth more than any check." Without a doubt. And I appreciate that
she acknowledged the power of her persona.

To be honest, I expect Oprah to use her show to reflect her own
point of view. It's called *The Oprah Winfrey Show*, not the *Generic
Infotainment Hour*. It would be virtually impossible, and probably very
dull, for an individually hosted show to be entirely neutral. I will go so
far as to say I think Oprah's entire program is political. Every moment
of it. From the topics she chooses, to the guests she invites on her stage,
to the side she leans toward on a controversial issue: These all reflect
her politics. We don't need to pretend that her show sits in some fantasy
neutral zone. If we expect her to be entirely evenhanded, she'd have
to erase herself, her award-winning personality, from the equation. It's
her passions that have helped her become as magnetic and interesting
as she is. I don't think it's appropriate to ask her to uphold journalistic
integrity on a talk show. I've read many people's complaints about her
lack of neutrality during the campaign, but I think maybe C-SPAN is
a more appropriate venue to obtain their information.

I've come to the conclusion that many of Oprah's guests are either
superhuman, highly emotionally evolved, or in complete denial. I
understand they are chosen to tell their stories because their cases are
extreme, and Oprah and her producers feel that we can learn something from them. I'm speaking specifically about the guests who have
gone through horrible tragedies and are able to find positive lessons in
their painful situations. For instance, a man whose wife and youngest

son were murdered, only to discover it was his oldest boy who master-
minded the crime. Instead of being eaten up by anger, he forgave his
son. Or the woman who was almost burned alive by her abusive and
jealous husband. She appears to be the gentlest, kindest, most positive
woman I've seen. She doesn't show the least bit of resentment. The list
goes on. On *Oprah*, we see guests transcending anger, sadness, fear,
and guilt. We're told to look to them as examples of how we might live.
Oprah will frequently highlight them so we are able to set the bar for
our own responses to difficult situations.

An interesting discussion has arisen on my blog about how we deal
with painful feelings. Recently, I was comparing myself with a woman
who insists she has no anger about her own diseased body. I really
admire her and find much inspiration in her words. But the more I
watch, I begin to feel down about myself, wondering why I can't be so
evolved when it comes to handling my chronic condition. Most of the
time, I feel strong and positive, but I do have my moments when I feel
scared, resentful, and defeated. I put pressure on myself to rise up to
the behavior of these strangers, but always come up lacking. This is the
pitfall I've encountered more than once this year. Watching nonstop
inspiring stories, eventually they backfire on me and I feel terrible.

My readers have brought up a point that I've forgotten as of late: It
is human to feel bad every now and then. So why do we so rarely see
this less attractive step in the healing process on TV? As long as we
don't sit and wallow in our darker times, we can actually benefit from
experiencing difficulties. While I imagine it'd be fabulous to live my
entire life on the peaks, it's in the valleys that I gain the most growth
as a human being. And yet we are so terrified of pain, in general, that
many of us would rather steer clear of it than discover the reason it
exists or do the hard work it takes to let it go. Physical and emotional
discomfort are to be avoided at all costs. It's no surprise that the self-
help and pharmaceutical industries are booming. No one wants to suffer. There's a pill or a quick fix for just about everything these days. I
think our desire to find respite from discomfort is one of the reasons so
many of us tune in to shows such as *Oprah*. We seek any Rx she might
prescribe for our distress.

In my experience, when it comes to healing my psychic pain, I need to find my own path. It doesn't mean I don't ever first turn to outside influences for guidance. But sometimes I turn to external sources because I'm avoiding the hard work of healing myself, I might fear the truth, or don't trust my own intuition. I can learn from example, but no guru can yank me out of my suffering until I'm ready, no matter how many transcendent heroes are paraded on the TV screen in front of me. So while Oprah urges us to learn from her guests, I have to remember to stop comparing myself to these shining beacons of emotional health. I wonder what would happen if I plunged myself into a self-help vacuum. Would I be any less likely to evolve? Maybe I'd learn to be a little more self-sufficient if I wasn't so magnetized to those pedaling miracles and spiritual snake oil. I need to build myself an invisible set of those blinders that are usually worn by horses. I could stop comparing myself to others and block out anyone or anything that lowers my self-esteem. Or maybe I could just cancel my cable subscription.

September 2008 Accounting

Date	Assignment	Cost	Time	Notes
9/1	Read *O* from cover to cover. *(LO)*		4h 0m	There was so much stuff to make life easier that I got overwhelmed!
9/2	"Go get your XM radio." *(SHOW)*	107.93	1h 0m	Radio and service
9/2	"Take the friendship quiz." *(WEB)*		0h 5m	This directive came in an e-mail. It turns out Grace and I are good at being friends. Shall we continue?
9/3	Get Rolfed. *(WEB/SHOW)*	130.00	1h 30m	I was looking for a way to help ease the chronic pain I have in my back. Because of the segment on the show (with Dr. Oz getting Rolfed) and the info on the website, I decided to get Rolfed. It was intense. Helpful. I will continue, although it is an investment. **(O)**
9/5	Get Burt's Bees Eye Cream and Ageless Night Cream. *(WEB/SHOW)*	40.88	0h 30m	I checked online about how to care for skin in my 30s. Rewatched Earth Day show from April where Burt's Bees was promoted. Cost is minus 10 bag refund. (30 minutes to research and buy; I will use regularly) **(O)**
9/10	"Watch this show and e-mail me about it." *(SHOW)*		0h 5m	Oprah was referring to the next day's show about why men cheat.
9/10	"Download the whole thing for free on Oprah.com." *(SHOW)*		0h 5m	Oprah was referring to Elizabeth Smart's book *You're Not Alone: The Journey from Abduction to Empowerment.*

9/11	Take online test Is He Cheating? (WEB)		0h 10m	Seems my marriage is crackin' up. Odd. I thought we were pretty happy. So did my husband.
9/11	"You need to find out if GPS tracking is legal in your state." (SHOW)		0h 30m	I see that it is legal to use in cases of domestic violence where the offender breaks a restraining order.
9/11	"Going out to work every day, which every man does who is responsible for his family, after a while men feel taken for granted that they are doing that...so there needs to be some acknowledg-ment of that." (SHOW)		0h 0m	I wish I also received acknowledgment for my part in bringing home the bacon. (O)
9/11	"The truth of the matter is, men do need to be made to feel like they're winners. They do need to have themselves built up." (SHOW)		0h 0m	Check. Make Jim feel like winner. (O)
9/11	Download M. Gary Neuman's The Truth About Cheating. (SHOW)		0h 5m	Downloaded
9/11	"...when you read it, you're gonna feel that." (SHOW)		2h 0m	Didn't need Oprah to tell me I was going to feel angry. I just am.

(cont.)

September 2008 Accounting (*cont.*)

Date	Assignment	Cost	Time	Notes
9/15	"Please don't turn away." *(SHOW)*		0h 0m	Referring to how difficult the show about Internet predators would be to watch.
9/15	"Imagine if it was your job, five days a week, to screen pornographic photos and videos of children — to see them fondled and raped — to hear them pleading for help." *(SHOW)*		0h 0m	I did this, but just for a split second as I cringed at the thought of having this job. Those folks are amazing souls.
9/15	"Prepare yourself for this: The latest form of entertainment for online predators is where you can see *live*, on demand, rape and molestations." *(SHOW)*		0h 0m	Ugh.
9/15	"You should be disgusted enough…Are you disgusted enough?… We should be disgusted enough to stop talking about this and actually do something. Our action plan is next, and you can do it before dinner tonight."		0h 5m	I wrote to Illinois Senators Barack Obama and Dick Durbin. Oprah.com had all the tools to make this simple for us to do.

	"We can legislate so there is enough money to begin to do something about it" (referring to the "PROTECT Our Children" Act). And "you only have a few days" (because the Senate is going on break soon). "We need to put pressure on our U.S. senators to bring the 'PROTECT Our Children' Act to the floor. And not just bring it to the floor, we want it passed." *(SHOW)*			
9/16	"Ten deep breaths. Morning. Night. Got that?" *(SHOW)*		1h 10m	5 minutes a day (took 2.5 in am and 2.5 in the evenings) for 14 days
9/17	Make paella. *(SHOW)*	124.59	2h 30m	I made the paella on October 2. (bomba rice: $14.95; paella pan: $34.99; seafood: $18.70; chicken drumsticks: $5.57; chicken sausages: $13.37; vegetables: $11.21; chicken stock: $7.98; saffron: $5.99) I think recipe was off. Turned to soup.
9/18	"We're going to go read the book." *(SHOW)*		0h 45m	I finished M. Gary's book.

(cont.)

September 2008 Accounting (*cont.*)

Date	Assignment	Cost	Time	Notes
9/19	"And for you at home, if you haven't seen Céline in concert: you must." *(SHOW)*	122.52	5h 40m	Sigh. (60 minutes to organize...this had to happen 3 times! Tried the first time for Chicago, then Indianapolis, then after the concert was canceled, I had to do it again! 160 minutes to travel: 120 minutes at concert)
9/19	"Sit back with your box of tissues." *(SHOW)*		0h 0m	I'm not counting the time on this, since I was already watching the show highlighting teenage Filapina singer Charice.
9/19	Change bedroom pillows if we "have the same pillows that you got married with. That is just wrong." *(SHOW)*		0h 5m	I got rid of the old ones.
9/19	Read *The Story of Edgar Sawtelle* by David Wroblewski (and don't read book jacket first). *(SHOW/BC)*	18.26	12h 0m	Enjoyed it, even though I've never owned a dog.
9/22	"Go online to preorder your copy today." *(SHOW)*	23.10	0h 5m	Ordered Thom Filicia's *Thom Filicia Style: Inspired Ideas for Creating Rooms You'll Love.*
9/23	"We need Suze Orman now more than ever." *(SHOW)*		0h 0m	Okay

9/23	"Go to Oprah. com for more of Suze's advice on how to survive these tough times." (SHOW)		0h 5m	(O)
9/25	"As long as you have a husband, you can have as many cats as you want." (SHOW)		0h 0m	Whew! Guess I can keep my kitties. My marriage has validated me as a pet owner.
9/26	"Go see Miracle at St. Anna." (SHOW)	8.50	2h 40m	Spike Lee's movie. War. Hard to watch.
9/29	"Everybody out there...is giving you their love and support right now." (SHOW)		0h 0m	Took a moment to send good, hopeful thoughts to the pregnant heroin addict.
9/29	"So, if you or somebody you know needs help with addiction and finding treatment in your area, call the National Drug and Alcohol Addiction Hotline." (SHOW)		0h 0m	At this time, this doesn't apply to anyone I know of...but it's a number I'll hold on to. (O)
9/30	"You have to do your own self-test." (SHOW)		0h 5m	Breast self-exam (O)
9/30	O magazine (LO)	4.50	0h 5m	O!
Through-out Month	Watch every episode of Oprah. (LO)		22h 0m	22 shows

(cont.)

September 2008 Accounting (*cont.*)

Date	Assignment	Cost	Time	Notes
Through-out Month	Do Best Life Challenge exercise. *(BLC)*		6h 0m	80 minutes a week for 4.5 weeks
Through-out Month	Take *A Course in Miracles (WEB/ SHOW)*		7h 30m	approx. 15 minutes a day for 30 days
MONTHLY TOTAL		580.28	70h 45m	
YEAR-TO-DATE TOTAL		3,631.60	1009h 58m	

ONGOING PROJECTS

- "Reinvigorate your appearance with some great advice on how not to look old…"
- "Rethink your eating habits with some absolutely delicious and utterly original meals…"
- Use cloth and reusable bags at grocery store. No more plastic.
- Change lightbulbs to energy-efficient bulbs
- "I think in terms of investment, it's the best thing you can ever give yourself is to have beautiful surroundings."
- "I would just say to anybody, whatever secret you're holding, live your own truth."
- Sharon Salzberg meditation
- Make your rooms personal.
- Best Life Challenge exercise and diet guidance
- "I do want you to start thinking about, as I have started thinking about, how much you consume. I mean, like every time you throw away a paper towel. Every time you are, you know, wasteful with food in your house…just think about how much you really need."
- "Get a lift when you come in the front door."
- "I want you to savor every meal."
- "I want you to pay attention to how happy women get that way."
- *A Course in Miracles*
- Declutter home/life.
- *A New Earth* meditation
- "With the arrival of spring, I hope you, too, will reconnect with nature."
- "When you think that you're going to get in a car and drive, I want you to think about this mother holding her daughter's head on the side of the highway. That's the thought I want to come to your mind before you go to get in the car after having even one drink."
- "Stop defining yourself by what you see—or think you see—when you look in the mirror."
- "Everybody think about this: On the way to work or on the way to do whatever you do during the day…how many negative things…the negative tape that's playing in your head all day long about yourself. *I can't do that, I shouldn't do that, I'm too fat, oh look at my thighs…*"

- "I think we should be open like Horton."
- "Alexis Stewart talks candidly about trying to get pregnant on her radio show *Whatever,* on Martha Stewart Living Radio. Tune in to follow her progress there."
- The YOU: Staying Young Aging Quiz
- Learn to accept all people.
- "Stop saying that." (re: using the word "just" to describe ourselves)
- Take Dr. Oz–recommended vitamins and supplements daily (vitamin D3, folic acid, fish oil).
- Rise and Shine—how to wake up less stressed.
- "Be sure to check him [Dr. Oz] out on XM156, Oprah and Friends, and also on our section of Oprah.com. Keep those questions coming."
- Ten Secrets to a Better Love Life

Accounting Abbreviations: *LO* = Living Oprah Project Task, *SHOW* = *The Oprah Winfrey Show*, *WEB* = Oprah.com, *MAG* = *O, The Oprah Magazine*, *BC* = Oprah's Book Club, *BLC* = Best Life Challenge, **(O)** = ongoing project

OCTOBER:

Isn't it ironic?

Time spent this month: *52 hours, 11 minutes*
Dollars spent this month: *$461.04*
I've always wanted that windswept look: *When having a portrait
taken, Oprah says, "Every woman needs a fan!"*
Words that stuck: *"If I could ask Oprah Winfrey a question it would
be: When do you sleep; when do you have fun; when do you have
time for yourself?"—E-mail from reader Carole Lieberman,
Woodland Hills, California*

SOMETHING IS changing.
    I have been asked dozens of times this week, by online readers
as well as by friends and family, if I am thrilled that my year of Living
Oprah is entering its fourth quarter. Even my yoga students happily
chirp, "The end is in sight!" I don't think many people realize that
I'm really torn about the completion of the project. I am excited at the
thought of having my life back and devoting my time to priorities other
than Oprah's. And it is true that, up until recently, I was quite focused
on the light at the end of the tunnel. But I'm a bit worried about what
life will bring afterward, as I've grown accustomed to this way of living.
While I was pretty resistant to following the leader at the beginning of
the year, I've eased into it. The decision-making part of my brain has
been idling, and I worry it might be difficult to fire it up once the New

Year rolls around. I tell people that everything will snap back to normal on January 1, but it's pure bravado. The truth is, I'm concerned.

I'm not going to lie, I'm looking forward to freedom from watching the show every single day. I'm so saturated by every topic, by the repetition, I feel a bit bruised. Recent topics have me down in the dumps. I have learned that the world's economies are in dire straits and I can't afford a single luxury. I now know that if I'm not vigilant, I'll age long before my time. I understand my husband could cheat on me at any moment. Oprah's become my personal Chicken Little, and I'm feeling a bit like the sky is falling.

I've unconsciously dug my heels into the dirt. There's a part of me—a very surprised part—that doesn't want this to end. What I've discovered, much to my embarrassment, is that I have warmed to the day-to-day ritual of giving my power over to Oprah. In many ways, I live risk free. I can't make mistakes in entertaining, in my relationships, in my diet. After all, I didn't make any of my choices—Oprah did.

I do believe I'll eventually be able to emerge from this year, able to experiment and think for myself as I did in the past. I'm just not so certain it'll be as easy to shed the Living Oprah skin as I would like. I've read that it takes 21 days to start a habit, but I never looked into how long it takes to break one. I think it'll be tough, but healthier for me the sooner I can stop this momentum. That's the difficult part. Example: I know that french fries are bad for me, they give me a belly-ache whenever I eat them, and I feel crummy about myself once my plate is empty. And yet I love them, and in unhealthier days, I used to eat them a lot. It's still really difficult to turn them down because they are so comforting and make me feel really satisfied in the moment. Eventually, I had to concede that they were doing more harm than good in my life, so I gave them up. I mourn their loss, their salty deliciousness. But it was for the best.

I have a suspicion that in 2009 a certain television talk show will be my new deep-fried nemesis.

I'm not immune to stress, but I am a yoga teacher and have studied meditation for years. I do have some tools at my disposal to bring myself to a more peaceful mind-set. Usually. They're just not doing the job like they did before this project. Of course, I have never battled so many layers of insecurity as I have this year. My priorities used to be simpler and rarely conflicted with one another. I find myself daydreaming about my time at Kripalu. I miss that peace and quiet and hope I'm able to find the same sense of well-being once Living Oprah is over.

I don't want to beat a dead horse, but I am overwhelmed by trying to keep up with Winfrey. I'm having a difficult time finding balance when I'm racing to keep up with everything she thinks are "musts" in our lives. So that is why I am struck by the irony at the top of this morning's episode, when Oprah tells us, "Today's show is for anybody who feels or has felt overwhelmed....It's your wake-up call. *Slow down.*"

I imagine that Oprah could use some rest, relaxation, and rejuvenation as well. It doesn't appear that even she is able to take her own advice when it comes to achieving balance. There's no way she could have the success she does, with so many irons in the fire, without spreading herself thin. She even stated in last month's "What I Know for Sure" column, "I AM OVERWHELMED!" She explained why. "Too many answers that need to come from me. Trying to do too many things at once. Flying back and forth from Africa to Chicago to California to New York. Doing. Doing. Doing."

Oprah's success is spectacular. Admirable. But at what cost to her? And if she's feeling overwhelmed, why is she foisting so many "musts" upon her audience for whom she genuinely seems to care? I doubt she wants us to feel the same way, unable to concentrate and with scant time to stop and smell the roses.

Oprah is lucky. When she finally realizes she needs downtime, she's able to take an entire day away from it all and retreat to one of her magnificent homes. Not many of us have the ability to step away from all our responsibilities for a whole day, but at least we can step back. And when we do, I hope many of the women I know who compare themselves to the Queen of Talk will reconsider the energy they spend attempting to live up to her ideals. Many of her ideals are not...ideal.

Much of *O*'s focus this year has been on self-care. I wish I could look into a crystal ball to predict whether Oprah will lighten up on the projects with which she is involved. I doubt it. Work is to Oprah as french fries are to me. Her multiple ventures may have started as snowflakes of ideas, but they've become an avalanche. Unstoppable. If she doesn't plan to ease up on herself, that's her own choice, but perhaps she'll consider limiting or filtering her dispensation of lifestyle guidance on her audience. I hope so, because the more I think about this, the more a little exasperation creeps up on me. I'm a wee bit upset that her "best" lifestyle broke her down, yet I'm still following all her advice. It might not be the case of the blind leading the blind, but it's certainly the stressed leading the stressed.

But is it working? This is the second question people inevitably ask me. Is Oprah's advice making my life better?

Well, if one judged me by outward appearances, they'd probably come to the conclusion that following Oprah's advice really works. I've got a publisher for a book I never expected I'd write; I have thousands of smart, hilarious, thoughtful readers on my website (I'm up to 144,225 visits!); I'm looking cute in a tame, O magazine kind of way; and I'm thinner. Some consider this pretty successful and, satisfied with the answer, won't dig any deeper. Society tends to judge us by our exterior, so many people assume that I have been rewarded with success by following Oprah's advice.

If you lived inside my head, however, you'd see I am almost always a stressed-out, insecure, exhausted mess. Everyone keeps reminding me that I should be having "fun" with this, and those words are like fingernails on a chalkboard. I'm not so sure how they'd expect this year to be a big party. I barely see my friends, I'm bleeding money, I am always busy, busy, busy, and I've allowed so many TV experts to poke at my marriage, there's a lot of mending to do. Most people don't stick around for this response, however.

Once the project is over, I'll have to see if the pros outweigh the cons, but right now I would choose my mental health over my smaller dress size.

I think when I began this journey, I inadvertently tripped and fell down the rabbit hole. Unlike Alice, I'm not saying "curiouser and curiouser!" as I drop. I just keep thinking "surrealer and surrealer." Case in point: At this moment, I'm in a limousine, being driven from LaGuardia Airport to Dylan's Candy Bar in New York City. I'm slated to appear tomorrow on NBC's morning cornerstone, *The Today Show*, to talk about my project. But first, I have to fulfill an assignment. Back in January, Oprah told us, "I say if you're going to New York, see the museums, of course, and then go by Dylan's Candy Bar." And for the record, we were told to hit the candy shop nine days after signing our Best Life Challenge contract. Dylan's is the boutique of sweets owned by the daughter of apparel legend Ralph Lauren. I never thought it'd be a suggestion I'd have to follow since I had no plans to travel to the Big Apple, but since NBC flew me in and I've already visited a myriad of museums, I am taking the opportunity to pay a call today. When I step inside, I see it's a really big store filled with lots of candy and children. I'm no television doctor, but I'm pretty sure they're all high on Pixy Stix, pupils dilated, begging their beleaguered parents for more of everything. It is a total hoot that I've been given the chance to check this item off my list. And while Oprah told us only to visit, I do buy Jim a small bag of penny candy for about $15.

And now I'm watching myself as I go through the motions of checking into my hotel, steps away from Rockefeller Plaza. I unpack much of my Oprah-suggested booty to give to the producer at NBC as they plan to use these items as props on the set. I hang up the "must-have" clothing that I've been asked to wear tomorrow morning on the show. Black tailored trousers, crisp white shirt, cashmere sweater. I am still not entirely at ease in these clothes and wish I could wear something that makes me feel good about myself. I understand why I've been asked to dress this way, I just wish I didn't feel like an impostor in costume.

I chat with my mom and Jim on the phone, assuring them I am cool as a cucumber and don't feel the least bit anxious. They are both quite impressed with my serenity. As am I. I practice some yoga in my tiny room, have a soothing cup of tea and a hot shower. When I'm satisfied that I am completely relaxed, I climb into bed and spend the next seven hours staring at the ceiling. It turns out cucumbers don't sleep. Cucumbers totally freak out when they're going to be on national television. Yoga and tea don't help cucumbers at all.

Early the next morning, I am already up and at 'em when I receive my wake-up call, my bedside clock blasts, the alarm on my cell phone rings, and my mother telephones to make sure I'm awake. I'm up, I'm up. Overly tired but fueled by adrenaline, I get dressed. It's the first time I've ever worn my Brooks Brothers crisp white shirt outside of the house and I must say, I understand why Oprah loves it. It looks super and there's not a wrinkle in sight. It also costs around the same as the rest of the outfit combined, including my shoes. I grab my purse and head over to the NBC building.

As I walk past security, I think about how Oprah does this every day. It's wild to imagine how one could become accustomed to speaking to millions on a daily basis. Of course, she would probably say the same thing about going to work and teaching people how to put their ankles behind their heads. I stroll past the onlookers outside the NBC building, and no one gives me a second glance. I love the renewed anonymity of being out of my own neighborhood. Getting lost in the hustle and bustle of New York in the morning actually relaxes me. I check in with an NBC page and am told to wait in a small greenroom, where I'm seated with two political pundits I see all the time on Sunday morning news shows. One, a far-right conservative, and the other, a well-known liberal, are chatting easily, although they are never so genteel on camera. Awaiting their moment to go on, they munch sandwiches and get their caffeine fix (the Republican sipping a Diet Coke, the Democrat polishing off a coffee). It's clear they are at home on the talk show circuit. On the other hand, I feel like the country mouse, visiting her city mouse cousin.

A producer calls my name and brings me downstairs to a bigger greenroom. This one is loud and filled with people moving and talking a mile a minute. I'm told to sit and wait until makeup, hair, and wardrobe can see me. There's more food here, but I'm wearing my crisp white shirt and I'm terrified I'll spill something on myself, so I pass.

As I await my turn in the makeup chair, I sit in this frenetic room, alongside the Harlem Globetrotters, a grieving family whose daughter was brutally murdered, a slew of male calendar models, Santa Claus, and the Dallas Cowboy Cheerleaders. Oh, joy — nothing makes me feel prettier and more secure about my physical appearance than being surrounded by gorgeous women in skintight hot pants. I regret that I didn't wear my Spanx underneath the tailored black trousers mandated by Oprah.

Look! There's the handsome cast of a new television show, ready to promote its premiere. I also hear the telltale voice of one of Oprah's regular style experts emanating from one of the private dressing rooms devoted to celebs. What a coincidence she's on this morning. I'm concerned she'll see my outfit and tell me I've done everything wrong. Publicly. There's a guy sitting next to me on the couch showing off some medieval rings he's brought to the show. I ask what he'll talk about on camera and he says he is not going to be on camera. I guess the rings are to be the guest and he's their chaperone. That should be a quick interview.

Surrealer and surrealer.

The crazier it gets around me, the calmer I become. There's something about the chaos and the noise and the basketball players flirting with cheerleaders that acts as a sedative, and I feel my body relax into the big couch.

I have to give a shout-out to Reggie, Oprah's makeup artist. While I might not be wild about the copious amount of false eyelashes he glues on her, I found his advice very helpful this morning when I put my face on. Earlier this year, I purchased makeup suggested on Oprah's show, website, and magazine, but I really didn't know what to do with it. Although I am confident in my ability to put on special-effects theatrical makeup, I didn't think my appearance on national television would be the right time to make myself look like a wrinkled crone or the Phantom of the Opera. I want to feel pretty when I sit across from dreamy Matt Lauer. I got online and found Reggie's Makeup 101 lesson and did my best in a short amount of time. One disappointment: He teaches that we need at least three colors of lipstick to create the perfect lip, and I only had one hue. Who knew?

When I sit down in the makeup chair, a lovely staffer tells me my makeup is already perfect. She barely has to do a thing to my face. I am so happy I did everything correctly, I consider writing Reggie a thank-you note. I am beaming. I wonder if this means I'd also be good at paint by numbers.

The rest of my time in the studio flies past. I am steamed and ironed and fluffed and lint-rolled. From the security guards to the pages to the producers and crew, everyone is incredibly kind to me. One of the guys on the crew bashfully mentions he is reading Oprah's new Book Club pick and loving it. Most people give me a wink and a nod and a supportive pat on the back. I'm not feeling nervous at all, but I think my out-of-body experience is keeping me from quaking in my boots.

While I'm waiting to be brought on set, Matt Lauer gives me a wave. He's reading some notes (about me, I think, prepping for the interview) and munching on a cookie. Oh, Matt. It's not even 8 AM. I'm hooked up to a microphone by the sound guy as I'm seated on the couch. I'm amazed how comfortable I am. I've been watching this show for years, and their set has become a satellite extension of my living room. It feels weird that it doesn't feel weird to be here.

Suddenly, we go live and I force myself not to look at my image in the monitors or read along with the teleprompter.

I'm allowed to talk about my project, answer some fun questions (Do I think other people should trying Living Oprah? No way!) and some challenging ones (regarding my choice to vote for Oprah's favored candidate in the primary), and clear up most misconceptions people might have about the purpose of my year (I swear I'm not an obsessed fan!). Matt (we're on a first-name basis) says that they contacted Oprah's people, and a spokeswoman from Harpo, Inc., has given *Today* a quote. (Yikes! I didn't know that was coming.) "Her blog takes a novel approach to being a fan. She certainly takes brand dedication to a whole new level." I don't know if that means that they are acknowledging that I'm trying to understand Oprah's fan culture from the inside, or if they think I am vying for the presidency of her fan club. I decide to file that one for later.

The interview ends just as I feel I've gotten warmed up. Matt is hilarious, welcoming, and fun to talk to. Cohost Meredith Vieira is really kind to me off camera.

She asks, "Why aren't you Living Vieira?"

I tell her maybe next year.

After I'm detached from my microphone and grab my purse, I'm ushered out of the building. I find my phone and dial Jim to see what he thought of the interview. As I hear his warm hello, I begin to take in what is happening around me. The crowd outside the studio is waving at me and calling out, "Hey, Oprah Lady!" A man reaches out to shake my hand. Then another. I entered the building completely anonymous and am leaving it as someone whom people want to talk to and touch. What is it about TV that instantly makes someone more interesting? I am just as boring as I was when I entered the studio. Maybe more so.

Later in the morning, people who have seen the show ask if I'll pose with them for pictures. I do, because as I still haven't entirely recovered from my out-of-body experience, I am not as protective of my personal space as when I'm in my body. One woman holds up a copy of *O* magazine when our photo is snapped. For the rest of the morning, people shout out to me across the street, talk to me in elevators, and pat me on the back as I pay for my salad at lunch. Geez! How many people watch morning television? I am so relieved when the limo picks me up in front of my hotel to bring me back to the airport.

Noticing the mini hubbub as the car pulls away from the curb, the driver looks at me though his rearview mirror, "You famous or somethin'?"

"No," I say.

He stares a moment longer, then readjusts his mirror. "Yeah, me, either."

After I check my bag at LaGuardia, I walk to the gate and one woman yells out that she saw me on *Today* and loves my leopard-print flats. I become a little paranoid, careful not to do anything to embarrass myself in public. I want to spit out my gum but can't figure out a way to do it gracefully, so I keep chewing until it becomes bitter, stiff, and slightly nauseating. Finally, I scoot to the bathroom and get rid of it. I feel watched and ridiculous for feeling like I'm being watched. I hide behind my sunglasses, wishing I hadn't pooh-poohed the oversized frame trend this year.

Mercifully, just a few hours later, I'm back home as if nothing happened. Jim taped the *Oprah* show I missed this morning, and I sit cross-legged on the floor watching. I'm wearing my sock-monkey pajamas, eating the sushi that he and my friend Jefferson have ordered. We talk briefly about *Today*. I tell them that almost everyone who called, texted, or e-mailed after the show asked me how tall Matt Lauer is. Jim and Jefferson laugh and then ask me how tall Matt Lauer is. The conversation quickly turns to other matters, like the upcoming Céline Dion concert and our to-die-for spicy tuna rolls.

I am relieved everything is back to normal.

Once again, I can't tell if life is imitating art or vice versa. This morning Oprah encourages us to follow our passions and have faith that our hard work and zeal will lead to a paycheck. She doesn't want us to waste our time at jobs that suck our souls. Unless, I suppose, it is our goal in life to have our souls sucked. In which case, she'd probably support us.

She motivates us by saying, "Find out how to get paid for doing what you love."

And "Following your passion, allowing yourself to be paid for what you love will give you a meaningful life, you know?" And "Do what you love and the money will come."

I know lots of folks (me included) who would be more than happy to *allow* themselves to earn a paycheck doing what they love. Most of them are entirely receptive to financial reward for their hard work, and in their defense, I must say Oprah's statement has rubbed me the wrong way. I feel she's insinuating it's our fault if we're not making a living in our fields of choice. I'm upset by her words and want to argue with them, but as I've just signed my first book contract as a result of following my passion, I feel like a huge hypocrite. Still, I can't help myself. Hypocrisy be damned! While I do agree that the world is full of possibility if we work hard and stay focused, I also think a key element in the alchemy of success is luck. We can work our butts off and keep our eyes on the prize, but this component of the success puzzle is not always under our control. It does help to be in the right place at the right time. What I think is special about Oprah is that she figured out how to identify her wave and ride it. That's what I think many of us really need to learn. How to recognize opportunity and take advantage of it, understanding that the window might be open for only a short time.

The reason I want to lay out my opinion is I've heard from women who feel pretty low because, no matter how hard they work and sacrifice to make their dreams come true, they aren't seeing a payoff. I think we have to consider that the formula for success is complicated, unpredictable, and not entirely in our control. I don't think Oprah agrees. "I don't believe in luck," she says. "I think luck is preparation meeting opportunity."

We all talk about how it is amazing that Oprah pulled herself from humble beginnings to mind-blowing success. But we should also realize that when *Oprah* became a syndicated talk show in 1986, she was just 32 years old. That's pretty early in life to get your dream job. Plus she got her first position in the industry she loves at age 17. She didn't have to wait with bated breath, keeping her fingers crossed when it came to career. Unlike Oprah, many of my blog readers, and many of the women in my life, are one or two decades further into their hunt for elusive success. When she says, "Do what you love and the money will come," these can be inspiring words, but might also feel like a kick in the shins for some folks exhausted by hard work and lack of monetary reward.

It seems to me that many of the country's most successful businesspeople don't believe in luck, and they attribute their high status to their hard work. Does this mean they think they've worked harder than those of us lower down the economic totem pole? If so, do they consider themselves more deserving of success than those struggling to make ends meet? I don't know. I guess it's also possible that Oprah and I simply have different definitions of luck. Perhaps it's pesky language getting in the way once again.

On July 11 this year, I was at Café Selmarie in Chicago with Grace, eating our favorite sweet potato fries with chipotle dipping sauce. These, by the way, are what I'd choose if I could have just one food for the rest of my life. I should mention that these are not actually fried, but oven roasted. I don't want anyone to think I'm cheating on Bob Greene. I love them, and the café that makes them, so much that I convinced Jim to name our recently adopted kitten Selmarie in their honor. Our server approached our table and sheepishly asked, "Are you the Oprah Lady?"

I froze like a deer in the headlights. I was still anonymous at this point, and the article in the *Chicago Reader* had just hit the stands. Because I was so uncomfortable at being recognized, I did what I always do when I'm feeling awkward: I started babbling. Even though I knew the poor waitress had to get back to work, I couldn't get my gums to stop flapping, and I think I told her my entire life story. When she finally, gently, extricated herself, Grace and I started to laugh. My eager-to-please dial must have been set to maximum power. Being recognized by a stranger was one of the oddest experiences of my life.

And it continues, especially now that people know my name and have seen my face.

The recognition makes me a bit panicky, and I try to pretend it's not happening. I've never before been on the business end of a pointing finger, and it's odd. This afternoon is gorgeous and sunny. I walk down the familiar sidewalks in my neighborhood to do a few errands. A woman rolls down the window of her SUV and yells, "Did Oprah tell you to buy those jeans?" Why, yes, yes, she did. I do my best to identify the voice and peer into the window as the driver rolls it back up. I'm pretty sure she was a complete stranger.

Pardon the drama, but I feel my identity slipping away. Initially, this was intentional. I got the ball rolling when I decided to follow Oprah's plan for living rather than listen to my own intuition. Since the beginning of the year, life has been feeling decreasingly vibrant, which makes sense as I'm really just living as a faded version of myself. This has become more and more uncomfortable for me as the months wear on. And now, when I'm addressed as the Oprah Lady, I feel like I'm being stripped of even more of my individuality. I don't have any power over this and I don't like it. This by-product of my experiment isn't a component I expected, and while I do not relish it, I suppose it speaks to the effect of turning off one's intuition in order to travel with the herd.

While it's important to allow complete transparency on my blog, when I'm faced with offline recognition, I have a strong urge to protect my privacy. But it'll detract from the project if I construct a wall between my personal and public lives. For now, I'll pretend it's not happening and go about my project as if people weren't calling "Hey, Oprah Lady!" at me from their SUVs.

I make a mental note to wear my headphones whenever I leave the house.

I'm sweating, pedaling away in front of the television. My bike—my beloved Gary Fisher that I've converted into a stationary bike by attaching it to an indoor trainer—has become a regular fixture in the living room this year. I can frequently be found cycling in the mornings as I watch *Oprah*. I've attached a little basket to the handlebars so I can have my remote control, a notebook, and my cell phone (with Internet access) within arm's reach. I can do my BLC exercise, make notes on the show, and check my blog all at the same time. I wish my exercise could also generate the electricity to power the television. Now that would be handy.

I've just reread an e-mail from my good friend Jefferson—Yoda of all television knowledge in my world. The subject of the note is today's episode, which has been quite a mystery. The promotions for the show have hinted that we'll learn all about Oprah's favorite to-die-for gadget, and Jefferson has discovered online that the device is the Amazon Kindle. This makes sense as Oprah loves to read.

For those of you not in the know, the Kindle is an electronic reader. It's wireless, like your cell phone, and can download a gazillion books or periodicals from Amazon.com for a cost of approximately ten bucks per book. It weighs as much as half a human hair, has cured cancer, makes a perfect soufflé, and will bring peace to the Middle East. At least that's what it feels like as Oprah launches into her promotion of the gadget. You can only get it at one place: Amazon.com. Her excitement is so fervent, she must make one thing clear: "I personally—let me just say this—I have no stake in the Kindle. I know it sounds like I do." I wonder what the frenetic energy must look like in Amazon's warehouses right now. I hope CEO Jeff Bezos made sure there were extra portable defibrillators in the packing area before the announcement. We all know that every time Oprah announces her love of a product, it flies off the shelves. And today her long endorsement is like an infomercial that I might see in the wee hours of the morning when I'm watching television, too stressed by this project to sleep. I feel as if I can read her audience's collective consciousness as they giddily hope she'll give each of them her favorite toy (she does).

I have a really weird premonition that she will send me one, but I dismiss it as quickly as it enters my mind. I am actually embarrassed by my ego, and I pedal a little faster. Why on earth would Oprah give me a present? Her staff has never contacted me or communicated the least bit of interest in my project. I doubt they'll start by sending me a rather expensive gift. Oy! Robyn, get ahold of yourself. Oprah says, "I'm sorry I couldn't get you all one at home, too." I giggle and say to the TV screen, "No worries, Oprah. No gifts necessary."

The phone rings and I snatch it out of my basket, certain it's Jefferson. The caller ID reads THE OPRAH WINFREY SHOW. I immediately stop riding my bike and break into a very cold sweat. How on earth did the show get my number? I start to get a little paranoid and wonder if I'm the victim of a prank. I fight my desire to look out my blinds to see if someone's watching me. I normally allow calls to go to voice mail when I'm working out or if the show is on, but it seems I've developed a case of alien hand syndrome and I hit the talk button.

It turns out there is an employee of the *Oprah* show who has been deployed to deliver a present to me. She's at my old address a few blocks away. Without thinking, I give this total stranger the location of my new home and wonder if I've also developed alien mouth syndrome. It dawns on me they must have my number and address from my application for show tickets earlier in the year. I make a note to myself to be more careful about the information I dole out online.

I'm suddenly mortified about my tiny little apartment, the bike I've dragged in front of the TV, the piles of laundry I've folded but haven't had time to put away. I've worked too hard on decorating my home this year according to Winfrey to allow anyone from the *Oprah* show to see it in a state any less than perfect. I'm apprehensive about their judgment. I see the employee pull up a bit past my building, and I fly downstairs to meet her before I have to let her into my home. I realize I'm sweating profusely and am a mess. When I work out at home, I do not dress as if I might be hosting one of Oprah's staffers. In fact, I should thank my lucky stars that I'm even wearing pants.

The gal who approaches is young and unsmiling and I feel completely awkward around her. She gives me a package, which I notice is wrapped exactly as the gifts were that Oprah just handed out to her audience moments ago. I know, without a shadow of a doubt, that there is a Kindle inside. I make some clumsy attempts at expressing my gratitude and ask her to give Oprah my thanks.

She raises a perfectly arched eyebrow and says something along the lines of, "We know how much you love the show."

I'm put off by this. Maybe they do think I'm one of their superfans, after all.

Her voice is flat. I can't really get a read about what she thinks of me, but I can tell she doesn't want to linger very long. I chuckle uncomfortably. She doesn't even give me the hint of a grin. I'm feeling really dorky now, my heart pounding in my chest. I bid her farewell and she says a curt good-bye and we leave each other. She heads to her car and I bound up the stairs so I can hyperventilate in the privacy of my own home.

Surrealer and surrealer.

I open the foil paper and feel like Charlie, anticipating a golden ticket within the wrapping of his Wonka Bar. It's a Kindle all right, and I automatically fall in love with it. The only thing I enjoy more than a cool gadget is a *free* gadget. There's a typed note, with an actual signature, on personalized stationery that accompanies the present.

Enjoy Robin [*sic*],

Wanted to save you a few dollars on this one!

Thanks for watching.

Oprah Winfrey

But wait. My cloud of excitement dissipates and I remember that on this morning's show, Oprah told us that we should get a Kindle "if you can afford it." I check the notebook in my bike basket and read that quote I transcribed in a shaky hand as I pedaled earlier, "if you can afford it." If I am to literally follow all of Oprah's advice, without bending her words to my benefit, I have to buy this device on my own, when and if I can. I haven't accepted any other monetary or material assistance from outside sources so far. I probably shouldn't start now. I place the Kindle lovingly on my couch and stare at it for a while, not wanting to play with it and become too attached.

I start to think about the project and how I'm trying to remain as unbiased and open as possible. Can I maintain my neutrality if I keep this expensive item? Would people question my findings and opinions if I accepted such a decadent gift from the very woman I analyze on a daily basis? The Kindle retails for $359, and this one contains a special $100 gift certificate for downloads. While I am certainly no journalist, I know they aren't supposed to accept gifts from their subjects. The reporter from the *New York Times* who came to my home this summer insisted that she pay for her own lunch because of the newspaper's policies. I feel I should maintain the same integrity.

By now, everyone reading this book should know what I do next: Call Mom. She has me read Oprah's note to her five times and is thrilled that I'm having such an exciting morning.

Then she says, "It's a shame Oprah didn't spell your name right."

I tell her that I'm freaking out because I don't think I can ethically keep the gift, but at the same time wonder if it's ever ethically correct to return a present. I've never done it before and certainly never to the Queen of Talk. I mean, doesn't *everyone* want Oprah to give them a treat? It'd be so much easier to just keep it. I want it. Oprah wants me to have it. And frankly, it's too expensive for me to afford on my own right now.

My mom takes a breath and gently says to me, "No matter what you do, you'll choose the right thing."

Oh, come on! What kind of advice is that? Clearly someone's taken over the body of my opinionated mother who even has a strong point of view on the subject of neutrality. We don't speak for a little while, but she stays on the phone with me as I pace. You'd think I was trying to decide whether or not to give Oprah one of my kidneys, not make a decision regarding a piece of plastic with a motherboard. Finally, although it hurts my fingers to type this, I decide I can't keep the Kindle. It just wouldn't be right. I tell my mom that I'm going to send it back.

"Oh, thank G-d," she exhales. "I was worried you were going to keep it."

Yup, that's my mom.

I call a messenger service to send back the package within the hour and sit down to compose a note to Oprah on my laptop. I hadn't intended to contact her directly during the course of this year, but I can't return her present without explaining that I don't mean the least bit of offense by my actions. It's not perfect, but it's the best I can do.

Dear Ms. Winfrey,
I was so pleased and touched this morning when I received this Kindle from you. It was such a thoughtful gesture, I was literally speechless. And if you knew me personally, you'd know "speechless" is rarely a term that could describe me. As grateful as I was, as I am, I felt I had to return the gift.

Please understand that this is in no means an insult or a show of ingratitude. It is not intended in that manner at all.

The issue is, when I started my Living Oprah project, I decided to follow some rules. One of the most important was that I did not receive any outside contributions as they might conflict with my research. So, no sponsorship, no advertising, no grants, no gifts, or any other financial assistance.

I admire you so much as a woman who has "stuck to her guns" over the course of your career. And it is in that spirit that I've decided to stay true to the mission of my own work and give this lovely Kindle back. Don't get me wrong—I did hold it lovingly for a few minutes before I decided it wasn't the right thing for me to keep it.

You did say on the show that we, at home, should get one if we could afford it. And I will be able to do this. Maybe not this month. But certainly in the next.

I hope I have made my intentions clear. I am in no way spurning your generosity, simply acting in a way I know will maintain the integrity of my project.

All the very best to you.

Thank you,
Robyn Okrant

When I go to print out the note, I flash back to a discussion I had last night with Jim, who told me he forgot to get toner for our printer. I stare at the red light blinking up at me and decide not to panic. I should handwrite the letter, anyhow. It's much more personal that way. I delve into my desk drawer and discover most of my notecards are silly and kitschy and, although I love them, none of them sets the appropriate tone. I briefly consider writing on one of my fun Wonder Woman greeting cards, but dismiss the thought. I should be professional and sincere, not irreverent. I finally settle on the simplest stationery I can find.

I transcribe what I've written on the screen. When I'm about half-way done, I remember that during a rerun back in January, Oprah shared that President Clinton told her to always write one-page letters so people can easily frame them. I get it in my mind that I should also try to write my note on one page. Certainly it won't be framed, but it'll be easier for her office staff to photocopy and poke fun at a single-sided document. I'm just doing my part to boost office morale. Only problem is, I start to run out of room. What started off as neat and legible at the top of the page turns into tiny, cramped chicken scratch at the bottom. It looks more like the manifesto of a lunatic than a thank-you and apology note. Maybe I should start again. Then the doorbell rings and I almost jump out of my skin. It's the messenger, waiting downstairs for me. I can barely afford the service as it is, and if I make the delivery woman wait, I'll have to pay a penalty charge. I decide to throw the crazy-looking note in with the Kindle. The messenger gives me a nod, shuts her car door, and drives off with the package. For the second time this morning, I head up the stairs to my little apartment, shell-shocked. With every step, I feel alternatively certain about my decision and incredibly doubtful.

Because of the day's events, it's challenging to follow Oprah's advice to "Get a lift when you come in the front door." I pause to look at the photos in my entryway. I hung them because they always make me happy: one of my parents bundled in warm clothing on a fall day in Lincoln Park, and one of Jim and me on our blind camping date, eating pancakes I cooked over a propane stove. My blood pressure begins to mellow. I lock the door behind me and take some deep, slow breaths, trying to see the true size of this event in the grand scheme of life. While I'm nervous about what my readers will think of my decision, I believe I made the right choice for myself. I look at my bike and remember I still haven't finished the morning's workout, but I don't even consider jumping back on to pedal. It's early afternoon and I'm exhausted and drained. I decide to take a hot shower, make a cup of tea, and lose myself in a great book made out of good old-fashioned paper.

The feedback from my readers about the Kindle Debacle, as I now refer to it, has been mixed. Some folks are angry I've given back a gift from Oprah and others are proud of my decision. At first I jump in and try to answer every comment, but then I realize I will never make everyone happy. This blog has grown into a healthy community, and it's not my job to police it any longer. Although, frankly, I can't wait for the debate to settle down as I think it clouds the purpose of my project and I'd like to refocus.

I learned from this experience that many people harbor deep hope that they'll receive a present from Oprah Winfrey. I'm not making light of this because it's with honest desire that some viewers dream of Oprah's gifts, support, and attention. She's positioned herself as a modern-day Santa, and countless fans long for her generosity. I've heard from many women who clamor for a piece of Oprah in the form of a gift. The material goods she hands out transcend their actual monetary value and are revered for their connection to the talk show host. Whether it's a car or a cupcake, it feels as if I'm witnessing a personal religious experience when guests have gifts bestowed upon them by Oprah.

Luckily for her fans, Oprah is very generous. She genuinely appears to love making people happy by giving them things. While I might find the crazed behavior of her audience disturbing after they receive their prizes, I find Oprah's action of giving to be heartfelt. I do wish what I saw in return was gratitude, not adoration, but most of our cultural responses to celebrities are exacerbated by the thrill that their stardom provokes. For instance, while my mom swears she never threw underwear onstage at a Tom Jones concert, some women did. Would we toss our panties at our favorite barista at the coffee shop? No way! Besides being a health code violation, it's absurd. We don't get as excited about one another in civilian life as we do with celebs, no matter how tasty someone makes our latte. It is no surprise that there is so much disparity between the haves and the have-nots when many of us are complicit in bolstering the idea that some people are more worthy of having lingerie flung at them than others. I say we should all just toss our underwear at one another, without discrimination, or stop doing it altogether.

October 2008 Accounting

Date	Assignment	Cost	Time	Notes
10/1	Read *O* from cover to cover. *(LO)*		4h 0m	
10/1	Get a mammogram "if you haven't done it already." *(MAG)*		0h 0m	Already done!
10/1	"Please take the time, if you can, to read" Nicholas Kristoff's column in the *New York Times* about livestock rights. *(MAG)*		0h 5m	Interesting op-ed piece. I'd like a more in-depth story. I think maybe he has a book?
10/1	Oprah says we gals are too judgmental of each other and we should support our fellow women instead of criticizing them. *(SHOW)*		0h 0m	I think this is absolutely true. I aspire to be entirely committed to this. I will tread very carefully for the remainder of this year, staying very conscious of my intentions toward other women. **(O)**
10/1	Go to Oprah.com and visit the message boards to follow up on today's show (about a woman who was so busy, she didn't realize she left her baby daughter in the backseat of a hot car all day; the baby died because of the woman's negligence). *(SHOW)*		0h 15m	*Yikes!* Oprah's message boards are brutal.

(cont.)

October 2008 Accounting (*cont.*)

Date	Assignment	Cost	Time	Notes
10/2	Prepare home in order to complete "have friends over for *Across the Universe* viewing" and "make paella." *And* make sangria from Oprah.com recipe. *(SHOW/ WEB)*	52.07	1h 0m	Cleaned the house, set up for viewing party, postparty cleanup. (Made sangria from Oprah's website, too!)
10/3	Read Maya Angelou's *Letter to My Daughter*. *(SHOW)*	16.50	1h 45m	I read this in two sittings. It's simple. You can really hear Angelou's voice. Some were nice, some I didn't agree with entirely, still a nice read, and there are a couple good quotes I'll keep.
10/6	"That is the real lesson — is because you carry the poison with you. The cost of not forgiving is to the person who is holding on to whatever it is… and so, that's why you let go of it, so you can free yourself." Because of Oprah's advice, I searched for assistance on her website and did the "Meditation on Forgiveness" by Jack Kornfield, which is on Oprah.com. *(SHOW/WEB)*		0h 25m	The guy's voice made me a little crazy, but I thought it was helpful.

10/6	"One of the reasons I was interested in telling this story on the air is not just for us to be voyeurs, but for each person who is listening today to look in your own life and ask: Who do you need to forgive?" *(SHOW)*	0h 10m	I wrote for a bit—came up with a few people I might need to forgive. Just holding on to a little bit of resentment about them...just acknowledging this took weight off my shoulders. I didn't think I even held grudges anymore.**(O)**
10/8	"Ask yourself, *What can I live without?*" *(SHOW)*	0h 15m	As I walked around through life today, I took note of what I didn't need. This will be an ongoing project. I do want to say just because I don't *need* something doesn't mean I can't have it. This is usually the way I look at these things—as if I need to go cold turkey. Frankly, there are some luxuries that improve my daily life and I'm not so sure I'm willing to give them up. **(O)**
10/8	"We need to shift the way we think about living our lives. And it really is about bringing us all back to living within our means." *(SHOW)*	0h 0m	This was going great until I needed a health procedure and back brace that wasn't within my means and I could only pay for it with credit. **(O)**
10/9	"Be nice." *(SHOW)*	0h 0m	I'm on it! **(O)**

(cont.)

October 2008 Accounting (*cont.*)

Date	Assignment	Cost	Time	Notes
10/10	"Okay, we're going to stretch" (to release the physical tension that gathers due to stress over money). *(SHOW)*		0h 45m	This is hilarious. Every time I freak about finances, I've been stretching. I even did it in public when I got a much bigger bill at a restaurant than I thought I'd be getting. The silliness relaxes me, more than the actual stretching, I think. **(O)**
10/10	"You're going to love it." *(SHOW)*	17.00	1h 29m	Oprah says I'll love the animated children's movie *Madagascar*. I'm not excited.
10/13	"Be sure to check out Suze on Saturday nights on CNBC." *(SHOW)*		2h 0m	I did this two Saturdays in a row. It wasn't so bad. It's not exactly what I think of as Saturday night fun.
10/14	"Vote at the grocery stores" to show how I feel about cruelty to farm animals. *(SHOW)*		0h 0m	I'm doing what I can. It's so much more expensive to shop this way that I've had to take some other things out of my cart. **(O)**
10/15	"We need to learn to be more civil to each other." *(SHOW)*		0h 0m	'Nuf said. **(O)**
10/15	"I also think this is very rude, so don't do it to me anymore. People say this to me all the time, 'Do you remember meeting me?' And then they go, 'What's my name?'" *(SHOW)*		0h 0m	Okay. I can't imagine it'll ever come up, though. **(O)**

10/15	"Ask yourself this, Are you rude?" *(SHOW)*		0h 0m	I've gotten 100 percent better about not using my cell phone when I am ordering coffee! **(O)**
10/15	"Be more gracious to everybody." *(SHOW)*		0h 0m	Why, thank you for this advice! I appreciate it! **(O)**
10/19	"Read the article. Such a great article." *(SHOW)*		0h 10m	Halle Berry article on Esquire.com.
10/21	Read *My Stroke of Insight* by Dr. Jill Bolte Taylor. *(SHOW)*	16.47	4h 0m	Oprah said to do this if we have a family member who had a stroke. I have.
10/22	"Whether you're a parent or grandparent, aunt or uncle, I hope you'll pass some of them along to a child you love." *(SHOW)*		0h 2m	Nothing was funnier than my 3-year-old niece's blank look as I taught her about fiscal responsibility before she opened her Christmas presents.
10/23	"Find out how to get paid for doing what you love." *(SHOW)*		0h 0m	This felt exhilarating to hear. **(O)**
10/23	"Following your passion, allowing yourself to be paid for what you love will give you a meaningful life." *(SHOW)*		0h 0m	Well, I am following my passion. And I'm allowing myself to get paid for what I love. And I know the universe will shower me with salary any moment now. Any moment…Universe?… **(O)**
10/23	"Do what you love and the money will come." *(SHOW)*		0h 0m	See above. **(O)**

(cont.)

October 2008 Accounting (*cont.*)

Date	Assignment	Cost	Time	Notes
10/24	"Take a breath, everybody." (SHOW)		0h 0m	Oprah wanted us to breathe and relax and know the economy will be fine.
10/24	Buy a Kindle reader "if you can afford it." (SHOW)	359.00	0h 5m	Couldn't afford it at first. Saved up! Bought it on 12/29/08.
10/24	"You are really going to love yourself when you do this." (SHOW)		1h 0m	Make Chicken Pot Pie from Cristina Ferrare's recipe (made on 11/28 for family during Thanksgiving weekend). My parents bought ingredients. Wouldn't tell me how much they spent.
10/27	"Every woman needs a fan!" (to make us look great in portraits) (SHOW)		0h 0m	*Hilarious.* I had the photographer turn on a fan during the photo shoot for this book. You can't tell because my hair's so short, though.
Throughout Month	Watch every episode of *Oprah*. (LO)		23h 0m	23 shows
Throughout Month	Do Best Life Challenge exercise. (BLC)		6h 0m	80 minutes a week for 4.5 weeks
Throughout Month	Take *A Course in Miracles*. (WEB/SHOW)		7h 45m	approx. 15 minutes a day for 31 days
MONTHLY TOTAL		461.04	54h 11m	
YEAR-TO-DATE TOTAL		4,092.64	1062h 54m	

ONGOING PROJECTS
– "Reinvigorate your appearance with some great advice on how not to look old..."
– "Rethink your eating habits with some absolutely delicious and utterly original meals..."
– Use cloth and reusable bags at grocery store. No more plastic.
– Change lightbulbs to energy-efficient bulbs.
– "I think in terms of investment, it's the best thing you can ever give yourself is to have beautiful surroundings."
– "I would just say to anybody, whatever secret you're holding, live your own truth."
– Sharon Salzberg meditation
– Make your rooms personal.
– Best Life Challenge exercise and diet guidance
– "I do want you to start thinking about, as I have started thinking about, how much you consume. I mean, like every time you throw away a paper towel. Every time you are, you know, wasteful with food in your house...just think about how much you really need."
– "Get a lift when you come in the front door."
– "I want you to savor every meal."
– "I want you to pay attention to how happy women get that way."
– *A Course in Miracles*
– Declutter home/life.
– *A New Earth* meditation
– "With the arrival of spring, I hope you, too, will reconnect with nature."
– "When you think that you're going to get in a car and drive, I want you to think about this mother holding her daughter's head on the side of the highway. That's the thought I want to come to your mind before you go to get in the car after having even one drink."
– "Stop defining yourself by what you see—or think you see—when you look in the mirror."
– "Everybody think about this: On the way to work or on the way to do whatever you do during the day...how many negative things...the negative tape that's playing in your head all day long about yourself. *I can't do that, I shouldn't do that, I'm too fat, oh, look at my thighs...*"
– "I think we should be open like Horton."
– "Alexis Stewart talks candidly about trying to get pregnant on her radio show *Whatever*, on Martha Stewart Living Radio. Tune in to follow her progress there."
– The YOU: Staying Young Aging Quiz
– Learn to accept all people.
– "Stop saying that" (re: using the word "just" to describe ourselves).
– Take Dr. Oz–recommended vitamins and supplements (vitamin D, folic acid, fish oil)
– Rise and Shine—how to wake up less stressed.
– "Be sure to check him [Dr. Oz] out on XM156, Oprah and Friends, and also on our section of Oprah.com. Keep those questions coming."
– Ten Secrets to a Better Love Life
– Get Rolfed.
– Burt's Bees Eye Cream and Ageless Night Cream

(cont.)

- "Going out to work every day, which every man does who is responsible for his family, after a while men feel taken for granted that they are doing that...so there needs to be some acknowledgment of that"
- "The truth of the matter is, men do need to be made to feel like they're winners. They do need to have themselves built up."
- "Go to Oprah.com for more of Suze's advice on how to survive these tough times."
- "So, if you or somebody you know needs help with addiction and finding treatment in your area, call the National Drug and Alcohol Addiction Hotline."
- "You have to do your own self-test" (re: breast self-exam)

Accounting Abbreviations: *LO* = Living Oprah Project Task, *SHOW* = *The Oprah Winfrey Show*, *WEB* = Oprah.com, *MAG* = *O, The Oprah Magazine*, *BC* = Oprah's Book Club, *BLC* = Best Life Challenge, **(O)** = ongoing project

NOVEMBER:

Guess who's coming to dinner?

Time spent this month: 72 hours, 53 minutes

Dollars spent this month: $260.03

Most challenging assignment: "Live with cellulite. Be happy."

Most enjoyable assignment: "Get rid of your toxic friends."

Words that stuck: "Oprah really loves grated orange zest. I think it might be her favorite food. Who uses that much zest?"—My aunt Rayna, after she cooked several Thanksgiving recipes from Oprah.com

I'VE DEVELOPED a new talent: I can recite the script from the Lowe's commercials along with Gene Hackman's voice-over. I've seen and heard these ads so often during Oprah's show, I know his intonations—every nuance of his line readings. I am able to perform this trick with several of Oprah's sponsors, and after I watch each episode, I find myself humming jingles as I go about my day. If there is an advertising edition of Trivial Pursuit, I highly recommend you purchase it and ask me to be on your team. I'm a ringer.

I can also tell you what's on sale each given week at Old Navy and Target. I'm a walking, talking circular. I'm not allowed to wear cargo pants this year, because they supposedly make me look old, but I sure know where they can be purchased at a low, low price for a limited time. Twice I've dragged Jim downtown to shop for items I've seen sandwiched between segments of the *Oprah* show. I never liked to shop before, but these bright, sassy commercials are turning my repulsion into compulsion.

This is one of the more surprising by-products of my daily viewing of the show. Oprah's advertisers have become integrated into my daily intake of television. While I prefer to mute or fast-forward through the commercials during the rest of my TV-watching time, I think it's important for me to absorb the full *Oprah* experience along with millions of other viewers. These ads become an extension of the show itself.

The *Oprah* audience is mainly female. Oprah.com says "Women outnumber men in the audience by a ratio of 19 to 1," and women drive most of the purchasing for their households. If I were an advertiser, I'd covet the opportunity to be part of Oprah's hour. When I see an ad for a product or service during the show, it is inextricably connected to the Queen of Talk herself. It's almost as if Oprah is personally urging us to join Jenny Craig when those commercials play between segments of her episodes about weight loss. And doesn't she want us to buy new tools from Lowe's when she does a program about home makeovers? For a nation of susceptible TV viewers who have limited funds, it feels like a dangerous concoction to mix TV's most influential woman and advertising.

Oprah has aired many episodes this year about fiscal responsibility. One of her experts, Suze Orman, has read us the riot act about chilling out when it comes to throwing our hard-earned dollars around. The country's economy is circling down the drain because many of us are spending money we don't actually have. Oprah and her panelists have urged us to be smart with our finances and to save. We've been informed about our hostess's distaste for waste. She recommends that we stop to consider what we can live without. And yet it's the nature of the television business that we don't follow her well-meaning advice. To keep shows on TV, we must put money in advertisers' pockets or else their dollars will dry up and our favorite shows will be canceled. I am dubious when television shows tell us to stop spending. I can't help but think about Philip Morris's Youth Tobacco Prevention Department or their QuitAssist® program. When I first heard about these, I just about fell out of my chair. Will Duncan Hines sponsor a diabetes support group next? If I hadn't quit smoking back in 1997, the frustration I now feel over this corporate game-playing might make me reach for a cigarette.

November 3, 2008
I love my vulva!

Oprah told me I should.

I'm so relieved her new sexpert, Dr. Laura Berman, has convinced Oprah to use anatomical terms for a woman's body. If I never hear the word "vajayjay" again, it'll be too soon. I don't want to pretend I've always been above embarrassment when it comes to discussing my body. When I was a preteen, I used to call the entire space below my navel and above my knees my "area." In Oprah's defense, at least "vajayjay" strongly insinuates the word "vagina" when used in context. "Area" could imply just about anything that takes up space. But hey, I was 11.

Oprah widens the sexual horizons of the daytime talk show audience. While I find her discussions pretty tame, it's the nature of the beast that daytime television falls behind prime-time TV in raciness. The kids are home, after all. Oprah seems ready to break through the constraints of what's socially acceptable to discuss before the kiddos' bedtime. The sex-related shows contain warnings galore so concerned parents can turn on the DVR or whisk their children out of the living room and throw them in front of World of Warcraft on the computer instead. You know, so they don't have to learn the evils of human sexuality.

I really appreciate the frankness of these shows. I would prefer they go even further in-depth, but I suppose baby steps are in order. Some of my blog readers were none too happy about such shows playing before the sun sets, but as a child-free woman, I say bring on the openness!

Oprah's audience emulates her. I think it is her responsibility, as someone whose goal it is to empower women, to display as much comfort with the human body and sexuality as possible. Shame often surrounds the topic of our bodies and sex, so the more Oprah can let her guard down, the more we will. I know this is a tall order for someone who comes from a background of sexual abuse, so I appreciate and admire her growth in this area. One small step for woman, one giant leap for a mostly female viewing audience of millions.

Speaking of viewing, tonight I am in my bathroom, squatting over a hand mirror. Oprah and Dr. Berman have urged us to familiarize ourselves with our genitals. I surprised myself when I thought back and realized I haven't done this since I still played cassettes on my boom box. I am not very intimidated by the assignment, but it is taking me ages to find a hand mirror. Once I finally locate the necessary prop, I have a little private time in the bathroom. I can't help but sing "Getting to Know You" in my best Julie Andrews vibrato while I reflect upon my best side.

"Robyn?"

I leap about five feet in the air. I hadn't heard Jim come home from work, and I nearly step on the mirror as I hustle to put on some pants. "I'm in here!" I call out to him.

Jim pokes his head in the bathroom, where I've just managed to button my jeans. For some reason, instead of telling him what I've been doing, I pretend I've just used the john and I flush the toilet and wash my hands.

"How was work?" I ask him. Then I recall another assignment I was given this morning and throw my arms around his neck, kissing him deeper than our usual peck hello. I count down in my head.

"10…9…8…7…6…5…4…3…2…1."

I let him go.

He looks pleasantly surprised and asks what brought that on. I tell him Oprah advocated that women kiss their partners for ten seconds every day. He looks bummed out that it was Oprah, rather than he, who inspired the smooch. Immediately, I regret killing the moment.

In the following days, I can't help imagining Dr. Berman and Oprah nodding enthusiastically as Jim and I kiss for our allotted seconds. While my husband is initially eager about this assignment, I'm kind of bored. It is making make-out time not so fun for me, and it's not an overstatement to say I actually start to dread kissing my own partner, whom I adore and who is truly quite kissable. While I count down our kissing seconds in my head, I am certain Jim is counting down the days until this project is over. I'm hoping the new year will immediately erase Oprah's presence from my bedroom.

Spontaneity is nonexistent lately. Oprah told her audience, "The first thing you need to do in preparing for sex . . . is wash yourself. . . . I'm just assuming that everybody has taken a shower." Jim looks entirely confused every time things get steamy between us and I run to the bathroom to get clean. By the time I dry off, his mind is elsewhere. Maybe next time I should bring him with me. We think about Oprah's advice every time we feel the least bit romantic, and this threesome is not enhancing my marriage. Her guidance has been helpful in many other aspects of my life, but Winfrey is no Spanish fly.

November 12, 2008
I've signed another contract. Oprah's guaranteed a clutter-free home if we follow the plan laid out in the Oprah's Clean Up Your Messy House Tour program. Oprah must know how to keep a house clean — from the photos I've seen of her various homes, her living space appears to be impeccable. I've come a long way as a housekeeper since the beginning of the year, but I've still got miles to go. I imagine Oprah and I have different methods and requirements when it comes to cleaning our homes.

Okrant:
Organize kitchen cabinets.
Spend ten minutes each day decluttering closets.
Stop accumulating kitchen gadgets.
Make sure drawers aren't a struggle to close.

Oprah:
Hire housekeeper.

The Oprah's Clean Up Your Messy House Tour is a mobile program that sends fleets of adorable VW Beetles around the country to help people like me. I don't want an army of latex-gloved strangers in my home, so I'm not applying for direct help, but I am signing my contract and following the rules. The program is six months long, and it's the first time I've been confronted with the concrete question about whether I'll continue any of this once my year ends in 49 days. Not that I'm counting.

This is one area of my life I'm hoping to maintain. It's nice to have breathing room in my small home. The cats have more fun when there are piles to hide behind, but it makes me feel stressed, distracted, and embarrassed. Jim even uses the word "declutter" now. It's like our new hobby: our boring but satisfying hobby. Still, I've had this avocation for less than a year. Will the habits of decades be broken? My fingers are crossed.

Today I witnessed one of the reasons I believe Oprah has been able to build and maintain her popularity since 1986. I've already spoken about how her passion is magnetic, but so is her pain. Today she informed us of the passing of her beloved cocker spaniel Solomon. She shared her grief with us. She wept and so did I. Her pain recalled the loss of pets in my past. I don't wish such sadness on anyone, but Oprah's ability to display her deep emotion makes her so much more accessible to me. It is her unguarded feelings that allow her audience a heartfelt connection to her. While some believe her lifestyle makes her unable to relate to the average Jane, it is in times like these I think we are able to reestablish our bond, if we desire to maintain one. Sure, she's guarded about many things that I wish she'd make more transparent, but in the moments when her boundaries dissipate and we see her express pain, embarrassment, joy, and excitement, she becomes human once again.

I think of Martha Stewart, also a media magnate and self-made success who has capitalized on her own passions. I've learned a lot of practical advice from her. In fact, my own interests fall more in line with Martha's expertise than Oprah's priorities. I believe Martha to be a strong teacher and a skilled, clever, and enthusiastic craftsperson. Yet, while she's shared her marvelous hints about creative housekeeping over the years, she doesn't have the same personal emotional connection to her audience that Oprah maintains. Martha appears more subdued and self-protective than Oprah. She doesn't yell guests' names like Tarzan or burst into an "ugly cry." (Oprah's self-proclaimed "ugly cry" is just what it sounds like—an unrestrained display of genuine emotion, complete with tears, snot, and running mascara.) I get the sense that Martha is perceived as a contained and controlled authority figure, while Oprah is embraced as everyone's BFF.

After today's show, even I wanted to give Oprah a comforting hug. I've never felt as if Martha needed my hug, but I'm not offended. It's way too dangerous to hug a woman with a hot glue gun in her hand, anyway.

My family rocks.

Not in a "my dad lays down the beats while sister makes her guitar gently weep" kind of way. It's more of a "I can't believe my family supports me so much they're allowing me to hijack their favorite holiday" sort of deal. I am incredibly grateful to be part of this gene pool. For the most part, we all enjoy one another's company and support each other's endeavors. I'd have to push pretty hard to cause them to turn their backs on me, but I might have finally discovered a way to test their limits. It's a little something we're all calling Oprah Thanksgiving.

They've allowed me to kidnap our tried-and-true (and much loved) turkey day menu and replace it with recipes I've gathered from Oprah's show, magazine, and website. Usually, our family is mighty laid back when we converge upon my mom and dad's home in New Hampshire. For my relatives who enjoy watching television, there is parade, football, and National Dog Show viewing. As we watch the well-groomed pups prance around, my family asks what happened with Oprah's advocacy of Pennsylvania's Dog Law early this year. I inform them it passed last month. There is a brief cheer before everyone returns to planning their Black Friday shopping strategies. There is eating and there is more eating. And there is a lot of sitting around, relaxing, catching up, and laughing. It's loosey-goosey, and everyone looks forward to it all year. This year, I'm surprising everyone with activities suggested in Oprah's various media. This enforced structure is either going to be a hit or a groaner.

Our holiday is loosely collaborative. My dad makes the turkeys, my mom and my aunt Rayna cook the myriad of side dishes and bake desserts. And by "bake desserts," I mean buy them. The remainder of us pitch in when we are asked or allowed. This year, we're going full-out potluck. Oprah.com tells us to "share dinner duties." My mom and I have gone through all the Thanksgiving-specific recipes on the website and in *O* to plan the menu, and I've doled out the responsibilities accordingly. I was a bit shy about asking my relatives to bend to Oprah's will, but for the most part, they jumped at the opportunity to be part of my project.

Now it's time for our big dinner, and we're all sitting around my parents' dining room table oohing and ahhing. Everyone looks ready to dig into the meal, but they have to put up with me taking photos and video of the table before we eat. Luckily, the novelty of Oprah Thanksgiving hasn't yet worn off, and everyone remains patient and plays along, smiling for the camera. Then I notice a few folks taking stock of what is missing from the table. Sure, the new dishes look like fun, but will we survive without our much-beloved brisket? And where the (insert explicative here) are the mashed potatoes? I better green-light the start of this meal before there is a mutiny.

No one will tell me exactly how much they spent creating their recipes. I, of course, kept track of my receipts for the sake of the project, but my family refuses to tell me their expenses, insisting it was their duty to bring the dish and so it's none of my business what they spent. Still, I would wager my two beloved cats that they spent far more than usual. I know this because of the extensive ingredient list for each recipe and because there isn't a can of cranberry sauce or a french-fried onion–coated green bean casserole in sight. And, most telling of all, the good china and silver came out.

Here's a little compare-contrast list of the usual Okrant family turkey day versus Oprah Thanksgiving. You'll note I stayed in people's comfort zones, lest they revolt.

Okrant	Oprah
Green bean casserole with french-fried onions (Did somebody say cream of mushroom soup?)	Slow-Roasted Green Beans with Sea Salt and Olive Oil (Nice. The goopy soup and onions were missed fiercely, though.)
Green salad (with countless bottles of dressing for everyone to choose from)	Festive Holiday Salad (Really nice. Restaurant-y.)
Relish Tray (kosher pickles, black and green olives. My sister and I wipe this out before the meal begins.)	Bacon-Nut Stuffing (I loved this. I was the only one, much to my delight. More for me.)
Canned cranberry sauce. (Can't help it, I think the ridges from the aluminum can make it taste delicious.)	Cranberry Fruit Conserve (This was a family favorite!)
Mashed potatoes (homemade, hand-mashed. Adored by my family. Even eaten on leftover turkey sandwiches the next day, along with a slice of cranberry sauce.)	Roasted Rosemary Potatoes with Garlic and Shallots (We loved this side dish. And we learned where the shallots are in the supermarket. Those suckers are expensive and hard to peel, but delicious.)
Roast turkey (two of 'em. There's lots of us and we require major leftovers.)	Classic Roast Turkey (Good. Needed to be babysat more than our usual birds.)
Gravy. (Created by Team Gravy. My cousin Steven and I even wear T-shirts with the Team Gravy logo on them while we whisk. Ridiculous? Yes. Classy? No. Fun? Totally.)	Turkey Gravy (I'm biased, but I think Team Gravy puts this to shame.)
Sweet potato casserole. (Yes. With the mini marshmallows. A classic.)	Thyme-Roasted Baby Carrots (Another fave. We don't usually break out the fresh herbs, but it was great.)
Baked sweet potatoes. (Because not everyone likes mini marshmallows.)	Sweet Potato and Pecan Pie with Cinnamon Cream (I didn't eat this one, but nobody liked it. It sounded delicious, but there were lots of grimaces.)
Pumpkin pie, pecan pie, apple pie (all slathered with spray whipped topping. I never understood my family's fondness for this, but I support their right to enjoy pressurized "dairy" food.)	Low-Fat Pumpkin-Banana Mousse Tart (Everyone says it's blah—but still the best of all the desserts. I stay mum as my cousins break out the spray whipped topping. Do they carry the stuff in holsters?)
Baked apples (There's always *someone* on a diet in my family, so we like to have some dessert alternatives available.)	Cream Cheese–Chocolate Chip Cookies (not on the Thanksgiving menu, but my aunt threw them in the mix for people to munch on. People took one bite and left the rest on their plates.)

I think there were positives and negatives about dinner, but overall, I found it really fun. I especially enjoyed going grocery shopping with my mom, dad, and Jim on Wednesday. It was like a scavenger hunt. Also, it's nice to think and eat outside the box every now and then. Ruts are safe and comfortable, but a breath of fresh air is much appreciated. After we polish off our meal, we all agree that next year we'll bring back the carrots and, without a doubt, those rosemary potatoes. I could sleep on a bed of those suckers and be content.

Between our delightful dinner and our disappointing dessert, we play a little icebreaker getting to know you game that was suggested on Oprah.com. Jim is responsible for copying the questions suggested on the website onto small cards, and while everyone digests we are meant to answer such things as:

- How do you want to be remembered?
- What would you do with a million dollars?
- What is your mission?

A couple of these Oprah-approved questions are asked, but then Jim rebels and sneaks in some deeper, more meaningful queries.

- What's the most naked you've ever been in public?
- If you could commit one crime without being caught, what would it be?
- Would you rather be locked in a room with a tiger or lick the foot of a homeless person?

This is when the party really gets started. I can say without a shadow of a doubt I am learning more about my father than I ever knew before. Why must he be so descriptive with his answers? It's a possibility I might be in therapy for many years to work through it all.

The game itself appears to be a form of training wheels for families without a lot to talk about. My family, never at a loss for words, definitely enjoys the activity but is eager to get back to our own conversations once the game is over. Everyone eats a bit of dessert, but not much of it, and then scatters around the house to nap, catch up, watch football, or plan their shopping excursions for the next day.

I run upstairs to put together the hostess gift Oprah has suggested on a recent show about how to have a thrifty holiday. She thinks one of the nicest things a person can receive is a personal note of gratitude.

She says, "The words from your heart mean more to people than anything you can buy."

As someone who has kept meaningful notes since childhood, I totally agree and am excited to create this gift for Mom. Earlier in the day, I gave everyone a card on which to write a note, and I've just gathered everyone's missives. I am putting the finishing touches on a collage-covered box (smothered with images of Oprah) to house the cards. I'm a little worried that my mom might think the gift is corny but am pleasantly surprised when we present the box to her. She is touched by the thoughtfulness. I give all the credit to Oprah. Although, to be honest, a couple relatives grumbled a bit about having to write their sentiments on paper. I think sometimes folks feel a lot of pressure to be eloquent, but my mom had no complaints.

As the family starts thinking about leftovers, I have to go to my old room to watch a tape of today's *Oprah*. My dad sweetly recorded the rerun earlier this afternoon so I could spend time with the gang. As I grab my notebook and a pen and hit play on the VCR, I hear my family bursting with laughter downstairs. I get suddenly and unexpectedly sad. I am upstairs, watching TV and taking in all of Oprah's words, unable to spend precious time with my family. It dawns on me that much of my year has been the same: watching TV, following advice, trying to find my elusive "best life." All the while, my "real life" slides past in a blur.

November 2008 Accounting

Date	Assignment	Cost	Time	Notes
11/1	Read *O* from cover to cover. *(LO)*		4h 0m	
11/3	"Love your vulva." *(SHOW)*		0h 0m	Oh, I do. **(O)**
11/3	Kiss Jim for 10 seconds every day *(SHOW)*		0h 10m	Daily **(O)**
11/3	Look at my genitals in a hand mirror. *(SHOW)*		0h 5m	Yup. Still there.
11/4	Vote. *(SHOW)*		0h 10m	I love Election Day.
11/4	"Nobody should watch alone." *(SHOW)*		5h 0m	Invited friends over to watch election.
11/6	"Private invitation: Shop the all-new Oprahstore.com!" *(E-MAIL)*		0h 15m	I came, I shopped, I did not spend.
11/6	"There's seven seconds in this film that will change your life forever." (movie: *Seven Pounds* with Will Smith) *(SHOW)*	12.00	1h 58m	We saw it. Weren't sure which 7 seconds were supposed to be life-changing, though.
11/6	Watch Oprah on *30 Rock*. ("Tune in tonight!") *(SHOW)*		0h 30m	Check.
11/10	See movie *Australia*. ("It's a definite must-go-see.") *(SHOW)*	20.00	2h 45m	Longest. Movie. Ever.
11/10	"We're gonna start callin 'em bikkies, too!" *(SHOW)*		0h 0m	For the remainder of 2008, I will call cookies "bikkies" like the Australians do. Oprah finds it fabulous.

11/11	"Live with cellulite. Be happy." *(SHOW)*		0h 0m	Trying. Not poking my butt in front of the mirror anymore. That's a start. **(O)**
11/12	"I want you to look around your house right now. Is it messy? Is it disorganized? Are there piles of stuff lying everywhere?" *(SHOW)*		0h 1m	No. It's lookin' pretty good.
11/12	"So, if somebody shows up at your door and says, 'Peter sent me,' do not let them in." *(SHOW)*		0h 0m	Warning her audience about fakers pretending to be with the Oprah and Peter Walsh Clean Up Your Messy House Tour. **(O)**
11/12	"If you're ready to clean up your messy house... sign up at Oprah.com and join our tour. You'll receive monthly homework assignments. Don't overwhelm yourself. Don't try to turn in your assignments early. Just stay with the program, okay?" *(SHOW)*		8h 10m	10 minutes a day **(O)**
11/13	See *Marley & Me*. *(SHOW)*	21.50	2h 0m	Oprah said I will "love" *Marley & Me*, starring Jennifer Aniston and Owen Wilson. Saw it.

(cont.)

November 2008 Accounting (*cont.*)

Date	Assignment	Cost	Time	Notes
11/18	"So, the next time you're walking down the street and you see someone who looks different, like seven-foot-tall Brendan...don't just stop and stare or pass by and then, you know, whisper to your friends. What he wants you to do is look him in the eye and say hello." *(SHOW)*		0h 0m	I'm doing this—but have to say, if I'm walking down the street in my back brace and someone says hello because of it, I'm going to be very uncomfortable. **(O)**
11/19	See *The Curious Case of Benjamin Button.* *(SHOW)*	11.00	2h 46m	Well, Oprah did say it was *the* movie to see.
11/21	"The first thing you need to do, in preparing for sex, I say, is wash yourself....I'm just assuming that everybody is taking a shower." *(SHOW)*		0h 30m	I'll let you guess—did I take just one very long shower before sex, or lots and lots of super short ones?
11/21	"And what this says, everybody, is that you constantly have to work at it. And the most important thing...is that if you're thinking that it's going to just naturally happen, you are mistaken." *(SHOW)*		0h 0m	Regarding sex and long-term relationships **(O)**
11/24	"That's who you call. Call Lowe's!" *(SHOW)*		0h 3m	I called to ask about chairs. This was the last assignment I completed on 12/31.

11/25	"Get rid of your toxic friends." *(SHOW)*		0h 0m	**(O)**
11/25	"So, everybody needs to stock their shelves with beans" and "Add more beans to your diet. And they're cheaper, too." *(SHOW)*	39.63	0h 45m	soooomaaaaanyyyyy beeeeeanssssss
11/26	"You must rinse well, inside and out…and then pat it dry and place the turkey in a large roasting pan." *(SHOW)*		0h 5m	Ew.
11/26	"If you have a friend who has a dog, you must give them this book. And you write the inscription to the person and their dog. And they will love it." *(SHOW)*	25.75	0h 30m	Bought, inscribed, and wrapped *The Story of Edgar Sawtelle*, a novel by David Wroblewski.
11/26	"Take Cristina Ferrare's step-by-step cooking class online on Oprah.com." *(SHOW)*		0h 25m	Watched video of Ferrare making turkey, gravy, sweet potatoes, biscuits, cranberry sauce, creamed spinach, stuffing, and pumpkin pie. I'm salivating.
11/26	Make Pumpkin Chiffon Pie. *(SHOW)*	4.93	0h 45m	Done on Christmas as my aunt already made a pie for Thanksgiving. ($1.19 pumpkin, $2.49 crust, $1.25 sugar… sister-in-law provided the remainder of ingredients)

(cont.)

November 2008 Accounting (*cont.*)

Date	Assignment	Cost	Time	Notes
11/27	"First, my thrifty idea for a hostess gift: Create a gratitude box. Give out the notecards to all the guests and then ask them write a special note to the host. And then put all the notes in the box." *(SHOW)*		0h 45m	Mom loved it.
11/27	Play getting to know you game. *(WEB)*		0h 45m	Jim led the game, my whole family played.
11/27	Oprah Thanksgiving *(WEB)*	105.23	7h 30m	This was a drop in the bucket, costwise. It was all I was allowed to contribute to the dinner financially. My mom can give you a better idea of the price tag. (time was for planning, shopping, prep, cooking)
11/28	Give *Inconvenient Truth* to friends and family. *(SHOW)*	19.99	0h 15m	It was actually hard to find someone who hadn't seen it.
Through-out Month	Watch every episode of *Oprah*. *(LO)*		20h 0m	20 shows
Through-out Month	Do Best Life Challenge exercise. *(BLC)*		5h 20m	80 minutes a week for 4 weeks
Through-out Month	Take *A Course in Miracles*. *(WEB/ SHOW)*		7h 30m	approx. 15 minutes a day for 30 days
MONTHLY TOTAL		260.03	72h 53m	
YEAR-TO-DATE TOTAL		4,352.67	1137h 2m	

ONGOING PROJECTS

- "Reinvigorate your appearance with some great advice on how not to look old..."
- "Rethink your eating habits with some absolutely delicious and utterly original meals..."
- Use cloth and reusable bags at grocery store. No more plastic.
- Change lightbulbs to energy-efficient bulbs.
- "I think in terms of investment, it's the best thing you can ever give yourself is to have beautiful surroundings."
- "I would just say to anybody, whatever secret you're holding, live your own truth."
- Sharon Salzberg meditation
- Make your rooms personal.
- Best Life Challenge exercise and diet guidance
- "I do want you to start thinking about, as I have started thinking about, how much you consume. I mean, like every time you throw away a paper towel. Every time you are, you know, wasteful with food in your house... just think about how much you really need."
- "Get a lift when you come in the front door."
- "I want you to savor every meal."
- "I want you to pay attention to how happy women get that way."
- *A Course in Miracles*
- Declutter home/life.
- *A New Earth* meditation
- "With the arrival of spring, I hope you, too, will reconnect with nature."
- "When you think that you're going to get in a car and drive, I want you to think about this mother holding her daughter's head on the side of the highway. That's the thought I want to come to your mind before you go to get in the car after having even one drink."
- "Stop defining yourself by what you see—or think you see—when you look in the mirror."
- "Everybody think about this: On the way to work or on the way to do whatever you do during the day... how many negative things... the negative tape that's playing in your head all day long about yourself *I can't do that, I shouldn't do that, I'm too fat, oh look at my thighs...*"
- "I think we should be open like Horton."
- "Alexis Stewart talks candidly about trying to get pregnant on her radio show *Whatever*, on Martha Stewart Living Radio. Tune in to follow her progress there."
- The YOU: Staying Young Aging quiz
- Learn to accept all people.
- "Stop saying that" (re: using the word "just" to describe ourselves).
- Take Dr. Oz–recommended vitamins and supplements (vitamin D3, folic acid, fish oil)
- Rise and Shine—how to wake up less stressed.
- "Be sure to check him [Dr. Oz] out on XM156, Oprah and Friends, and also on our section of Oprah.com. Keep those questions coming."
- Ten Secrets to a Better Love Life
- Get Rolfed.

(cont.)

- Burt's Bees Eye Cream and Ageless Night Cream
- "Going out to work every day, which every man does who is responsible for his family, after a while men feel taken for granted that they are doing that...so there needs to be some acknowledgment of that."
- "The truth of the matter is, men do need to be made to feel like they're winners. They do need to have themselves built up."
- "Go to Oprah.com for more of Suze's advice on how to survive these tough times."
- "So, if you or somebody you know needs help with addiction and finding treatment in your area, call the National Drug and Alcohol Addiction Hotline."
- "You have to do your own self-test." (re: breast self-exam)
- Oprah says we gals are too judgmental of each other and we should support our fellow women instead of criticizing them.
- "One of the reasons I was interested in telling this story on the air is not just for us to be voyeurs, but for each person who is listening today to look in your own life and ask, Who do you need to forgive?"
- "Ask yourself, What can I live without?"
- "We need to shift the way we think about living our lives. And it really is about bringing us all back to living within our means."
- "Be nice."
- "Okay, we're going to stretch" (to release the physical tension that gathers due to stress over money).
- "Vote at the grocery stores" for how I feel about cruelty to farm animals.
- "We need to learn to be more civil to each other."
- "Ask yourself this, Are you rude?"
- "Be more gracious to everybody."
- "Find out how to get paid for doing what you love."
- "Following your passion, allowing yourself to be paid for what you love will give you a meaningful life."
- "Do what you love and the money will come."

Accounting Abbreviations: *LO* = Living Oprah Project Task, *SHOW* = *The Oprah Winfrey Show*, *WEB* = Oprah.com, *MAG* = *O, The Oprah Magazine*, *BC* = Oprah's Book Club, *BLC* = Best Life Challenge, **(O)** = ongoing project

DECEMBER:

Light at the end of the tunnel

Time spent this month: *64 hours, 59 minutes*

Dollars spent this month: *$429.17*

But I don't even like sandwiches: *"A panini maker is the thing to have."*

Wasn't all my 2008 Best Life work enough? *I see several promotions telling me to sign up for the 2009 Best Life program.*

Words that stuck: *"Can we take a vacation now?"—Jim at midnight on December 31*

I PREFER a marathon to a sprint. The everyday minutiae that went into the first eleven months of this project were right up my alley. At times, it was an exhausting test of my endurance and sometimes surprisingly frustrating, but I rarely considered removing my nose from the grindstone. And yet, as I enter the last month of Living Oprah, I feel as if I might not have enough fuel in my tank or willpower to get me to the end of the year. In the grand scheme of things, 31 days are only a drop in the bucket, but I'm just plain tired.

Hindsight is 20/20 and I've just realized a severe error in my earlier planning. Back in January, I decided to leave the fun-sounding assignments, without date requirements, until the end of the year. I imagined December to be a joyride, filled with movies, fun little decorating and cooking projects, and easy items I might tick off my list with the greatest of ease. What a miscalculation. The problem is, there are so many of these tidbits, I am up to my eyeballs in to-dos. Additionally, I've adopted so many new behaviors due to Oprah's suggestions, my days are filled with new habits and tics, from the moment I wake up until I fall asleep at night.

Even in slumber, I'm not totally free. My recurring nightmare about rearranging the furniture in my home has been replaced by dreams starring Oprah Winfrey. I've dreamed about meeting her while I'm traveling by airplane, by El, and by bicycle. In these dreams, I'm always on the go, and she sits down across from me, next to me, or in the case of my bike dream, chases me in a car. I am feeling stifled and weirdly paranoid as she's now making appearances in my subconscious. When I wake in the middle of the night due to anxiety, I rush to my laptop and search Oprah.com for advice about how to catch some shut-eye. I've reached my saturation point, it's official. I've placed myself under Oprah's thumb 24 hours a day. It's a little like George Orwell's *1984*, but the clothes are more flattering.

There are moments I'm so tired I could cry, but there's no time for self-pity. I take some deep breaths and harden my resolve. I have to trust there are enough fumes in my tank to get me through to the end of the year. What I'm lacking in sleep, I make up for in adrenaline and caffeine. I'm behaving a bit frenetically. And although I make copious lists of what I need to accomplish each day, I inevitably misplace the list or leave it at home and find myself in the middle of a grocery aisle wondering if I'm there to buy eggs or toilet paper. I usually give up and buy both, which explains why we're eating so many omelets lately and my bathroom closet looks like an aisle at Costco.

It's getting harder and harder to keep up. I haven't felt this much pressure to look and act a certain way since high school. At least, as an adolescent, I had personal interaction with the sources of my peer pressure. It's so different to allow someone I've never met to guide my daily choices. I am also feeling quite isolated now as the clique I'm striving to join is entirely virtual. It's a really lonely feeling.

Jim admits he is ready for the year to end. He hasn't complained very often, but in recent days he's been talking about how much he is looking forward to 2009, when he'll see more of me. That makes me feel really lucky as I've worried I might have alienated him this year.

We seem to pass like ships in the night. And when we are home at the same time, I am usually worrying about unfinished projects, and things I should fix about myself or our apartment. Have I made my rooms "personal" enough? Would my new filing system pass Oprah's inspection? Would she approve of the tray I've chosen to fulfill her assignment to make my entryway table neater and more efficient? In addition to his discomfort from living under a microscope, I imagine it must also hurt Jim to know his opinions this year have taken a backseat to Oprah's. He might think I'm super cute in a T-shirt with a funny saying like NOSTALGIA WAS BETTER IN THE OLD DAYS. But it doesn't matter. If Oprah doesn't approve, I won't wear it. I totally understand the communications I've received from harried husbands and boyfriends of Oprah's biggest fans. It must be a bit emasculating to have your partner constantly striving to emulate celebrities, trusting Winfrey's opinions over your own.

I'm even confused when it comes to the line between my point of view and Oprah's. In the beginning, there was a distinction between Oprah's priorities and my own. I would follow her suggestions to the letter but didn't feel entirely comfortable completing the tasks. In fact, I frequently felt awkward. Yet, a couple months ago, I remember looking down at the leopard-print flats on my feet. They were once the bane of my existence, but now, I have to admit, they've grown on me. When I initially wore the clothing she promoted, decorated as she wished, or read the books she pushed, I didn't feel at home. Now I do. I can't decide if I became accustomed to Oprah's world, or if my entire aesthetic has truly changed. I look at myself in the mirror, admiring the perfectly arched brows I've groomed and plucked in accordance to the directions on Oprah.com. Nice.

"Are you about ready to roll?" Jim peeks into the room as he buttons his cuffs. We're already a bit late and still need to run a couple of errands before heading to a holiday party.

"One sec," I tell him, feathering together my three shades of lipstick. "How do I look?" I spin around, puckering, so he can check me out.

"Fine. I mean, good." He looks at the concern on my face. "I mean, isn't that what you wore the last time we went out? I said you looked good then."

"It's a multipurpose black dress." I try not to snap. "I can dress it up or down." He looks dubious. "I'm wearing totally different accessories." He nods. And then, as if prodded with a stick, "You look awesome." Whatever.

Speaking of wardrobe, just over a month ago, Oprah mentioned why she won't wear certain clothing: "I never go without sleeves because I have big, fat arms." She wears tight-sleeved outfits frequently, and I never once thought of her as having chunky limbs. Since she shared her own clothing rule with us, I've become concerned about my own choices. I examine myself in the full-length mirror, wondering about my body. I should probably be more careful about my belly. I'll never be accused of having abs of steel and think my midsection might be too big for the narrow belt I was planning to wear. There's no time to research my dilemma on Oprah.com. I tear off my dress and opt for one of the forgiving tunic tops and the dark-wash jeans Winfrey has encouraged us to have in our closets.

I grab my purse, and as Jim locks up the apartment, I slink down the front steps, self-conscious.

Oprah's weight is back in the news and she's chosen to put it there. She's clearly not as svelte this season as she's been in the past couple years, but I don't care how much she weighs. For me, the main issue is that she appears distracted when she's not happy with herself physically. While it doesn't matter to me what size she is, I enjoy her show so much more when she brings her A game.

With Oprah's blessing, her best friend, Gayle, has gone on a morning talk show to discuss Winfrey's body. Now *that* is an amazing friendship and a clear sign of trust. I wonder if there's anyone in my life I might set free in the world of morning television to discuss my weight. I guess a lot would depend on if morning television interviews still occur when hell freezes over. Winfrey's weight gain is being used to promote the new season of *Oprah*. Her struggle is a major marketing tool, utilized with abandon to attract an audience. I don't mean to belittle her trouble. It's a very real, very deadly roller coaster she's on with her health, but her show has been able to capitalize on it.

I wonder if this is why many people seem to feel her body is open to public criticism. Not only does Oprah talk about it all the time, but she discusses it in a setting frequently used for entertainment. Oprah's weight is like a character in a soap opera we've all been watching for decades. It's got a split personality, and we're drawn in to find out if it's playing the villain this season or the hero. Ads for next year's shows imply her weight will once again be starring in a major role. I feel sad and exhausted for Oprah. I hope she makes peace with her body soon and wish she would do so privately.

I have been reading endless statistics about women's dissatisfaction with their bodies. Like many of you, I've seen poll results online and in magazines showing that the majority of us are not entirely at ease with our weight. We're unhappy with our physical appearance, and we compare other women's bodies to our own. These statistics are no surprise to me. My own social circle reflects this. I don't think I've had a single friend, ever, who has not mentioned her body in a disparaging way at least once. Oprah, the televised version of our collective best friend, talks to us in the same way we talk to each other. It's such comfortable patter, like white noise, except far more damaging to our self-esteem. I think it's important to stop enabling each other to speak in this manner about ourselves. Including Winfrey. While she can be such a positive role model for women, she's also a perpetuator of this kind of talk. But, to be honest, I fall into the same trap.

In advertisements for shows beginning in January, Oprah states that she's ready to tackle her own behavior. Short of donning an O sweater and grabbing a pair of pom-poms, I'm really pulling for her. However, as I watch promotions for the Best Life Week coming up in January, I feel a little let down. It is implied these shows will be better than last year's. I've worked in marketing, I know that it's a necessity to utilize this language. "Bigger!" "Faster!" "More absorbent than ever!" Still, I can't help but feel like the year I've just spent Living Oprah was a waste if I only got the JV self-help guidance. I want the varsity team.

I'm so torn by this. I've been planning to take a break from watching the show in 2009. I'm desperate for some time off. And yet how can I turn my back on Best Life Week in January? I might miss something groundbreaking and life altering. I am hit with the memory of an old Oprah about compulsive gamblers. A gambler with an addiction to playing the slots will stay at the same machine with the obsessive hope that any moment she might hit triple sevens. She won't walk away because she fears that the next person to sit down will hit it big. I feel the same way. Even though I know watching the same television program every single day can't be too healthy, I don't want to turn away. What if the episode I miss is the Best Life jackpot? Sure, I'm dubious, but I still have a glimmer of hope. It feels like a pretty major gamble to turn away from the TV now.

"Holy crap," Jim says, shaking his head. "You're totally addicted."

"I'm totally not." I shrug it off, faking nonchalance. "I can stop anytime I want." That sounds so pathetic in my own head, I can't believe I said it.

Jim just sighs. He's been doing a lot of that lately. Maybe he's asthmatic.

December 16, 2008
I'm in Jefferson's car, heading to the United Center to see Céline Dion live in concert. I'm only an amateur meteorologist, but I'm pretty sure Chicago is in the midst of a blizzard. There are cars littered on the side of the highway, and the local news has warned everyone to stay safe and warm in their own homes tonight. Oh, how I wish this was possible for a myriad of reasons. *Reason one*: I'm heading to the United Center to see Céline Dion live in concert. *Reason two*: It's usually a 30-minute drive to the stadium, but we've been in the car over an hour and we're only halfway there. *Reason three*: Jefferson appears to regret his decision to accompany me tonight. He keeps saying, "We could turn around anytime you want. It's up to you."

I think I'm coming down with a cold.

Jefferson and I are pretty sure we know only one Céline song, the one from *Titanic* that played incessantly from 1997 to 2001. I was certain more people knew its lyrics than the national anthem. We try to come up with other torchy-sounding ballads that we might attribute to tonight's headliner, but we draw a total blank.

After we finally arrive and pay for parking, we trudge through the snow to the front door. Everyone else looks happy to be there, so we try to whip up some enthusiasm. I've never been to a concert this big, and I allow myself to be swept up by the energy of the crowd. Our seats, the cheapest I was able to procure, are about 35 miles from the stage and just steps away from an exit. These are the best seats in the house, we decide. This lightens our mood even further. The opening act, a comedian, is doing his shtick onstage. This guy is awful, but the folks around us are eating it up. I study them. Who are these people who are laughing at a Robert De Niro *Taxi Driver* impersonation ("You talkin' to me?") like it's the first time they've heard such genius originality? There are lots of women dressed to the nines who can't sit still in their seats, they are so excited. Accompanying them are their mostly male partners who obsessively check the time. Even though I'm Caucasian, I don't think I've ever been around so many white people in my life. It's creepy.

I look at my cell phone. It's about an hour later than the show was supposed to begin, but we haven't seen any indication that the concert is starting anytime soon. There are clearly tons of empty seats in the United Center. I bet the weather is keeping people home. Either that or a rampant outbreak of good taste has struck the Chicagoland area. The "comedian" is doing some sort of medley of impressions now: Pacino, Nicholson, Bill Clinton, and an unidentifiable voice that sounds like the love child of Ronald Reagan and Cher.

There is a group of women behind me who aren't paying the least bit of attention to the opening act. They are all chattering about Charice, a teenage singer from the Philippines who is Oprah's favored child prodigy of the year. Oprah's had the girl on the show several times to perform, and Céline has invited her to sing at Madison Square Garden. The women behind me love Charice. They love Céline. They love Oprah. They are gushing so much, I feel their collective adoration pressing against the back of my neck. I want to turn around and join the conversation, but Jefferson is elbowing me in the ribs.

"Look!" He's thrilled because he thinks he's spotted a black man in the crowd. He points: front row, aisle seat.

We are briefly excited by the diversity.

And the lights go down.

I spend the next couple hours entirely speechless. Jefferson and I are amazed. It turns out we don't know only *one* Céline song, we know *all* of them. Without ever intentionally sitting down and listening to an album, we've absorbed her music via the pop culture fabric that blankets our everyday lives. I've been listening to her songs for years without even knowing it. They definitely all sound similar to each other, but distinct at the same time, written utilizing some mysterious formula to a wildly successful pop ballad. Every single one has a hook that sinks into my subconscious and won't let go.

Much of this evening reminds me of Oprah. She, too, is so rooted in our daily lives, many of us don't even realize it. All through the year, I've heard from people who insist they never, ever watch *Oprah*, and yet they can quote her, they know about her girls' school in Africa, her campaign effort for Barack Obama. They know the names of her experts and their specialities, they recognize her best friend, Gayle, and of course, everyone knows Steadman. I witness Oprah's name spoken daily, reverently and irreverently on TV, in movies, in books, on products. Oprah Winfrey isn't just a name, it's a part of everyday speech used to describe qualities that range from wealth, philanthropy, megalomania, power, to generosity, materialism, strength, and the American dream. Like that song from *Titanic* that Jefferson and I can't stop singing on our drive home, Oprah's got a hook. But unlike *Titanic*, she has gotten more popular over time. She is not interchangeable, replaceable, or replicable. Not even tonight's impressionist attempted that feat.

I'm seeing a lot of Oprah-suggested movies. They're not all exceptionally good, either. Did she really sit through all of these and love them? Or was Oprah simply promoting a movie star guest's new project out of professional courtesy or obligation. These aren't films I'd normally select to view, but Winfrey's chosen my holiday season entertainment. Jim has been so sweet to accompany me to most of them. He studied film in college and would probably prefer something dark and existential to this marathon of animated kids' movies, so-called chick flicks, and two-hour dramedies about misbehaving dogs. One day we watch three movies in a row, and when we try to evaluate what we've seen, one plot runs into another and we give up.

My poor brain is overtaxed and overextended. I'm forgetting things left and right, which is unlike me. I actually stood my friend Nicky up for lunch. I felt horrible, and even more so because she was so understanding and sympathetic. My time feels so precious these days that I am mortified I've devalued someone else's. I'm usually early for everything and am a natural planner. That's all gone out the window. I don't know what end is up. If my home was truly a physical manifestation of my emotional and spiritual life, as it's been suggested on *Oprah*, I'd be living in a carnival fun house. Instead, my paper files are neat and organized, but my mind is muddled. I need a tiny Peter Walsh to be injected into my bloodstream, as in that classic sci-fi movie *Fantastic Voyage*. He needs to steer his fleet of itty-bitty VW Beetles into my head where his miniaturized crew can declutter my brain à la Oprah's Clean Up Your Messy House Tour.

Okay. I'm losing it.

I've been urged by Oprah to make a pumpkin chiffon pie recipe created by her friend Cristina Ferrare. It will be my dessert contribution to Christmas dinner at my in-laws' home. For a Jew married to a non-Jew, this holiday can be awkward for me. I don't have any Christmas traditions I can share, beyond the stereotypical Jewish December 25, Chinese food and a movie. I'm relieved Oprah's presented me with something I can make for the family.

I'm worried because the dessert recipe calls for uncooked eggs. With all the horrible stories in the news about salmonella outbreaks and other foodborne illnesses, I'm a bit concerned I might wipe out my husband's entire family with one tasty treat. Merry Christmas! I'm not going to lie—I'm relieved Oprah's told me only to make the pie, not eat it. So far, so good, though. Everyone's taken a few bites, and I haven't had to call poison control yet or use my CPR training. Nobody's falling over themselves with excitement, either. They tell me they think it's okay.

"It's not as firm as I thought it would be," says my mother-in-law.

"My favorite part is the crust," says my father-in-law, with a mouthful of pie.

The crust, incidentally, is the only store-bought part of the dish.

Jim and I have allowed Oprah to choose the gifts we'll be giving out this year. We're a bit broke and have decided to forgo holiday presents for each other, but the big unwrapping fest on Christmas morning is his family's tradition. I've gleaned some ideas from Oprah's show and have also done research on the website. One of the gifts she told us to give is her newest Book Club pick, *The Story of Edgar Sawtelle* by David Wroblewski. We are to write an inscription in it to the recipient as well as the recipient's dog. My sister-in-law, Linh, is a big reader and owner of a big dog, so she'll be opening that big book on Christmas morning. There was also a downloadable medley of free holiday music that Oprah's offered us for a limited time. I've burned a CD for Linh, but it turns out she already saw that freebie and made a disc of her own. I guess I'm not the only one who watches Oprah, then?

I decide to bake most of our gifts this year, based on holiday recipes from Oprah's website. In order to tickle everyone's taste buds but still give them something substantial, I choose an array of goodies to be presented in adorable stacked tins. While I began the process with the intention of fiscal and time restraint, it quickly snowballs into an exercise in excess, and we have to pull out the old credit card to buy several ingredients. Over the course of three days, I spend hours shopping, cooking, wrapping, and thinking about the rest of my to-do list the whole time. I have one week until the end of the year and miles to go before I sleep.

When I'm done, my kitchen looks like Christmas exploded, but I'm proud of what I've accomplished. I think everything looks terrific, and I can't wait for everyone to open their treats. I made three sets of the following:

- Apricot, Ginger, and Walnut Tea Bread (two loaves for each family)
- Dark Chocolate Bark with Pistachios, Sweetened Dried Cherries, and Pumpkin Seeds (I made enough for my husband to share with his coworkers. I'm very popular in his office now.)
- Deceptively Delicious Brownies (Yup, I went back to Jessica Seinfeld. These treats hide carrot and spinach purée within their chocolaty goodness!)
- Spiced Nuts (I thought the sweetness of everything else needed some balance.)

I hope I've presented them with something for everyone to enjoy. I'm holding my breath that they'll like it all and am hungry for feedback. This is odd. Where did the comfortable lack of accountability go? For months, I felt very little pressure because all my choices were made by Oprah, not me. But now I'm desperate for appreciation and acceptance of my gift. I am attempting to behave otherwise, because I want people to be honest with me about their reaction to the food, rather than concerned about hurting my feelings if they don't like their treats.

I watch my father-in-law feed something I've made to his dog, and I feel a little stab of pain. I feel ownership of these presents. What on earth? Clearly, this has all sunk in deeper than I had planned or expected. I am afraid that the distinction between me and performing Living Oprah has been erased. I never thought I would be susceptible to the absorption of this lifestyle. I wish I had been wearing an emotional hazmat suit the entire time to protect myself.

December 26, 2008

I might be bit of an emotional wreck, but my body is another story. The health advice I've received this year from Oprah has been plentiful. She's covered the bases, from what goes into my mouth to what should come out the other end. And I've got to say, I feel pretty good. Before the year began, I was already a regular exerciser, but I used my Best Life Challenge contract to keep me active, even when I wanted to play couch potato. Plus it encouraged me to test myself in new ways, to push myself further. It was empowering.

I completed my 21-day vegan cleanse, which did get me out of some eating ruts, nudging me toward the direction of more variety. Expanding my food options has equated to a more nutritionally well-rounded diet and definitely resulted in an increased enjoyment of my meals. And of course, every bite was savored. It was impractical and ridiculous at times, but more often than not, it was relaxing to eat in this manner. As a bonus, I felt satisfied at the end of each meal.

To assess my health toward the beginning of the year, I took the RealAge test on February 21. The RealAge program was developed by Dr. Oz and his partner, Dr. Michael Roizen. While Oz is a frequent guest on Oprah's stage, Roizen is usually seen in the front row of the audience, but rarely addressed. There's no mistaking who's Simon and who's Garfunkel in that relationship. When I first took the online exam, I found out I had a RealAge of 29.5. I was proud that a computerized quiz diagnosed me as spry. The results were followed up with suggestions about how I could pump some more youth and vitality into my cells. There were supplements to take, activity levels to achieve, and relationships on which to focus. I set a goal for myself to drop to a RealAge of 25 by the end of the year.

So now it's the night before my 36th birthday. As I repeat the Real-Age test, ten months after the first time, I can celebrate that I followed all the health guidance offered to me this year. However, as I fill in the blanks, I realize I have had one major weakness: stress. I improved many of my lifestyle choices. I've taken my fish oil pills and my vitamin D religiously. I've exercised, eaten right, meditated. But due to the pressure of the project and many of Oprah's assignments, my level of stress shot through the roof and my sleep got worse. I think this canceled out many of the positive changes I made.

When my results come in, it turns out I have a RealAge of 29.6. While it's not the outcome I was hoping for, I guess aging only 0.1 years over the course of ten months isn't too bad. At this rate, I'll be 30 by the time I turn 40. I'd like to see how Jim handles that candle situation.

At work, I tell a friend about these results. She knows how much work I've put into these assignments and jokingly mentions that my health has been a part-time job this year. She's right, it's been incredibly time-consuming, but I decide there's nothing wrong with making my health a priority. I am happier for it. I feel better. It might not be the way most Americans live their lives, but I don't think it's a bad idea to reconsider our priorities. I certainly feel more powerful for it.

The real hero of the year is my VCR. Poor little antiquated machine has been busting its sweet little motherboard to stick to my staunch schedule of recording *Oprah* and Oprah Winfrey–related shows. And today, on December 29, that brave little soldier gave its life for my project. No amount of shaking, tapping, or incessantly pushing the power button will resuscitate it. I've tried. Jim's tried. I only hope its next life is easier than this one. Rest in peace, Sony VHS Recorder, model #SLV-N77. You will be missed, good friend.

December 31, 2008
The credits are rolling on the last episode of *Oprah* for the year. Jim asks how I feel, but I can't tell quite yet. It's all a bit anticlimactic as I still have a few more items on my to-do list before the clock strikes midnight. I have watched 262 hours of *Oprah* over the course of the leap year. Even though this piece of the project is complete, I can't call 262 hours of television viewing a victory, any more than I call playing Wii a workout.

I jump up from the couch. No time to waste as there's still plenty to do. I have to get one more interesting, fabulous chair to put in my living room. This is a Nate Berkus piece of advice backed up by Oprah from months ago. While I've been bargain hunting quite a bit, right now I just want this item off my list as soon as humanly possible. Jim has volunteered to go pick up the seating I chose online from a reasonably priced retail franchise. Great. I'm lucky he's so amenable because I need to go pick up some pants I've had tailored (an Oprah must!) and dye my hair one last time with the *O*-recommended Perfect 10 hair color product. I'm going to end the year looking as young and fresh as Oprah's magazine advises.

Oprah's told us to "stock your shelves" with beans, so I've purchased enough cans to sink a small ship. Not only are they healthy, but she says they're a thrifty choice as well. She's been concerned about how the economy is affecting us and has been throwing out ideas on how to keep costs to a minimum. The legumes are still in grocery bags, sprawled on the kitchen counter. I make a mental note to stack them in my cabinets later tonight while hair dye is permeating my stubborn grays.

It's an odd day because there's a lot of running into and out of the apartment, and it's becoming farcical to fulfill Oprah's suggestion to "get a lift" every time I walk in the front door. Luckily, I have a new reason to feel happy during my latest entrance: a brand-new chair stands, resplendent, in its place in the living room. Jim stands just as proudly next to it. He tells me he wrestled it home on the city bus, which I find adorable, and I'm feeling so grateful for him right now. There's no time to gush, however. Before we have a moment to sit in the new chair, we're heading to make a donation to Chicago Books to Women in Prison. Oprah told us to organize a philanthropic project with our friends and neighbors. As books and reading are very special to me, I decided to make them the focus of my Big Give. I've collected paperbacks from friends and family, and we're about to drop them off at the not-for-profit's headquarters. Carrying bags bursting with books, we hustle to the train. It feels fabulous to be of service. Jim and I are thrilled we can help this terrific organization and agree to keep it up even when Oprah doesn't enforce our philanthropy.

On our way home, Jim insists we have time to stop for a late lunch, even though I'm buzzing to knock off the last couple items for the year. He takes me to Café Selmarie for sweet potato fries, and although I want to rush home, I savor every morsel. About six feet away from us, there is a table of people—we're guessing parents with their adult children and spouses—who keep pointing at me and talking about my project at full volume. They are discussing how they've seen me on TV, that I live in the neighborhood and teach yoga nearby. One woman starts regaling the others with items she's read on my blog. She's talking about me as if I'm not even in the room. I'm not exaggerating: She is so close I could hit her with my sourdough roll. At one point, the man I'm guessing is her father exclaims, "That's just crazy! She's crazy."

I begin to giggle. Jim asks me if I want to change seats so my back is to the group. Although I consider the offer, I feel it would appear rude, so I turn him down. We wonder if maybe we should stop coming here, but it's our neighborhood place. We have come here for years and have so many fond memories of the café and its food, but still, I don't want to be the latter half of "dinner and a show" whenever we drop in. While I'm slowly, agonizingly, chewing my last bite of food, fighting the urge to run back home with a bag over my head, I am comforted by the thought that this, too, shall pass. The year ends in less than nine hours, after all.

Make sure tailored pants fit like a glove: Check!
   Exercise: Check!
   Hang final pieces of decor on walls: Check!

Read *A Course in Miracles* at Oprah.com: Check!

Perform breast self-exam: Check!

Be nice: Check!

It's a few minutes until midnight. Every single item has been crossed off my list to the very best of my ability, but I can't believe it. I've pored over my notes, worried that I might have forgotten something. Jim and I have been running around for so much of the day, we look like we've just returned from the gym, all sweaty and stale-looking. We thought we'd have time to stop in at a couple of our friends' New Year's Eve parties, but we're tired and don't want to budge. We are so happy to be at home, cozied up on our couch, fondly looking at our new chair. (We can't sit on it yet as we've wrapped it, mummy-style, in double-stick tape to train the cats not to use it as a scratching post. They will be repelled by the texture of the adhesive, say several pet-advice websites.) Our annual New Year's Day party is canceled tomorrow. I'm so disappointed. We just didn't have enough time, energy, or resources to pull it together.

We have the TV turned on so we can watch the ball drop, but the sound is off. We need some peace and quiet. As the countdown begins, I grab Jim's hand and snuggle up closer to him. We're both holding our breath. When the clock strikes midnight, we kiss. This lip-lock is not mandated by Oprah, and it feels like a breath of fresh air. I burst into a couple little sobs and then some embarrassed laughter.

"Congratulations," he says, wrapping his arms around me.

I thought I'd be over the moon at this moment, ready to celebrate. Instead, I feel very mellow, in disbelief that I made it. I wish I could say something profound and extraordinary, but can't stop repeating a less-than-momentous, "Holy crap. Holy crap. Holy crap." I keep waiting for a switch to turn off in my mind so I can immediately separate myself from the project and begin to dissect and quantify it. No such luck. Like Scarlett O'Hara, I decide I don't have to figure everything out today and can let it go until tomorrow.

As we settle into bed for the night, Jim asks, "Are we sleeping in tomorrow?"

"Of course." I smile.

He turns out the light and we sink under the blankets. In under a minute, I hear his breath change as he eases into sleep.

Wait.

"Jim?"

"Hm?"

I give him a little shake. "Jim?"

"What is it?" he asks, wrapping himself around me, avoiding my freezing feet.

"Actually, can you set the alarm for eight forty-five? I think I should get up and watch the show tomorrow."

At first Jim is very still, and it's so dark in the room I can't make out his face. Then I feel him sit up in bed. The numbers on the clock glow brighter for a moment while he sets the alarm.

"Thanks," I whisper.

He burrows back under the covers and lets out a sigh.

December 2008 Accounting

Date	Assignment	Cost	Time	Notes
12/1	Read *O* from cover to cover. *(LO)*		4h 30m	
12/1	Listen to 2-part interview with *Sinus Relief Now* author Dr. Jordan S. Josephson. *(WEB)*		0h 11m	I had a sinus infection and looked to Oprah. com for relief.
12/4	"Don't let scammers and con artists make you their next victim." "Online buyers and sellers, I want you to beware." Because many scammers are sending around fake Oprah offers/sweepstakes, Ms. W said, "So, always check our website to confirm if an offer is the real thing." *(SHOW)*		0h 0m	Will do. **(O)** Will do. **(O)**
12/4	"Go to theoprahstore.com today." *(SHOW)*		0h 2m	I went.
12/5	"A panini maker is the thing to have." *(SHOW)*	70.85	0h 45m	I bought this but we didn't use it until May 2009.
12/9	And finally, an assignment about tomorrow's rerun: "Call your best friend and watch this together." *(SHOW)*		0h 5m	Called. Watched.

(cont.)

December 2008 Accounting (*cont.*)

Date	Assignment	Cost	Time	Notes
12/11	Makeup application— received bulk e-mail and was led to info on how to apply on Oprah.com. *(WEB)*	18.48	1h 0m	Didn't have all the makeup supplies necessary—who knew I needed to shimmer so much over the holidays? (2-for-1 sale at drugstore)
12/17	"Don't miss the hilarious, Emmy Award–winning *30 Rock*." *(SHOW)*		0h 0m	Already done!
12/19	"Go put your strengths to work." *And* "While you're waiting on something to happen, you're waiting on some miracle that's gonna show itself, and suddenly you don't have to do it anymore, it's always waiting on you. The universe is waiting on you." *(SHOW)*		0h 0m	Oprah is a perfect example of attaining lifelong goals. (**O**)
12/19	Buy goat milk. Oprah was impressed with it on show about Blue Zones. *(SHOW)*	3.69	0h 30m	I like it!
12/20	Happy Light *(WEB)*	119.99	0h 15m	Feeling down because of Chicago's gray and miserable winter. I checked out Oprah.com for guidance on picking up my mood. I'll use it this winter, even when not Living Oprah. (**O**)

12/20	Refill omega 3 fish oil pills. *(SHOW/ WEB)*	24.61	0h 5m	
Dec 23–25, 2009	Christmas gifts for in-laws (created treats from recipes on Oprah's website). *(SHOW/WEB)*	177.32	20h 0m	Next year, I'm knitting everyone a scarf. I gotta get out of the kitchen.
12/24	Sign up for 2009 Best Life program. *(SHOW)*		0h 1m	I honestly don't think I'll be following this once the Living Oprah project ends.
12/25	Green rice. *(WEB)*	14.23	0h 30m	This might have been too exotic for my parents-in-law, although my niece loved it.
12/26	Follow up RealAge test. *(WEB)*		0h 20m	I'm 29.6 in RealAge. That makes me 207.2 in dog years.
Through-out Month	Watch every episode of *Oprah*. *(LO)*		23h 0m	23 shows
Through-out Month	Do Best Life Challenge exercise. *(BLC)*		6h 0m	80 minutes a week for 4.5 weeks
Through-out Month	Take *A Course in Miracles*. *(WEB/ SHOW)*		7h 45m	approx. 15 minutes a day for 31 days
MONTHLY TOTAL		429.17	64h 59m	
YEAR-TO-DATE TOTAL		4,781.84	1202h 1m	

ONGOING PROJECTS
- "Reinvigorate your appearance with some great advice on how not to look old…"
- "Rethink your eating habits with some absolutely delicious and utterly original meals…"
- Use cloth and reusable bags at grocery store. No more plastic.
- Change lightbulbs to energy-efficient bulbs.
- "I think in terms of investment, it's the best thing you can ever give yourself is to have beautiful surroundings."
- "I would just say to anybody, whatever secret you're holding, live your own truth."

(cont.)

- Sharon Salzberg meditation
- Make your rooms personal.
- Best Life Challenge exercise and diet guidance
- "I do want you to start thinking about, as I have started thinking about, how much you consume. I mean, like every time you throw away a paper towel. Every time you are, you know, wasteful with food in your house...just think about how much you really need."
- "Get a lift when you come in the front door."
- "I want you to savor every meal."
- "I want you to pay attention to how happy women get that way."
- *A Course in Miracles*
- Declutter home/life.
- *A New Earth* meditation
- "With the arrival of spring, I hope you, too, will reconnect with nature."
- "When you think that you're going to get in a car and drive, I want you to think about this mother holding her daughter's head on the side of the highway. That's the thought I want to come to your mind before you go to get in the car after having even one drink."
- "Stop defining yourself by what you see—or think you see—when you look in the mirror."
- "Everybody think about this: On the way to work or on the way to do whatever you do during the day...how many negative things...the negative tape that's playing in your head all day long about yourself. *I can't do that, I shouldn't do that, I'm too fat, oh, look at my thighs...*"
- "I think we should be open like Horton."
- "Alexis Stewart talks candidly about trying to get pregnant on her radio show, *Whatever*, on Martha Stewart Living Radio. Tune in to follow her progress there."
- The YOU: Staying Young Aging Quiz
- Learn to accept all people.
- "Stop saying that" (re: using the word "just" to describe ourselves).
- Take Dr. Oz-recommended vitamins and supplements (vitamin D3, folic acid, fish oil)
- Rise and Shine—how to wake up less stressed.
- "Be sure to check him out on XM156, Oprah and Friends, and also on our section of Oprah.com. Keep those questions coming."
- Ten Secrets to a Better Love Life
- Get Rolfed.
- Burt's Bees Eye Cream and Ageless Night Cream
- "Going out to work every day, which every man does who is responsible for his family, after a while men feel taken for granted that they are doing that...so there needs to be some acknowledgment of that."
- "The truth of the matter is, men do need to be made to feel like they're winners. They do need to have themselves built up."
- "Go to Oprah.com for more of Suze's advice on how to survive these tough times."
- "So if you or somebody you know needs help with addiction and finding treatment in your area, call the National Drug and Alcohol Addiction Hotline."

- "You have to do your own self-test." (re: breast self-exam)
- Oprah says we gals are too judgmental of each other and we should support our fellow women instead of criticizing them.
- "One of the reasons I was interested in telling this story on the air is not just for us to be voyeurs, but for each person who is listening today to look in your own life and ask: Who do you need to forgive?"
- "Ask yourself, What can I live without?"
- "We need to shift the way we think about living our lives. And it really is about bringing us all back to living within our means."
- "Be nice."
- "Okay, we're going to stretch" (to release the physical tension that gathers due to stress over money).
- "Vote at the grocery stores" for how I feel about cruelty to farm animals.
- "We need to learn to be more civil to each other."
- "Ask yourself this, Are you rude?"
- "Be more gracious to everybody."
- "Find out how to get paid for doing what you love."
- "Following your passion, allowing yourself to be paid for what you love will give you a meaningful life."
- "Do what you love and the money will come."
- "Love your vulva."
- Kiss Jim for ten seconds everyday.
- "Live with cellulite. Be happy."
- "So if somebody shows up at your door and says, 'Peter sent me,' do not let them in."
- "If you're ready to clean up your messy house...sign up at Oprah.com and join our tour. You'll receive monthly homework assignments. Don't overwhelm yourself. Don't try to turn in your assignments early. Just stay with the program, okay?"
- "So the next time you're walking down the street and you see someone who looks different, like seven-foot-tall Brendan...don't just stop and stare or pass by and then, you know, whisper to your friends. What he wants you to do is look him in the eye and say hello."
- "And what this says, everybody, is that you constantly have to work at it. And the most important thing...is that if you're thinking that it's going to just naturally happen, you are mistaken." (re: sex and long-term relationships)
- "Get rid of your toxic friends."

Accounting Abbreviations: *LO* = Living Oprah Project Task, *SHOW* = *The Oprah Winfrey Show*, *WEB* = Oprah.com, *MAG* = *O, The Oprah Magazine*, *BC* = Oprah's Book Club, *BLC* = Best Life Challenge, **(O)** = ongoing project

JANUARY 2009:

Basking in the afterLO

Total hours spent Living Oprah in 2008: *1202 hours, 1 minute*
Total cost of Living Oprah in 2008: *$4,781.84*

I T I S January 1. I am recovering.

I have been passing the hours plopped listlessly in my living room, watching television and eating as quickly as I want. I am in full schlumpadinka regalia: sock-monkey pajamas, mismatched wool kneesocks, and a sweatshirt that could house a family of four. I'm so comfortable. And to top it off, Jim let me sleep in. When our alarm went off at 8:45 AM this morning so I could watch the first *Oprah* rerun of 2009, he did a little sanity check with me.

"Are you sure you want to do this?"

I whimpered but didn't fully awaken. He got out of bed and tucked the blankets around me. I don't remember falling back asleep, but I did wake up at almost 11 AM with a start. The show! I'm missing *Oprah*!

"Don't worry," Jim comforted me. He had recorded the show on our backup VCR so I could watch the tape in my own time.

What a man.

The rest of the day passes without pomp or circumstance. I feel tired. Empty. A little depression creeps in. I'm sure I just need to sleep and all will be better tomorrow.

*   *   *

It is January 2, 2009. I'm sitting in a café with my laptop.

As hard as I worked on my cozy, fully accessorized home last year, I had to get out of there or I was going to lose my mind. I couldn't stare at my fabulous chair or the mountain of *O* magazines in my living room for one moment more. I tossed the trusty old Mac in my backpack and passed by four coffee shops filled to capacity with other people also wielding laptops. There wasn't an open seat in sight. I laughed because today was supposed to be MY VERY SPECIAL, MONUMENTAL DAY: THE DAY I STARTED WRITING MY FIRST BOOK. It didn't even occur to me that everyone else might want to start their great American novel, too. Talk about humbling. For a moment, I stood in the cold, the weight of my computer pulling at my shoulders. I watched the writers tap happily on their keyboards as they sipped big-as-your-head lattes. Then I moved on down the street until I finally found a free chair in a giant coffee chain that apparently doubles as a playground.

I've been sitting here for about an hour.

My forearms are sticking to the table, and in order to drown out the ambient shrieking I've buried my earphones as far into my head as physiologically possible. I haven't produced a single word. As I stare at the blank screen on my laptop, fingers poised to type the moment I generate some clear thoughts, I replay this morning in my head. When I went through my ritual of showering, making breakfast, and packing Jim's lunch, I never suspected I would watch *Oprah*. Yet I still mechanically, unthinkingly turned it on. My father called during the show.

"Dad, can I call you back? The show is on."

He cleared his throat, "Seriously? *Oprah*? Is it a new episode?"

"No," I said, not taking my eyes off the screen. "Rerun. I wasn't wild about it the first time it aired."

My father asked, "So why don't you turn it off?"

I couldn't come up with an explanation that satisfied either one of us. During the first half of the show I did some dishes and neatened up around the house, but without realizing how I drifted there, I found myself sitting on the couch in front of the TV. I caught myself listening to Oprah with the same rapt attention I had during the project. I was ready to gather every drop of wisdom that spilled from her mouth. I thought I had the strength to turn this part of my mind off when the ball dropped at midnight. I had no idea how difficult it would be to work against the momentum I'd created over the past 366 days.

So I'm freaking out a little bit, and I'm feeling a little less powerful than I did on December 31. Way back then, about 40 hours ago to be exact, I wrote in my journal that I was looking forward to taking my power of choice back and dropping this cloak of conformity. But what I'm finding is, as hard as it was to get comfortable following the leader at the beginning of the project, it's even more difficult to stop the momentum. I created Living Oprah to explore a very specific type of compliance, but I never thought it might actually stick. I truly didn't think I'd be susceptible.

Nearby, two women are speaking in voices louder than my earphones can suppress. As if on cue, one woman starts talking about her vision board. She heard about their power on *Oprah* and by watching *The Secret*. I feel like I'm being punked and covertly look around to see if my friends are setting me up. She says her mother thinks it goes against their religion to put faith in the boards. I snatch the buds out of my ears. The woman's companion starts to answer, but the din rises in the café and I can't hear her response. Screeching children run around, super-powered by the sugar in their hot chocolate. Don't these rude kids know I'm trying to eavesdrop?

My first day of writing is not fruitful.

It is January 3, 2009. I am at the gym.

Last year, I came to fully appreciate how much regular exercise helps me focus, control my stress, and increase my self-esteem. While I no longer need to follow Bob Greene's Best Life program, I plan to continue this physical regimen for years to come. This morning I feel great after my workout, and as I change out of my sweaty clothes in the locker room, I overhear the television that hangs in the corner. Two morning news anchors are half joking, half speculating about whether Barack Obama might appoint Oprah as secretary of state. Two elderly women laugh as they peel off their swimsuits.

"Oprah?" one of them says. "She sells flowers and soap. What does she know about government?"

Flowers and soap? Stark naked, I rummage like a madwoman through my gym bag for pen and paper to write down the quote. I've never heard anyone trivialize the Queen of Talk in this way. Actually, in my experience, whenever people critique Oprah, they begin their sentence with a qualifier, such as: "Oprah does a lot of good in the world, BUT..." Only *after* acknowledging Winfrey's charitable works do they launch into their negative tirade.

Suddenly, I feel weird. I imagine how these women in the locker room would react if they knew I did everything the flower and soap lady told me to do for a whole year. They'd cackle me right out the door.

Later that day.
I am teaching my first yoga class of the year.

I approach a newer student who is holding tree pose. She's standing on one foot, her arms reaching skyward. I adjust her posture, guiding her to square off her hips.

She whispers, "Do you think Oprah will ask you to be on her show?"

I step back, shocked. She looks at me expectantly, and I'm at a loss for words, looking around to make certain none of my other students heard her question. I think of yoga class as a sacred space where we can leave our daily lives outside until our practice is complete. It is about each student staying fully focused on the connection between her or his body and mind. It is not the appropriate time to discuss the possibility of television appearances.

"Make certain your breath is full and controlled," I tell the class, more as a reminder to myself than them.

I am incredibly disappointed at how many people want me to speculate whether I'll ever meet Oprah, as if meeting Winfrey were the ultimate goal of my project, the blue-ribbon prize for all my effort. I suppose it hurts my delicate little feelings to think that people assume my entire year was a stunt to sit on her couch. I feel it minimizes the investment I made in exploring the cultural phenomenon of women following one celebrity's lifestyle advice. Also, the question seems absurd. Why would I create a yearlong critique to get into Oprah's good graces? After all, the results of my project could go either way. If all I wanted was to get on the show, I would have thought up a smarter way to do it. While I have seen guests on Oprah's show admit that, now that they've met her in person, their dreams have come true, that's never occurred to me. I've never based my dreams on the acceptance or acknowledgment of another person.

I don't know why I'm so sensitive about this. I've been just as cynical about others' ulterior motives. I guess this is a lesson. Judge not, and all that. At the end of yoga class, my students are lying peacefully on their mats and I start biting my cuticles. When did I pick up that disgusting habit? I sit on my hands and decide I'm the tensest yoga teacher this side of the Mississippi. I look at their relaxed bodies and it hits me that I have been wound tightly for too many weeks to count. I need to de-stress.

Once I get home from the studio, I head directly to my computer. I begin researching meditation and spa vacations in remote destinations — beaches, jungles, and mountains far away from magazine stands and American television. I have a terrible desire to get away from it all. Jim, ever the pragmatist, reminds me we're broke. We begin a vigil around the mailbox, hoping for the quick receipt of the first installment of my book advance.

I ask Jim if he regrets that I let a couple offers slide last year for documentary films and a reality television show based on my project. We have a good laugh. One person suggested the project could be called *Living Oprah!* That's Living Oprah with an exclamation point, to show how wacky I am.

When the first inquiry came in, I laughed out loud, thinking the guy was joking. My amazement quickly faded into disinterest. My project felt too dear to me to allow it to become a spectacle. Plus I have a control-freak streak. If this project was in the hands of a reality television producer, my life could be hijacked and edited into something I didn't intend. I cringed at the thought of being portrayed as a crazed fanatic or a mean-spirited Oprah hater. Blogging and writing a book about my year might not draw in as large an audience as a TV show, but at least I could retain my self-respect. And what if the show was a hit? I might have to live this way for years.

As if my main concern about *Living Oprah!* were the size of my paycheck, a friend assured me this had the potential to be a lucrative project. He might have been trying to convince me to do the show but only managed to make me feel dirty. I also imagined it would be the end of my marriage. Jim could handle the disappearance of his trusty television from our bedroom, but I don't think he'd stand for the addition of high-definition video cameras mounted on our headboard.

I told one producer I would be very interested in creating other projects with her company, but I wasn't interested in documenting Living Oprah for television. I imagined crickets chirping during an awkward silence on her end of the phone. She was very polite, in a don't-call-us-we'll-call-you kind of way, but her voice sounded as if I'd turned down a canteen of water in the desert. There's a scene in the 1968 movie musical *Oliver!* that takes place in the dining hall of a gothically depressing orphanage. Our little ragamuffin hero approaches a big brute who is ladling out gruel. Oliver holds up his empty bowl and asks for another serving. The porridge-slopping man says, "More? Nobody asks for more!" I felt similarly disdained when I showed my disinterest in a reality show. "TV? Nobody turns down TV!"

That was months ago, and now we're nearing a state of rationing the food in our pantry (thank goodness for all those beans Oprah told us to buy!) and starting to use our credit cards with a little more abandon. While I don't regret my decision, I can't help but allow myself to fantasize what the theme song to *Living Oprah!* would be.

I still spend a lot of time in front of the computer. I blog about the show and spend hours reading and responding to e-mail. I have read countless appeals from folks who look up to Oprah like a savior and consider her their last, best chance for help. These people are praying for the opportunity to have her shine her philanthropic light upon them. I feel blessed and cursed at the same time that I've been the recipient of a cross-section of her e-mail. Of course it isn't easy to e-mail Winfrey directly, and many solace seekers have a difficult time locating the Contact Us link at the bottom of the website. I suppose because my blog has the name *Oprah* in the title and an easy-to-find e-mail link, people send their notes to me, instead.

The scope of Oprah's charitable giving is wide. She has housed Hurricane Katrina victims and clothed out-of-date fashion victims. Her show highlights a myriad of people she's pulled up from the depths. I received e-mails questioning Oprah's motives in helping people in such a public manner, with her name attached to her acts of kindness. It is my sense that many wish she would appear more humble when she hands out aid, thinking that giving should be its own reward, not the accolades one receives for appearing charitable. Initially, I might have agreed with them, but now I do not. If people get help, who cares if Oprah puts her name on each project or foundation? The same marketing power Oprah wields to convince her audience to buy ice cream and fire pits also inspires people to give to charities and donate their time and energy. I've heard the criticism that Oprah's loyal fans are like robots — O-bots, if you like — programmed to allow Winfrey to control their every action. When it comes to helping others, I say bring on the automatons!

Yes, Oprah stamps her name on lots and lots of stuff. Yes, her brand is everywhere, and sometimes it feels oppressive to me, but when it comes to helping people in need, I will not waste my time and energy on sour grapes.

I am also the accidental recipient of e-mails from people who hope she'll promote their products, services, ideas, or talents. I receive the tiniest sampling of her mail, but it's overwhelming to see how many people hang their hats on the idea that Oprah might change their lives forever. Whoever filters Oprah's e-mail should receive a raise and a free daily massage. I imagine that it's a job with a high burnout rate. It's emotionally draining for me, and I receive only a handful or two each week.

I can't bring myself to ignore a single e-mail, even those that come to me mistakenly, and I've reluctantly fallen into the role of volunteer for Oprah. I always let the writers know I have no affiliation whatsoever with Winfrey. I wish them luck in their endeavors and direct them to Oprah.com. Sometimes people are simply requesting information about a product seen on the show. If I am able to help them out, I will. I once received a note after an episode with sexpert Laura Berman inquiring about the make and model of a vibrator seen on *Oprah*. As I replied with the requested information, I thought, "Oh, Robyn, you stooge, why are you acting like Oprah's help desk? She's got a massive staff to do this for her." But I can't stop myself.

People spend valuable time attempting to connect to Oprah, and I want them to know their e-mails aren't floating around in cyberspace. Also, I am oddly concerned they might feel Winfrey is giving them the cold shoulder if I don't write back and redirect them. They might never receive a note from Oprah or her staff in return, but at least the weight of responsibility is off my shoulders. I don't want anyone to feel so unimportant that their words go unacknowledged.

When she received the first Bob Hope Humanitarian Award at the Emmys in 2002, Oprah said, "The greatest pain in life is to be invisible. What I've learned is that we all just want to be heard."

Years ago, I shrugged off her quote, thinking it too narrow and simplistic. But her words definitely strike a chord with me now. After years of having yoga students approach me to share insights into their practice and how it impacts their daily lives, and after spending 366 days reading comments and e-mails from my blog, I believe she has a great point. I think people want to connect by sharing their histories, opinions, passions, and more. As a result of this project, I've cultivated a deeper understanding of how I may be more respectful of other people, not only by listening but by being fully present when they reach out and share with me.

When I reflect on my project, I feel I've done Oprah a disservice by wondering if she can truly understand the priorities of a real woman. Who am I, who is anybody, to define what it means to be a real woman? Does she put on makeup and do her hair before she leaves the house, or is she comfortable looking like a schlumpadinka in public? Is a real woman someone who stays home with the kids, or one who goes to work to support them? Is she a size 2 or a size 20? Does she have trouble making ends meet, or is she rolling in dough? Does she get her period every month, or is she kept awake with hot flashes? Does she have ovaries and breasts, or has she mourned their loss? Is she Oprah, or is she me?

I overheard a conversation at, where else, the café in which I love to sip and write. There were two women in workout clothes, with jogging strollers, diaper bags, and what seemed like 46 children (but in reality was more like 5). They drank their lattes and watched their tots ravage low-fat scones, getting more crumbs on the floor than in their mouths. As the moms compared chipped manicures, one bemoaned how tough it is for real women to get any "me" time because of the demands of raising kids. Well, it's hard for me to find time for myself as well, but I don't have any children. Does this mean I'm not a real woman? I'm pretty sure I am. Don't I have a vulva? I swear I saw it in a hand mirror quite recently. And I loved it.

It really steams my broccoli to be excluded from my gender based on lifestyle choices. I'm part of the club and no one's kicking this woman to the curb without a fight. I've witnessed gals stake their claim in reality, based on their dress size, sexual orientation, priorities, and abilities. To what end? How useful is this label when it can be used to validate us one day and exclude us the next? I'm going to put it out to pasture.

Since I'm on a roll, I'm also going to stop using the word "average" to describe myself. What the hell does that mean, anyway? It might assist advertising companies to generate new campaigns, but it doesn't really apply in the (yes, I'm going to say it) real world. I hear so many people that I consider extraordinary call themselves average that I think average is in the eye of the beholder.

Another term I'm going to strike from my vernacular to describe women is "normal." What a useless, boring word. Its only purpose is to create separation between myself and others. I've been told I'm not normal because, in yoga class, I can twist myself into pretzely-looking poses. I practiced diligently toward being able to place my body into those positions. How is working hard toward a goal *not* normal? Oprah's worked her butt off and can afford a private chef to make vegan meals for her. How is that not normal?

I've heard—and I'll admit that I've used—so much exclusionary language while performing this project, I'm allergic to it. One important lesson that's been confirmed for me this year is that we're mighty as a collective but appear petty and create an us-against-them sentiment when we use language to segregate ourselves from each other. You know that annoying "meow" sound that some members of the other gender make when we look down our noses at our sister women? Wouldn't it be supercool if it went the way of the dinosaurs?

Oprah might not relate to my priorities, my relationships, my life-style, or my needs, but she's every bit as *real* a woman as I am. What a yawner it would be if our gender wasn't an infinite patchwork of lifestyles. I'd love to start a rousing chorus of "I Am Woman," but my voice is less than inspiring.

I think I'll just hum.

I feel a lot of pressure to provide a black or white answer when it comes to the burning question, "Did you find your Best Life? Did it work?" I am having trouble quantifying the success and all the costs of Living Oprah. There are simple ways to do this, of course: by adding up my receipts and the columns of spreadsheets I maintained to track the time spent on each assignment. I can have the doctor weigh me, check my blood pressure, and I can take RealAge.com tests. I can tally the price of the must-have items in my closet. That stuff is easy.

However, there are less tangible results that are difficult for me to evaluate. I can't tell if my relationships with Jim, my family, friends, and students have been forever changed due to absence or strain. I don't know if the stress and sleepless nights were worth it. Also, what is my time worth? How about missed moments with those I love? Or energy spent feeling more insecure in my mid-30s than I did in my midteens? I can't put a price tag on these, and they don't figure cleanly into the bottom line. I battle with this. I would prefer a palpable sum of all the project's parts. As I look back at my year and grapple to formulate a solid conclusion, I feel as if I am up to my knuckles in a Chinese finger puzzle and the harder I pull, the more stuck I feel. I try to give my tired brain a rest and pick up a magazine (no, not *O*). A headline—"Lose 1 Dress Size in 2 Weeks!"—screams at me from the cover, and it hits me what a numbers-based society we live in when it comes to defining success. It's almost impossible for me to think outside that box.

I formed my career from my passion for yoga because it's a journey-based practice rather than one of destination. My yoga students have heard my old goofy joke a million times, "It's yoga *practice*, not yoga *perfect*." So I'm uncomfortable that my latent perfectionism reared its ugly head last year. This project made me so focused on results and clear-cut answers. While Oprah never says that our Best Life has to be based on numbers, she definitely highlights them on her show. We know how much money certain entrepreneurs made, how much weight Oprah lost and gained. We see material wealth and consumerism celebrated. We know how much her Favorite Things cost and how many audience members received a brand-new car. This is one of my major internal conflicts as I digest 2008.

While I do not believe my Best Life can be quantified, I was continually faced with test results that categorized me, defined me, and diagnosed me. This was a difficult contradiction for me to manage, and I never made peace with it. When it comes to health and wealth, basing success on numbers is mostly valid. But when it comes to happiness, or the health of my relationships, I found the formulas unusable in my own life. Everyone defines success and fulfillment differently, so I think multiple-choice tests are pointless, unless one also enjoys trying to mash square pegs into round holes.

When I was in graduate school, I took a class that focused much of its attention on virtual reality. I learned that while technology has developed to a point that most objects are uncanny reflections of real life, the least successful area of VR is recreating believable human beings. Visual media programming, for all its flexibility, is a rigid medium with which to work. Think about a pixel. It's a tiny square. It has sharp edges and angles. How can we create a realistic-looking person when the building blocks are not organic? If I were sculpting the human body, I'd opt to work with Play-Doh over Legos. Just as computer programming based on numbers and edges cannot create a completely believable human being in VR, I don't think all the numbers, tests, and formulas in the world can define me or guide me toward a happier, healthier, more fulfilling emotional life. While I might be nudged in the right direction, I do not believe I will ever find my own Best Life by these means. Human beings are too nuanced for one-size-fits-all advice.

Here's What I Know for Now: From the crown of my head to the soles of my feet, I know I'll never discover my Best Life when I am trying to live up to someone else's vision for me. I know it's fruitless to measure my happiness while using someone else's yardstick (or meter stick, for all you Céline Dion–loving French Canadians). And why on earth does happiness need to be quantified in the first place? IT CAN'T

BE. That is what I learned this year. I know I will never truly believe I am beautiful if I allow someone else's definition of beauty to impact my self-esteem. I know I will never have a truthful, honest relationship with Jim if I judge my own marriage against others' unions. The same goes for my friendships and my connection with my family. It is futile and exhausting for me to shape my life to meet anyone else's standards. And I know there is a hazardous divide between being inspired by others and being dependent on their guidance and approval.

I now fully understand, if only in theory, not practice, that I can't depend on outside sources to tell me who I am or who I should be. Of course, I knew this before I started Living Oprah. I'm not going to play dumb and pretend I had no idea that my own truth and beauty should come from within. Yadda yadda yadda. We all know this by now, don't we? The problem is, until last year, I was absolutely clueless how often I didn't trust my own instincts. I didn't know how many seemingly insignificant choices I made during the day—taking an online quiz, poking at my butt in the mirror, reading an article about how not to look old, coveting another woman's appearance, demeanor, or relationship—chipped away at my "best life." This project was a magnified version of my existing daily behavior.

When I was 14, I worked at a roadside ice cream stand. I could put away so much ice cream, dairy-producing cows shuddered in terror when my name was uttered in their presence. I was told the longer I worked there, the more I'd develop a distaste for ice cream. Didn't work. Total crap. I loved every single spoonful. Except for the rum raisin—that was pretty gross. Anyhow, while the saturation method didn't apply to a teenager bent on stuffing down her feelings with delicious frozen treats, it really hit home for me last year. I was filled to the gills with TV, magazines, and the Internet. I saturated myself in the attempt to march to the beat of Oprah's drummer and hang with the in-crowd. And you know what? It kind of tasted like rum raisin.

I learned less from following Oprah's advice than I did by watching her work. No matter what level of success she attains, she is never complacent: She continues to cultivate her brand and thrive. Yet she also struggles to find balance and self-acceptance, just like the rest of us. No amount of celebrity, wealth, or power changes that. So, frankly,

I think we can all give up hunting for the elusive path that will lead to our Best Lives. I think the very idea of attaining our Best Lives is a fairy tale that keeps us from being satisfied with our Real Lives.

I'm grateful that I was witness to Oprah's methodology this year, and while I might not agree entirely with her philosophy, I wouldn't trade my experience for anything in the world. Winfrey seeks to empower us. She said in her acceptance speech, when presented with her Lifetime Achievement Emmy, "And I want to continue to use television... I choose to use it in whatever way I can, we can, to make people lead better lives. To lead them to the highest vision possible for themselves. That is the goal."

I think this year of watching each episode of *The Oprah Winfrey Show*, reading every *O* magazine cover to cover, and referring regularly to her website gave me incredible insight into how I might achieve a happier, more fulfilling life. I truly believe my "highest vision possible" will never be found viewing a television show, flipping though a magazine, or in seeking the approval of others. In fact, I think the biggest compliment I can give Oprah is to acknowledge and appreciate all the lessons I learned from her this year, and turn off my TV.

ABOUT THE AUTHOR

Robyn Okrant is a writer, director, performer, and yoga teacher. She graduated from Bennington College in Vermont, majoring in Drama (both socially *and* academically) and holds an MFA in performance from the School of the Art Institute of Chicago. Robyn has produced, written, and directed many original pieces: from traditional stage plays to solo performances to sketch comedy to improvised full-length plays, and, most recently, short films.

She lives in Chicago with her husband, Jim, and two cats, Wasabi and Selmarie. When pressed, she'll admit to being a schlumpadinka at heart but thinks it's part of her charm.

You can visit the author at www.robynokrant.com.